Four Words

'I Like Book, Me'
ROBBIE WILLIAMS

'Stop F**king Texting Me!'
CARIDEE ENGLISH

'Take Yo Panties Off'
CRAIG ROBINSON

'Never Met Him Before'
ANONYMOUS

'Wait For The Movie!'
FRED

'Any Four Words? Emmm . . . '
LIMBER KIMBER

'Clothes Off. Dance On!'
ME

First published in 2010 by
Liberties Press
Guinness Enterprise Centre | Taylor's Lane | Dublin 8 | Ireland
www.libertiespress .com
info@libertiespress.com
+353 (1) 415 1224

Trade enquiries to CMD BookSource
55A Spruce Avenue | Stillorgan Industrial Park | Blackrock | County Dublin
Tel: +353 (1) 294 2560
Fax: +353 (1) 294 2564

Distributed in the United States by
DuFour Editions | PO Box 7 | Chester Springs | Pennsylvania | 19425
and in Australia by
InBooks | 3 Narabang Way | Belrose NSW 2085

ISBN: 978–1–905483–90–7

2 4 6 8 10 9 7 5 3 1

A CIP record for this title is available from the British Library.

Cover design by Ros Murphy
Internal design by Liberties Press
Set in Garamond
Printed by Scand Book

RanDumb

The Adventures
of an Irish Guy in LA

Mark Hayes

In no specific order . . .

Mum and Dad.

Thank You.
Firstly. For having me. Mostly. For everything else.

Remember. None of this happened to me.

And, to everyone else . . .

Book on!

PS If I was ever late. And kept you waiting. Apologies.
I can't keep time.

Contents

Pro. Log   9

Go On the Journey!   16

Moving On In   21

Where Does a Gay Horse Live?   24

Ladies . . .   29

Wingless Wonder   34

Hans in the Hills   36

Sweet Valley of Jesus   40

Dumb Bum   43

Trudging   48

Freddie Cougar   51

Crazy Town   56

McJob   61

A Hippie and My Leprechaun   66

Blood, Sweat and . . .   71

Everybody Needs Good Neighbours   77

Just Like Entourage   79

Acting Up   83

Free Jim!	87
Diet Coke Head	92
Bought a Bucket	96
Transformer	101
Waddling Fat Duck	107
Right On!	111
Ehh . . . Happy Birthday!	114
Sign What? Sweat Where?	120
Fear Not!	125
Hands Off My Sex Pistol	130
The Cable Guy	133
Spanglish, Sí? Eh? No? Sí	137
Obsessive and Clingy, I'm on the Rebound . . .	140
Lads' Night Out	144
A Messy Break-up	149
Aw Yeh	152
You Are Ricky Bobby!!!	153
Full of . . .	158
Who's Your Paddy?!	161
Mandatory Mandate	163
Ted! Do What to Who?	166

Did You Know . . . ? 171

I'm on a Plane 175

Sprung Broke 177

Forgive Me, Father 181

Naked Wrestling with the Cleaning Maid 183

Bang Smart Stop Dumb Go Flow! 187

Every Man Needs an . . . Orgy? 190

In the Shower. Singing. In French. Crying. Go! 194

Pumping. Spinning. Sweating. Oh Jesus, What Have We Done, Jim?! 198

Call Me, Bridget. Call Me, Prick! 204

Hollywood. Fight. Club 206

Chancers, Prancers, Dancers! 209

The Passion of Christ 212

Wow Factor 216

Fantastisch! 219

Stand Up. Sit Down 222

Oblivious to the Obvious 226

Implosions 230

In the Name of the Father 232

Googling. Crawling. Running 235

What Number Are You? 237

Do It for Me, Ricky, Please!!! 240

Breakdown? Breakthrough? 248

Hmmm. That Is Interesting 251

Adaptor 254

Brad, I Feel Your Pain! 257

Procrasti Nation 259

Write, Said Fred 261

Ninety-nine Red Balloons 262

Not So Happy Day 265

Wallow and a Plough 267

How to Tie a Tie? 270

Bring Back the Bubble 272

Gigging and DJigging 274

Books, Shows and Rocking Chairs 278

The Long Tail 279

On Tour 283

Vi-Ya? 287

V. Sa. Par. A. Noia 291

Hey Day. Not You. It's Me 294

Home. Come On Home 296

The Beginning . . . Things I Don't Remember 297

Pro. Log

Singing. Dancing. Prancing along. Pirouetting gaily through his youth. Always looking to perform. Jumping at any chance to be on stage. Seeking out the spotlight. Bursting into song at the first sign of rain. Speech and drama. School plays. Talent competitions. Anything creative. Watching *Fame* on repeat. Intent on making it as a performer. Hell bent on going to acting college in London. Honing his craft. Jazz hands. West End. Musicals. New York. Broadway. Name in lights. LA. Movies. Jackpot. Global. Icon. Maybe returning to his first love of singing. Best-selling albums. Always on tour. Always on the go. Energizer bunny. Bouncing along. Destined for greatness! Born to perform! Born to be a star!!!

Thankfully, he was not one of these annoying idiots growing up. Probably the one wishing that they would just dance their way off the nearest cliff. Perhaps sensing that while these folk gave the appearance of having talent, they were destined to end up as clowns in the circus. Or, for the few who could sing just above an average level, living the dream of performing cabarets on cruise ships. Audiences of OAPs. Half-asleep. Half-dead. Fully uninterested. Brave face. Smiling on the outside. Broken on the inside. Shattered dreams.

No, growing up he was just the normal kind of annoying idiot. Played some sports. Did the odd colouring competition. Making sure to stay within the lines. Played some more sports. Listened to music. Sang in his head. Along with a crowd. Never really getting an urge to burst into any sort of ad-hoc performance. You know, just for fun. Showed little interest in the arts.

Unless, of course, these all-singing, all-dancing, all-annoying wannabe stars happened to be all-right-looking girls. If so. Perhaps click his fingers. Clap a little. Creating a beat for whatever dance they were trying to pull off. 'Yeah! Great dancing. Wuu!'

More than likely, like anyone else when young, if asked – 'What do you want to be when you grow up?' – something along the lines of 'Actor! Actress! Acting! Movie star!' probably would have been shouted out. Along with the likes of 'Singer! Soccer player! Spaceman! Actually. An actuary!' (Never actually wanted to be a spaceman. Did actually want to be an actuary for a while. Had a thing for maths.)

Why would the likes of 'actor' be on the tip of most tongues. For the art? The craft? The acknowledgment from peers of outstanding performance? Highly doubtful. Wouldn't even consider the whole acting side of it. Actually act? Alien concept. However, the word, along with everything that came with it? Highly appealing. Fame. Fortune. Glamour. Women. What a life! What a generic dream. Only ever that though. Pipe dream. Never realistically considered it when growing up. Unlike, say, soccer player. Still a pipe dream. Closer to home at least. Probably still holds deluded thoughts he could make it there. If. Only. This. That. Maybe. Definitely. Deluded.

Not that his creative side never reared its ugly head. Back row of a school choir. Miming. Mouthing. Wording. Free pass out of class. On to college. Few half-hearted attempts. Wrote a few lyrics while his buddy strummed away on the guitar. Ingeniously realising that a lot of words rhyme with 'You'. And all the things you do. Strangely, the rest of the song seemed to be based around a mysterious 'Cat' that popped into his head. Sitting there, on the mat, looking at him. Why are you looking at him like that? Never made it past a first draft. Preferred to keep it raw.

Couple of years later, in an attempt to take his singer/songwriter ambitions to the next level, he bought that guitar from his friend. Cost. €100. Worth. €30. Max. Good friend. Brought the guitar home. Strummed it once. Twice. Three times a lady. *Wmmappfh* went a string. Broke. Nearly took out an eye. And that was the end of that. No clue how to actually play the guitar, never mind re-string one. Same buddy offered to buy it back a week later. For €30. Claimed it had gone down in value, seeing as technically, now broken. Yeah, technically he'd prefer to leave that guitar rot in his room. Telling people ever since, if they happened to see it, 'Yeah, play a bit. One of the strings *just* broke though. Otherwise, I'd play one of my own songs for you. Great one about a cat.'

Perhaps it was throughout the last few years of college when his interest in acting and writing kicked in. Distinctly remembers Al Pacino's performance in *Scent of a Woman*. 'Hoo-hah!' First time noticing an actor in a movie. Rather than just watching it as a movie on its own. *The Sopranos*. Having never watched it before, got the first five box-sets as a Christmas present. Barely left the house. Studying not only the acting, but also the whole production of the show. Engrossed. Analytical. Saving the last few episodes. Just to make them last longer. *Pan's Labyrinth*. Watching it hung over in the cinema. Going back the next day. Just to make sure. Unreal. Back again the next day with a group of friends. *Superbad*. Same again. Recurring theme. Hooked. Sparks. Flying. All the while, watching too many bad movies. Foolishly thinking that he could do better. Sparks. Lighting a delusional fire of grandeur.

And then sitcoms came into play. First year of college.

Watched an episode of *Seinfeld*. Didn't really find it funny. Didn't really pay much attention to it. Probably busy writing a song about a cat at the time. Final year of master's. Projects. End of year. Until then. Procrastinate. Time to kill. What's on daytime TV today? Reruns. *Seinfeld*. Over. And over. Every. Single. Episode. Religiously. Jerry Seinfeld. Larry David. Geniuses. Comedic zeniths. Suddenly waking up with thoughts that this was what he wanted to do. Mentioning it to a few people. Probably after a few drinks. All talk. All thinking. All in his head. All the time.

Finished his degree. What now? Do a master's? Why not. Master's. Done. And now? Hmmm. Not. A. Clue. Interested in translating documents for the Irish navy? No thanks. Delusions of grandeur. Pardon? How much? Offered a bucket of money. OK. Set up his own company. Out of the blue. Lost in translation. German gun manuals. Not really what he had planned. At all. Great. Time to delegate. Hired cheaper online translators to work for him. Which was handy. Freed up a lot of time. Tipping away. Odd email to them now and again. How's it going? Well. Good. Money flowing. Time going. Not flying. Just cruising. Drifting. Way of life. Automatic. Routine. Grand. Fine. Until one day, he was kind of bored. All the time. Decided to buy a few new T-shirts for himself online. Cheer himself up! When they arrived, he was still the same. Bored. Tired. Just doing the same thing. Saying. Thinking. Doing nothing.

Reread *The Alchemist*. Listened to Sigur Rós. Watched sitcoms. Watched movies. Ambitions started to burn once more. Sitcoms. Movies. No more saying this, that or the other though. All well and good having it as a nice idea. Safe in his head. Time he did something about it. Even if it didn't sound a bit realistic when said out loud. Probably as he'd absolutely no clue where to begin. No idea of the business. Alien. Clueless. What to do . . . Sat around. Thought about it. Googled it. Must've got bored. Wrote his own sitcom script. Life in college. What it's *really* like. Surely nobody has tried that before. Sure. Sent it to the main television station in Ireland. Went back to his routine. Television station acknowledged it at least. Showed a slight bit of interest. Delighted. However. In the end. Asked. 'Who are you? What have you done before? Translated what?' Thumbs down. No thanks. Rejected. Threw in the towel. Dumb dream.

Unfortunately, not exactly. Instead. Thought about it. It wasn't him. It was them. No original/good sitcoms were being produced in Ireland. Funk them. Funk Ireland. 'Do they not know how good this is? Title alone is brilliant! Can they not see the potential?!' He probably thought. On numerous occasions. Tempestuously. Dumbly. Ignoring the fact he expected his first-ever attempt at a script to be given the green light. Never even occurred to him as being unrealistic. Blissfully unaware. Either way, that rejection was the deciding factor to move to Los Angeles. In at the top. Go global if he was going to give it a proper go. Navy et al had supplied him with the funds. Now or never. Time to make his mark. Plus, it was LA after all. Not like he was off to an obscure farm in the middle of Siberia. For whatever dream may involve doing that. LA all the way!

Off he went. California on. One quick visit first to his buddies who were spending the summer in Santa Barbara. One last blowout. Physically getting closer at least. Now telling others of his plan. About to try his luck in LA. Still had no definite plans. Which is why the quick visit turned into a longer stay. Summer finished up. Friends flew home to Ireland. *Finally* he was on his way to LA. Just a quick trip to Mexico first for a week. Wedding in Cancún. Girl he knew was getting married. American. Used to live in Ireland. Invite out of the blue. Unexpected. Even more so, while at the wedding, boy meets girl. Boy actually likes this girl. New groom and bride invite him to San Francisco. Visit for a few days. Maybe a week. Maybe he'd meet the girl again. And he did. Without realising, those few days turned into almost three months. He was Dupree. Living with the newly married couple. Involved with the wife's sister. Out of the blue. Once again. Somehow he had re-entered the comfort zone.

Dreams. Ambitions. LA. On hold. Now living a different kind of American dream. White picket. Blond hair. Blue eyes. Back to cruising. Still planning to go to LA. Just no clue when. Did know that his visa expired around Christmas. Decided he needed to head back to Ireland for a while anyways at that point. Could go to LA after Christmas? But the girl in San Fran? Gave him a choice . . . LA or her. One or the other. Not just going to wait around for him. Can't have it all his own way. Nine times out of ten, plough on to LA. No second thoughts. However, boy actually *liked* this girl. Plus. In the dreaded comfort zone. Caught in two minds. Indecisive idiot. Maybe he could commute to acting classes in LA from San Francisco? Maybe. Compromise. Once his visa had cleared, he'd fly back to San Francisco first. Decide then. Whenever that may be.

Back to Ireland. Desire for LA. Back. Christmas comes. Goes. Got another contract job from the navy. Injection of funds. January shows up. Visa was good again. Time to make the call. Head saying LA. Body drawn to San Francisco. What to do? San Francisco first anyways. That plan was still on. Noticed that the conversations he had with the girl were a bit off. Something was up. Pressed. Found out. Girl was pregnant. What?! Oh sweet Jesus. Not his. Oh thank Jesus. Wait. What? Not his? How? Who? Girl hooked up with an ex on New Year's Eve. Oh right.

Boy. Hangs up. Phones back. Girl. Goodbye. Boy. Shell-shocked. Rattled. Down.

Thankfully, his maths brain kicked in. Took it as a sign. Pointing him on his way. Choice. Made. Not ideal. Not ready. Nothing else holding him back. Told no one about the incident. Booked a flight. Packed his bags. Two days later. On his way. Off to LA. Not really thinking that every cloud has a silver lining. Probably not thinking either that within a week he'd be hobnob-bing with movie stars, unwittingly being used as a drugs mule, or wearing women's clothes. (Silver lining?)

I have a friend. His name is Mark. This is his story. How he headed off. On a mission. Trying to become. An actor. A writer. Something. Just. Like. That . . .

Go On the Journey!

LAX. Bags. Rental car. Choice. GPS? iPod dock? GPS. iPod. Direction. Music. I'm a man. Know where I'm going. Even if I've never been here before. Give me music! One song in, iPod freezes. Good man yourself. And away I go. Bemused. Confused. Lost. For the umpteenth time. Good work. Ape. iPod unfreezes. At least the music is back. Lost in Hollywood. Listening to music. Wuu.

My plan. Not going as planned. Maybe just not a good plan. Land in LAX around six in the evening. By the time I got my bags, rented a car, and made my way into LA, there'd be no traffic. Plain sailing. Check out places to live. Pick one. Move in. Off to a flying start. Great plan! Booked my flight based on how bad traffic might be at that time. Good plan. Rented a car based on the selling point that it allowed me to hook my iPod up to the stereo. As it is *vital* that I can listen to one of my iPod mixes as I drive along. Vital. I'll take that over the other car. Who needs GPS? It would appear that I do. Clueless. Lost. Humming. Not part of the plan.

Phone rings. Howdy. Is that me in the hilarious little car? Blocking traffic? Don't think so. The PT Cruiser I'm in is pretty cool. Although I am kind of blocking traffic. At this point a black Escalade pulls up next to me. Tinted windows roll down. Blonde girl on the phone. Points at me. Nods. Do I know you? I do . . . The girl I emailed about the room! Ditch my cool car. Jump in the back seat of the Escalade. As if I stepped into a nightclub. Blue glow from the dash. Plush. Sound system pumping. Hot brunette driving. Hot blonde on the phone. Jess and

Layla. Smile sheepishly as they sing Journey's 'Don't Stop Believing' to me. On cue, I start clicking along. Yeah. Wuu. Go on the LA!

Decided to take that song as a sign. A hidden gem I liked to unleash at parties during college. Ignoring the fact that ever since *The Sopranos*, the song had been back in the mainstream flow, being overplayed by everyone. A sign. So when the girls turned around and asked me if I wanted to live with them, that song alone was the reason I said yes, straight off. Kind of. Seemed easy to get along. Bonus. Plus the fact that they were both models. Maybe that had something to do with my choice too. Maybe.

Maybe it had something to do with the previous places I'd checked out. Maybe. Neither really what I'd been expecting. After I booked my flight to LA, I looked up Craigslist for a room to rent in Hollywood. Weeded out the nut-jobs. Buckets of nuts. Lined up the best options. Three places in particular showed promise. Month to month. Available straightaway. Contacted each of them. Conversation. Back. Forth. Basic details. Age. Occupation. Likes. Dislikes. Send a photo. Visual point of reference. Plan was to have a quick look at each place, pick the one that suited me best, haggle the price, shake hands, take my suitcases out of the rental car, and move in. Straightaway. Fool. Proof. Plan.

First port of call. Two-bedroom apartment. Spanish lady. Spiritual. Funky. Tad off-key. Cackled. Still. Seemed nice. Really nice apartment. Except. As I got the tour. I realised. Only one bedroom. Which was cool. Place to myself. No. She was leasing out the bedroom. And she'd still live in the apartment. Probably sleep on the floor. Or the couch. Did it not occur to you to mention this quirk in any of the emails? No. Or that you live with your three cats? Who are the best friends anyone could ever need? So much fun. So full of life. So why didn't they move an inch the whole time I was there? Convinced one of them was dead. Just lay there. Staring at me with a glazed-over look. Maybe it was a 'kill me now' look. I was reassured that Pumpkin was not dead. Just resting. Pretending that I was, regrettably, allergic to cats, I made my escape.

Second port of call. Two-bedroom apartment. Legitimately. Mexican lady. Maria. Renting out her spare room. Found the apartment. Buzzed in. An older lady answered the door to me. Used the old, reliable: 'Oh, you must be Maria's younger sister.' Just looked at me strangely. Immune to my charm. Backtracked. Must be Maria's mother? No. Turns out. She was Maria. Pardon? You're Maria? Can't be. Maria's thirty. Long brown hair. Sent me a photo. Hazarding a guess, you're sixty? With short grey hair. Just shrugged her shoulders at me. Cackled. Acted as if it was nothing. Made it even weirder. Might as well have sent me a photo of her as a baby. Shrugged my shoulders with her. Continued on the tour.

Classy, sleek-looking place. Swimming pool. Gym. All in the complex. Ticked all the boxes. Except. Nail in the coffin . . . Her list of rules. No television. No loud talking while on the phone. No noise whatsoever after ten o'clock. No guests. And. No meat allowed in the fridge. Would you not have thought to mention any of this when we emailed? Those several emails back and forth. Remember when you emailed me your photo? And flirted with me? No? OK. As appealing as her rules sounded, I told her I'd have to sleep on it.

So. Maybe it wasn't just the power ballad that made me say yes to moving in with the two girls. Originally, I told the girls that I would be at their apartment at nine o'clock for a viewing. Another girl was going at that time to check it out too. It was now almost half eleven. They were on their way to a party. As a result, even though I wouldn't be able to see their apartment tonight, they needed to know if I would move in or not. There and then. Other girl was keen to move in. Didn't really click with her though. Prefer if it was to be me. Yes. Or. No.

Truthfully, they were my first choice all along. I'd seen photos. Of the apartment. Knew the place was nice. Spoke to them on the phone briefly. Seemed to get on well with each other. Reason I left their apartment until last was that the rent was by far the most expensive. By far. However, the thought of having a woman and her cats curling up at my feet while I slept, or, alternatively, living in a totalitarian time warp, were both less appealing than crippling rent. Funk it. Here to enjoy myself. Buy now, pay later. I'm in! Shook hands with the girls. Deal. Done. And. Dumb. Happy days.

Jumped back out of the Escalade. Girls drove off to their party. Sat back into my cool PT. Sigh of relief. Pleased as punch that I had found somewhere to live. Sorted. Except. Balls. Wouldn't actually be moving in until the morning. Not tonight, as I'd presumed and banked on. New problem cropped up unexpectedly. No longer lost. Now just nowhere to go. Stay with a friend? I know people living around California. In LA? Cat Woman. And Photoshop Maria. My pool of friends wasn't even a puddle. Hotel on. Where's the closest hotel? Actually. Where am I?

Feeling I couldn't just sit in my car at the side of the road, I started to drive. Aimlessly. Felt like a lost pigeon. Foreign land. Lost basic knowledge. Reborn. Re-programmed. New dumb state of mind. Couldn't even drive properly for some reason. Cars whizzing by. Yelping. Highly strung drivers screaming at me. From the comfort of their own cars. Could've at least rolled down the window at me. All I could see was their big angry heads. Angry mute muppets. Got the gist. 'Where do you think you're going?! What the f**k are you doing?' Don't ask me bud, I don't have a funking clue!

Eventually pulled into a Denny's restaurant. Might as well hang out here for a few hours. Ordered some dodgy food. Realised how much money I'd just committed to rent. Observed the weird customers floating in and out. Pretty soon I had a lovely, lingering, queasy feeling. Went back out to my car. Started to ring around and hunt down a room in any hotel that was somewhat close by. Almost two in the morning at this stage. Needed sleep. First three attempts. Fully booked. Jet lag kicked in. Wearily closed my eyes for a minute. Roughly thirty-seven seconds later. Out for the count. Asleep. Car park of Denny's. In a PT Cruiser. Living the dream.

Moving On In

Randomly woke up at God-only-knows what time. Thought I was in Ireland. Looked around. Thought I was drunk. Figured out I was asleep in a car. A sign saying 'Hollywood' up in the distance. Passed out again quickly before I let myself make sense of anything.

Woke up a few hours later, this time from the heat. Sweat. Bucketing. Brain woke up. Rang the girls. Got directions. Found the apartment. Dropped my bags at the front door. Drove back to the airport. Dropped off my rental car. Baffled by all the hidden charges. Man behind the counter was baffled by my accent. Ended in a frustrating stalemate. Taxi back to the apartment. Saw the apartment properly. Realised it's not really an apartment. More of a Spanish-style townhouse. Two-storey, enclosed gated courtyard outside. Saw that a few of my neighbours are ridiculously good-looking women. No wonder the rent is so high. Told that the complex is just like Melrose Place. Supposedly. Matt Damon lived in the exact same place when he first arrived in LA. Apparently. Marilyn Monroe lived next door. Handy to know, if I ever have small talk with him. Probably not her.

No sign of the two girls. Jess's ex is here though. Moving out. So I can move in. Bit of awkwardness as this is revealed. I don't think he understands my accent. Or else doesn't like the look of me. While he packs up his stuff, I unpack my bags. Try out my new sheet-less bed. Jet lag and car sleeping are not serving me well. One quick lie-down. Woke up again some time in the evening. This time from the smell of smoke. Forgot the girls had told me that they smoked in the house. Lied when I said this wouldn't be a problem. On paper, I just brushed it off. In reality, it's probably top of my 'Not A Fan' list. The other reason, along with price of rent, why I was skeptical about the apartment. However, will just have to build a bridge. Perks outweigh these two negatives.

Girls ask me if I want to go drinking with them, head to a party afterwards. It would be rude not to. I'll teach them some drinking games. Start drinking at about ten. Soon after, Jess gets a phone call from her ex. Goes upstairs. Layla and I bond over the music on my laptop. Can't beat a bit of Girl Talk! Stories are flowing. Somehow gets it into her head I sing a few of the songs. Not sure how. Her and Jess know a lot of the singers from the bands I am playing as well. Not wanting to prod, I take a mental note to come back to that. Even though I was bursting to hear more stories of who threw what TV out of what window when Jess broke up with him.

At about one bell, I notice that there's no still no sign of Jess. Around the exact same time, while I'm picking out a song, Layla throws the head at me. Eyes closed. Mouth open. Goldfish-style. I stare intently at my laptop screen. Where is that song I really need to find?! Thinking I must not have copped on, the goldfish dives in again. I pretend to be drunk. Clueless to what's actually going on. I need another booze. Kitchen on! Act. Dumb. Easiest. Option. Numerous reasons why I acted oblivious. Numerous. Top five:

Perhaps subconsciously rattled after the whole recent pregnancy situation.

We now live together. In the long run, would just be awkward.

I prefer brunettes. A brunette.

Night is young.

I can think of four reasons. Obviously not drunk.. Enough. Yet.

Return with boozes. Layla has an embarrassed vibe. Tells me she's going to bed. Should I mention reason number four to her? Nay. Leave it off. Ciao ciao. What do I do now? Jet lag has me wide awake. Drink has me wanting to get drunk. Feels like my night is just beginning. Raring to go! Unfortunately. No clue where to go. No one to call. No one to go out with. Cat Woman? Nay. Could go Solo Joe. Maybe. And then. Bizarrely. It started to rain. Cats. Dogs. Men. Buckets. What the funk?! It rains in LA? Thought I left that behind in Ireland. Only one option. Booze on. Finish off the slab of cans on my own while watching re-runs of *The Hills* on MTV. Delighted when I see my street at one stage. Eventually fall asleep. Drunk on the couch. Dreaming about living the dream.

Where Does a Gay Horse Live?

Today has been a full day. Of nothing. Yet still littered with incidents. Woke up, made some breakfast, put on some music, and thankfully found the match I was looking for on TV. Everton against Liverpool. FA Cup. Sign off for a flurry of deliveries for the girls. Suitors are on the prowl already it would seem. Big bouquet of flowers arrive. I give them to Layla, who comes pottering about. Nothing said about last night's little head-throwing incident. Happy days. Sweep on. Getting ready to go meet a friend who's in town. (A guy she used to date. Or is now dating? So soon?! God only knows, ambiguity seems to be the name of the game). Mentions to me that they were having a party later on. Be ready. Really want me to meet all their friends. Wuu huu, more models all the way! Just as she walks out the door, mentions that 'It's so funny that you're listening to that song'. Eh, yeah. Hilarious? Didn't get it. Tad hung over. Charity laugh. Back to the match.

Half-time. Nil all. Full time. 0–0. Extra time. Scoreless. Penalties looming. Around this time, Layla returns to our abode. With her friend. I'm on the edge of my seat. Barely notice. C'mon Everton! Point Layla in the direction of the pile of shoeboxes that were just delivered for either her or Jess. Quick hello to Layla's buddy. Too engrossed in the match for long formalities. Just as he sits down next to me and asks me to explain the offside rule, Everton score. I jump. For joy. I jump. On him. Yelping with delight. Confused, he half-heartedly joins in. Embracing the celebrations. Obviously I take this as a queue to jump up on him some more. Hug him. Sing 'Championes' in his ear. All that.

At this point, I kind of recognise him. Isn't he . . . aren't you . . . it is . . . the lead singer of the band I was listening to earlier. You are Spoon! Ha, great start to my second day. Everton win. Converted Britt to the Blue side. Five-minute chat about music. Goodbye hangover, hello front foot! And then I got the third-wheel feeling. Hung in there for as long as I could. Gibbering on. Ah shur I'll leave ye at it. Go venture off for myself. Explore my surroundings. Get my bearings. More importantly, go get a George Foreman grill. No toaster or grill in the house. Everyone needs a George.

Originally my plan had been to live in the heart of LA. At the core. Downtown. Right in the hub. Epicentre. Walk out my door and everything is just there. My original plan. Until I found out there's no real centre to LA. A complete sprawl. Downtown is crap. Office buildings. All right. Next plan. Where's the best place in the sprawl? Quick bit of market research. Told West Hollywood was the place to go. One girl I knew, who used to live in LA, told me: 'You would *really* love living in WeHo, right up your alley.' WeHo had a nice ring to it. Got the nod.

Thanks to the gods of Google, I had found a prime location. Sunset Boulevard is at the top of my street. Santa Monica Boulevard one street below me. Clubs, bars, shops, cinemas, gyms, coffee places, everything you might want, all close by. Likes of Chateau Marmont, the Laugh Factory and the Standard Hotel are all right at the top of my street. Walking distance. Handy. Especially as I quickly realise that nobody else walks anywhere. Streets to myself. Hustle. Bustle. Nada. No New York. Not even a San Francisco. Everyone drives. No matter how close they are to where they want to go. Drive-across-the-street kind of thing. Only other people I met walking more than one block on my mission to buy a George were homeless folk. Although there was that Filipino guy actually.

Decided to do a loop. Ralph's on Sunset would hook me up with George. Down to Santa Monica first for a look. Walked one way. Bits and pieces. Walked the other way. Bits and bobs. Just go buy the George. I know where I'm going. I'll take this short-cut. And obviously, ended up in a weird little alley. Not sure where I was going. So I asked the Filipino guy who was hanging around down the alley. Friendly chap. Asked where I'm from. Shrilled with delight. Claimed to be Irish. Or an Irish man. Or wanted to be Irish. Or wanted an Irish man. Not really too sure what he said. Seeing as he had at first informed me that I was 'lost' down Vaseline Alley. Vas-e-line Alley? Weird name. Gave me a knowing wink. Oh Jesus. Filled in the gaps. Figuratively. Quickly giddied up out of the alley. Before we could 'Irish kiss goodbye'? Sweet Lord. Where's Ralph?!

Few blocks later. Find Ralph's. No sign of George. Ask a shop assistant to help me look. As I am repeating myself (accent has been both a help and a hindrance), a girl overhears and says she's looking for the same thing. Come join the hunt! I stumble upon the grill section, picking up a George, and wave them over. Shop assistant asks to look at my one and then gives it to the girl. Looks like that's the last one. Which now . . . *my* one? Sorry, no, *her* one. Was I not here first? He doesn't care. I see then that the girl looks familiar. Look out the window at the big billboard I walked by on my way in. Plugging some chick-flick movie that just came out. Penny drops. Same girl, Isla Fisher. Taking off with my George. Not even the obligatory 'No, you take . . . No you . . . No, I insist!' I let it go. Although. Not even an Irish kiss goodbye!

Celeb encounter of some sort I suppose. Virginity broken. And then walking home, I decided to check out the Mexican restaurant at the top of my street. Order up. Find a seat. Food on. Tap on the shoulder. Girl at the table next to me. Asks for the salt. No problem. Let me get it. Turn around to get it from my table. Realise. I recognise her. Turn back again. Rihanna. How's it going?! Pardon? Salt? Oh yeah. Forgot about that. Apologies for turning around again just to gawk and eyeball you. My bad. Smooth.

And then. On the way home. Stall at the top of my street. Stopped to buy a bottle of water. Another guy doing the same. Both of us then walking down my street. Again, I recognise him from somewhere . . . the dude from *Superbad*. Two of us strolling along. Drinking water. While he was devouring an ice cream as well. Eat up bud! Side by side. Great buddies. Equals! Except. He's made a few class movies and I have . . . yet to make mine. As I turn into my building, I feel like I should say goodbye to him. After all . . . water buddies. Wave the bottle at him. Gives me a strange look. Half-heartedly shakes his bottle back. Go on the water! This is a great neighborhood!

Another thing about WeHo. Quite apparent. Quite a lot of guys in my neighborhood. Quite friendly guys. Guys with poodles. Guys with waxed eyebrows. Guys with pink pants. Guys with jumpers around their shoulders. Guys walking like peacocks. Guys saying 'Heeey' and 'Mmhmmm' as they walk by. Smatterings of ridiculously good-looking women. However. Mostly. A. Lot. Of. Guys. Rainbow flags everywhere. Someone said something about 'Boys Town'. Hmmm. Interesting. Wait. Wait. There we go. Hello penny. Now I get it . . . WeHoooo. Makes sense. Might explain why *Superbad* gave me a dodgy look. Probably thought I was cracking onto him. Either way, plenty of good-looking women around to keep me happy. Plus, I already found myself slouching less as I walked around. Posture on!

Overall, I'm a fan of WeHo. Cool place. Hot women about. Places within walking distance. Like a little village. Full of the Village People. Star-spangled. Buckets of well-known people. Various letters, degrees and numbers. Just get used to that I suppose. Still pretty cool though. Unlike that Salt and Peppa joke I might've made earlier. Few celeb stories to ring home about at least. Big news. Especially when you're from Ireland. Good to find all this out today I suppose. Early doors. Acclimatising in full swing. Hence, there shall be no more pointless name-dropping. I hope. Nor stories of guys trying to slap me on the ass. Again, I hope. As long as I avoid certain alleys, I should be good.

And just in case you were wondering about the party, it was a mighty . . . letdown. Met the friends. All dudes. Twenty guys smoking in the sitting room. Drinking my booze. No women. No hot models. No party. Went to my room. Early night. Listened to some Bon Iver. 'Blood Bank' has been on repeat. Not a good sign. Tomorrow night. Out and about. Boozing. Big time. Badly needed. Might get onto George, Ralph and Fillipe. Lads' night out!

Ladies . . .

Big day. Main goal. Buy sheets for my bed. Using my hand towel as a pillow and bath towel for a blanket was getting a bit unrealistic. A damp bed is never fun. When I mentioned this to the girls, they invited me along to Santa Monica to go shopping with them. Seemed they wanted to buy me a pair of proper jeans anyways. Not that they don't like my style, I'm told. More that they just absolutely hate my jeans – loose-fitting, not too baggy, not too skinny. Skinny is the new look. Or the look they like. Honestly, I can't stand skinny jeans. Probably because I can't stand comfortably with them on. However, when in LA. Sell your soul. Off to Santa Monica we go!

Simple enough shopping agenda . . . Buy me sheets. Buy me jeans. Perhaps stroll around Santa Monica. Should be fun. Painless shopping trip. Girls just have to call into one shop first. Forever 21. Just grab one thing. Which seems to take forever. Four hours and countless shops later, I'm deliriously wondering when I might see sheets. Don't care about jeans. At all. Need sheets though. *Finally* we get to the shop. Where I can buy . . . a proper pair of jeans. Girls laden me with a mountain of denim. Shoo me off to the changing room. Shoes off. And realise that the jeans are ridiculous. Some are so skinny I literally can't pull them up past my knees. Added to this struggle, gay shop assistants keep popping their heads in the changing room curtains to see if I'm OK. One guy in particular does it a bit too often. Lingering looks. Leering. In fairness to the really hot female shop assistant in there, she stayed professional. Didn't bother me once. Nice of her.

Eventually I managed to zip up a pair of jeans. Girls love them. Chanting. 'Buy them! Buy them! Buy them now!' To keep the girls happy and speed up the process of culling this shopping trip, I nod in agreement. Maybe I might wear them if I ever have to paint the house. Something like that. Plus, and far more importantly, they are only $10. As I make my way to the counter, Layla spots another pair. Oh my God. They're almost as nice as the ones I have! In fact, yes, she thinks they may be even nicer! Yeah, mayb— spot the price tag, $180. Ha, no, no, I think the ones I have already are my favourite. Bullet. Dodged.

Final port of call . . . buy sheets. Jess knows the perfect shop. Boutique place she visits. (Sheet boutique?) Within ten minutes I'm carrying sheets, pillows, candles, duvets, rugs, comforters, throws, fancy hand towels, fancy washcloths, matching towels for guests, robes, slippers and a book. Called *Interesting Thoughts*. For people to read. If I ever get guests in my bathroom. Only $30. Exactly what I needed to buy. Decide to sit down and let the girls look for another elusive type of pillow I might need. As I'm chilling out, I notice the prices of all the items in my basket. At least $1,000 worth of goods. Cheapest towel is $50. I have my own towel. I don't need any of this crap. Even the sheets are ridiculously expensive. $250 for sheets? Or is that just for a pillowcase? I ask an assistant. Counting threads? Pardon me?

Funk that. Across the road I spot a Target. Say nothing to the girls. Slip over. Grab sheets, couple of pillows, $50, and away I go. By the time I get back, Jess is at the counter with all my goods. Ready to buy? Anything else I wanted? Seems to be let down when she sees my Target bag. Did I not like the sheet boutique? Decides to just buy all the stuff for herself so instead. Which gave me the impression she was going to buy the stuff for me all along. Her treat. Good work by me. Book of thoughts would've been a nice touch. Still though, sheets are sheets. Can't go too wrong with them.

Bonded with the girls today at least. Most of the time. Mentioned to Jess that she looked a bit like Kate Moss. Did not go down as well as I'd assumed it would. Seeing as they both unwittingly dated the same guy at the same time before. In my defence, what are the odds?! Saved the day by complimenting her dress sense. Funky as funk, with a rock and roll twist. Blue boots. White dress. Leather jacket. Russian-style fur hat. Somehow, all worked well. Really well. I also knew she was a model. A proper model. Just didn't expect to walk past a store and see a huge photo of her in the window. Well, her head. Looked good though. Moved out to LA about six months ago. Relocated from New York after being offered a role in a movie. Really cool chick. Appears to know a lot of well-known folk. And has more than a few eye-popping stories.

Layla knows Jess from modelling in New York. Long blonde hair. Slim. Hot. Flirtatious, to say the least. More all-American look. White tank top and cut-off denim jeans. Still finding her feet in LA. Model. Maybe wants to be a singer. Maybe an actress. Maybe something else. Not sure. Ambiguity is ongoing theme. Only moved here a month ago from New York. She and her boyfriend had been staying in the room I'm in. Boyfriend paying the rent. Until. Last week. Split up. He left. She can't afford rent. Now pays no rent. While she sorts her life out. That's where I came in. Even though I can't really afford the rent either. Not sure where my feet are. And have no clue what I'm doing. Let's ignore that. She's going to sleep on the couch. Or share Jess's bed. Lucky her. Not having to pay rent, and all. Obviously.

Neither girl actually told me their age, now I think about it. Early/mid-twenties? Must be a model thing. Actually five of us in the house . . . Tubin and Bowie as well. I have no clue as to what kind of dogs they are . . . Small one? My first thought whenever I meet any dog is if it is going to be the one who decides to attack me for no reason (blame childhood experiences for that, I think). Thankfully Tubin and Bowie are small and cool. Unobtrusive. Chilled. One aspect I've yet to grasp, however, is the way girls go berserk when they see them: 'I seriously can't handle how cute these dogs are. Seriously. I can't handle it. I might just die. Oh my Gawd! So fricking cute.' Happened a lot today. After five times, the sheen wore off. General consensus is that they are cute dogs. Who get a lot of attention. A lot. Perhaps I'm jealous. Per-haps.

Shopping. Finally. Done. Home. Shower. Wallowing over. Sorry Bon Iver, not tonight. I'm heading out! Suss out the bars nearby. Rebound around the place. Bounce on! Girls? Too tired? OK. Which way should I go? Down the street. Down I go! First bar. At the bar. Order a drink. Sip. Sip. Two free drinks sent over to me. Compliments of those two guys. At the other side of the bar. Cheers lads. Nice of them. Nice fellows. Both have good posture. Interesting. Looked around. Noticed. A lot of guys in this bar with good posture. Peacock style. Tested the water . . . cheers everyone. All gave me a 'Heeeeeey' back. Good work by me. Rebounding is going well. First bar. Gay bar. Drinking on my own. Screams out the exact kind of message I was hoping for. Bar man see me comprehending all of this. Points me in the right direction. Chug. On my way.

Second bar. Barney's Beanery. College/sports bar. Not exactly what I was looking for either. But. At least a few women here. Pretend to look for friends at the bar. Fun solo drinking. Find a bar stool. Booze on. Two girls next to me spark up a conversation. Friendly girls. Jolly-looking. Remind me of Roseanne Barr.

Funny women. Realise they seem to be together. Buy me a shot. Buy me another one. Invite me to a party with them. Back at their place. Just the three of us. Just the three of us? That's no party! Oh. Right. Innuendos are being thrown at me. Few more shots are being thrown down me. Still very friendly and too jolly-looking. So I politely throw their innuendos away.

Drinks. Flowing. Mingling boots on. Meet a few girls. Ladies. Top o' the morn'. All fans of the Irish accent. All buying me whiskey. All because 'It's an Irish drink!' Six chunky shots later. Teaching them all made-up Irish dancing. Which unfortunately was my last definitive memory of the night.

I do know this. Next morning. Woke up. In my room. Half-naked. Half-wearing inside-out women's clothes. Highly confusing when still highly drunk. Girls burst in my door. Laughing at me. Why the funk am I wearing women's pants?! Explained. Skinny jeans I bought yesterday . . . Women's jeans. Oh right. That's how they're so skinny. All the guys wear them. Presumed I knew. I did not. I also didn't know why I would try them on at whatever hour I got home either though. Probably as I am an ape.

And the reason the girls were laughing at me? Seeing as I slept next to my bed. On the floor. Using my unopened sheets as a pillow. Why did I not sleep in the bed? Good question. I'll go with being a drunken ape. And I am a sheet head. Turns out, you actually *can* go wrong with sheets. My bed. Fit for a king. My sheets. Fit a queen! WeHoooooo!

Wingless Wonder

Strangely hung over all day. Strange, for a foreign country. Making me over-think it was a downer hangover. Ugh. Boots. No. Can't be wallowing still? Don't think so. In LA. Cop the funk on. Probably down to it raining on and off. That's it. Just SAD. Ha, c'mon sun. Sweat the booze out of me like a good man. Please. *Danke*. Day on the couch. Reining in flashbacks. Thinking about my nights out thus far. Timid enough. Boozing at home. Asleep on the couch. Wrong girl made the move. Timid. Last night, started off in a gay bar. Ended up in women's pants. A little less timid, but not really what I was after.

Kind of had a feeling I knew why. Something which first cropped up in Heathrow, waiting for my flight to LAX. Flying solo. Not always ideal. In the airport. Need to use the bathroom. However, no one to mind my luggage. Lugging suitcases into a cubicle. Not ideal. Flying solo is needed though. Can't sit and wait for others to come along all the time. Guitar over the shoulder and away you go time. Still, for certain things it would be better to have a buddy around. Would be handier while watching soccer matches. We could take turns in explaining all the rules, all the time, to friendly, yet uninterested, Americans. Minor issues really.

Only major downside of flying solo is the lack of a wingman. Or at least a buddy to go out boozing with. Obviously make friends over time. Initially a bit of an inconvenience though. Until then, two options really:

Sit around. Be bored.

Get up. Go out. Adventure on.

Only one option so really. Just deal with being lumped into the 'weirdo on his own' category. Although I do prefer solo clubbing to solo pubbing. Walking into a bar on your own, not meeting anyone in there, feels a bit like getting a table for one at a restaurant. Up there with sober dancing actually. As if a spotlight is shining on you. Glaring. Highlighting it all. Self-aware. Even though you know that nobody else is looking, or cares. Still awkwardly dancing. Clubs allow you to float around with far more ease at least. Innocuous. If anyone asks, pretend your friends are over there. Over where? Over there. By the other bar! Oh right. I like to over-think things. Moving on. Time to get rid of this hangover. Only one cure. Besides *The* Cure. Obviously. Oh Jesus. I need a drink.

Hans in the Hills

First Saturday night in LA. Big one. Shop. Beer. Booze on. Laptop pumping out songs. TV keeping me company. Crack open first can. Cheers! A toast. With myself. To myself! Crazy Saturday night party has begun! This was fun. Drinking from a crate of beer on your own is fun. As long as you're going to meet your buddies afterwards. Otherwise . . . Ahh, great fun. Drink more. Care less. About an hour later, good to go. Google (my new best buddy) recommends I check out Kress, a club right in the heart of Hollywood.

Taxi. Hollywood Boulevard. Pull up outside. Place is *swarming* with people. Talent. Unreal. Great call. Good man Google! Pretty big queue. Not a fan. I had a plan. Mosey my way over towards the barrier by the entrance. Opposite side of the queue. Pretending to look for someone. Is, eh, Joe around? Spot a guy with red hair holding a clipboard. Time to bluff. Wave him over. Hiya buddy! I met you last week, didn't I? Picks up on the Irish accent. He's Irish as well! Well, kind of. His Dad is one-third Irish. Maybe his grandparents. Who knows, who cares, we're both Irish! Plan works a treat. If you're just one Irish guy on his own, it's far easier to get into places, no matter what size queue. And to think you doubted flying solo?! In I go. Even lets me in for free. Won't lie, I thought I was great walking in.

Skipping the entire queue has other perks as well. A girl with another clipboard asks me if I'm going upstairs. Sometimes it's better to say less, nod more. Wraps a wristband around my arm. VIP. Happy days. Rooftop is VIP, basement is the normal club part. Up for a look. Layout is ridiculous. 'Panoramic views of all

Hollywood' as one idiot said to me. Maybe I said it to myself actually. Class décor. Funky lighting. All that crap. Cool place. Bit too cool. People are in their own groups. Sitting at tables. Being cool. No one else is really mingling. VIP seems to be where the cool people go to look cool. Like most places really. I try to fit in. Half-drunk, strolling around, saluting strangers. Sore thumb. Quick confusion with a girl who I think is offering me a drink. I'd love one, cheers. Turns out she's a cocktail waitress. Now I'm saluting people with my 'Big Pink Dink'. Costs me more than two crates of beer. Tastes non-alcoholic. Wuu.

As much fun as it was in VIP, I decided it was time to slum it. Basement. Club. Tunes are belting out! As I'm strolling around like I know where I'm going, a remix of 'Dancing With Myself' kicks in. Go on, the Billy Idol! Maybe that cocktail did have booze in it. Especially as I get the urge to go dancing, a rare occurrence. Either way, away I go, fist pumping in the air! Dancing with myself! Where are all the girls in Tokyo?! Go on LA! Go on LA girls!!!

One thing leads to another, and by the time the club is finishing up, I'm at the bar with a new group of buddies. Valley girls. Ha, this is brilliant. I thought the Valley was a myth! Calling them all Jessica and Elizabeth. They can barely understand my accent but the next thing I know I'm invited to their party. Sounds like we're dancing! Pardon? Say goodbye to my buddies first? Over where? Which bud— oh yeah. Went over to a group of random dudes sitting at a table finishing their drinks. Wished them a good night. High-fived them. Told them I was off. Left them pretty confused. See ye lads! Now where's this party? How are we getting there? One of the Sweet Valley High girls is driving. Did I not just do a shot with you a while ago? Three shots actually? No, OK, drive on!

Outside. Cold air. Bit hazy and foggy from here on in. I remember weaving through streets, uphill, on the way to the party. Turns out it was on in the Hollywood Hills. My first party in the Hills, wuu huu. Which, when you are drunk, is the greatest thing ever. Particularly being flanked by three girls from the Valley. Party on in a mansion. Huge! I remember thinking there was a lot of marble. Along with arches, chandeliers, staircases, and a big lit-up pool outside. Wandering off on my own. Couple of bars inside. DJ. Security. Hipsters. Suits. Women. Stereotypes. All over the place. The works. Lines for the bathrooms were ridiculously long. Presume people had weak bladders. Although maybe they actually did, in fairness to them. Seeing as they were all openly horsing into plates of white sugar while queuing up. Also not entirely sure but I *think* at one stage I walked into an orgy room upstairs as well. Or else it was just the bedroom where the naked people were hanging out. Not entirely sure. Decided to have a look at the pool outside.

Discovered another DJ playing outside. Along with another bar. Told to tuck in. Help myself. Jack. Pot. Don't say that to an Irish man. 'You're Irish?! Me too, tuck in!!' Call me Tucker. In I jumped. Happy days. Standing at the pool. Drinking out of a bottle of champagne. Overlooking the rest of LA. Thinking that this was like a scene out of *Entourage*. Think I was texting a few buddies at home that exact thought when a flamboyant little Italian man interrupted me. Introduced himself. Owner of the mansion. Fashion designer. Told me he was Irish. Didn't believe him. Although I did believe him when he said he loved Irish men. Just a weird vibe I got. Or maybe I got the weird vibe when he asked if I wanted to go upstairs and do drugs with him. Maybe that was it. Don't think he believed me when I told him I wasn't into drugs. Or having sex with men. Common misconceptions. Thankfully the Valley girls showed up. Whisked me away in time. Apologies John Lucky, I'm off. Pardon? Oh, sorry, Gianluca. Cheers Jan!

Unreal party all the same. Fun was had. Fake. Shallow. Drunk. Brilliant. Straight out of the movies. Just with an Irish ape floating amongst it all. Who then floated back into the night with the girls. Off to Sweet Valley High for yet another party. And then . . . eh, then the Big Pink Dink must've finally kicked in! Duu.

Sweet Valley of Jesus

Holy Mother of God. Woke up. Startled. Lost. Absolutely. Clueless. What's going on? Where am I? Why am I naked? More specifically, exactly whose bed am I in? Sat up. Looked around. Quickly figured out two things:

Still drunk.

Not fully naked. Remembered to put one thing on at least.

Ahem. Mouth parched. Chugged whatever concoction was in the mug next to the bed. Looked like water. Hoped it was water. Water turned into wine. Merely topping myself up. Surveyed the scene. Two beds in the room. Lots of photos on the walls. Lots of photos on the bedside drawer. Typical college girls' room. Oh yeah. Memory. I'm in the Valley. Suddenly get a call 'Come downstairs, Irish man!' Finish off what I now think was a mug of wine. Find my clothes. Hunt down my socks. Head downstairs. Check out my new Valley friends.

Walk into the kitchen/living room area. Realising I'd a little bit of a problem. Two girls were sitting on the couch. Another girl was in the kitchen. Realising the problem. Right about now. Funk. Think. Quick. Think! No clue of their names. That wasn't the problem though. Whose bed did I just wake up in?! Because if I figured that out, I could get a better idea as to exactly which girl I had . . . ahem. Oh Jesus. Not. A. Clue.

Kind of remember that I left the club holding hands with

one of the girls. Leaving the party in the Hills, I don't think it was the same girl. Party in their house. Bit of a blur. I do know. Wine. Vodka. Whiskey. Flowing. Other specifics? Non-existent. Constantly getting names wrong. They didn't care. Irish accent. I think. Chatting with one girl in the kitchen on my own. Perhaps chatting with the first girl from the club upstairs then though? I definitely remember my *ménage* suggestion getting rebuked. Girls can be so selfish at times. Sharing is caring.

Definitely wasn't the girl in the kitchen. Although there would've been no complaints. Just no blonde flashbacks. Unfortunately. Rule her out. Definitely one of the girls on the couch. Did not help at all that they looked very alike. In my memory bank, almost identical. Brown hair. Tanned. Brown hair. Tanned. Both looking at me oddly. Probably as I'd just been standing in the kitchen surveying them both. Without speaking. Eventually rattle out 'Morning girls! Eh, where the funk am I?' Turns out they like my accent just as much today. Not just a drink-related perk.

Both girls on the couch are in a great mood. Not so much the girl in the kitchen. Perhaps it was blondie after all? Oddly, both girls on the couch are being nice to me. Maybe they're just drunk as well. Flashbacks start to creep back into head. Definitely fooled around with both girls on the couch. Separately. Just no clue. Who was the final port. Back to where I am. Quickly get the rundown. In a valley. I know that. How do I get to We of the Ho? Taxi. Might take a while. Maybe their other roommate will give me a lift. Going that way after work. Will I give her money for gas? Perfect.

For the next twenty minutes, I dodge any specific questions or details about last night from the two girls on the couch. Concentrating on getting to know the third girl. I thought subtly getting her to spell the other girls' names might help me remember. Laura and . . . Lauren! No wonder I was on a slippery slope. Still clueless. Thankfully, I'm saved by the bell. More by the horn. Roommate. Finished work. Outside. Sweet Valley High girls, it's been a pleasure. We shall meet again! Bit of an awkward moment as both girls on the couch tell me I have their number. I will text ye both. At the same time. With the same text. Ciao ciao.

That mug of wine had me perked up. Postponing my inevitable cruel hangover. Flying form on the way home! Get on really well with the girl who is giving me a lift. Really funky chick. Likes cool music, wants to bring me to a few clubs she thinks I'll like. Sounds like a plan! Also helps that she's quite good-looking. All-American. Hot body. Cool dress sense. I'm a fan of her funk. And her funky-looking sunglasses. Pull up outside my house. Thanks for the spin. Starts to rattle off her number so I can call her. Only now do I realise my phone has died. While inspecting it, she takes off her sunglasses. This is the first time I have seen her eyes. And you know what they say . . . 'It's all in the eyes'. As she turns to face me, I notice that she has the laziest left eye I have ever seen in my life. Laziest. Ever. Did not expect that. At all. So I think I kind of gave a shocked, inquisitive look as she turned to face me full-on. I did feel bad. But I couldn't take my eyes. Off her eye.

In the end, I actually didn't get her number. Or give her mine. Blocking traffic. Cars beeping. All a bit rushed. Let's Facebook each other altogether. Thanks again for the spin. Wine wore off. Anyways, I would've felt bad doing it to Laura. Or Lauren.

Dumb Bum

Here's an amazing revelation that struck me in the face today. When I'm hung over, I am dumb. And. I am a bum. Dumb. Bum. Life is going as planned. Absolutely wrecked all day yesterday after my fun and frolicking the night before. Have an early night, then wake up fresh and ready to go! Ready to go do something productive! Would've been the right thing to do. However. I am. A dumb bum. Managed to let myself get over-tired and stay up until three in the morning, staring at the TV. Well worth it. Woke up. Wrecked. Probably more tired than when I went to sleep. Slow Monday morning. Although, I don't really think I ever saw the morning. Bad way to start the week. Quickly got worse.

Physically paying rent, handing the cash over, feels like someone is kicking me in the groin. Quickly followed by a punch in the sphincter. For five minutes. Especially when it's more than I budgeted for. And having committed to at least two months. Verbal contract. Chunk of a lump. Not planning on working. Got suckered in. Slightly sickening feeling. Regret. Despair. Disaster. Self-loathing. Followed by constantly readjusting my budget. Fooling myself. Reassurances built on some sort of belief. Thankfully, once the sixth minute arrived, all was good. Where there's a will, there's an LA! Or however that works. I'll figure something out. Still have a payment from the navy to come through. Safety net. No need to worry about it for another month.

Rent incident ensured it was a great morning/brunch/lunchtime. Focused me at least. Decided on something. Before acting classes started up. I would look for a job. Part-time. Cheap and cheerful. Keep me tipping over. Until the big break comes along. Pay for my nights out. First port of call. Obviously. Hunt down any Irish bars in the area. Thank God for Google. I would be lost without it. And as for Craigslist . . . Up there with one of the greatest sites of all time. Found me my apartment. My wonderful new home. Now supplying me with a few leads for bar work and the likes. All you need to get you set up in a new place. Google. Google Maps. Craigslist. Three Amigos.

Jess headed out for the day. Off to an audition for a movie. Which I thought was pretty funking cool! Amazing! Exciting!!! Bambi eyes. However, my bubble of excitement was burst. No big deal. Everyone has them. Just an everyday occurrence in LA. Layla relayed this information to me. Who was at home for the day as well. Looking for a waitress job. Amazing. Far more exciting than a boring audition. Must get some info from Jess later on. Figure out how and when I'll be able to head off to my own auditions! Bam. B!

Instead of staying in the house all day. Myself and Lay Diddy Lay headed off with our laptops to a coffee place. Fool ourselves into thinking the change of location would make us more productive in our hunt. I hankered for Starbucks, but Lay Diddy was hearing none of it. Apparently Coffee Bean is the hot spot around here. Coffee's coffee, but Coffee Bean is slightly nicer. Somehow. And if sitting around posing is your cup of tea, then you will fit right in. Sounds good. Should be like a duck to water!

Coffee is coffee but the whole ordering process is turning out to be an ordeal. Especially for a dumb bum like myself. Problem is that people struggle to understand my accent at times. Lots of the time. Taken at least a week for the two girls to comprehend the gist of what I'm saying. Still can't understand me on the phone. Ordering coffee can be a bit of a joke. Why do they insist on needing my name? People won't just let me order a coffee. Leave it at that. If only they would. If only . . .

'Hey there! How are you today? Fabulous day, huh?!'

'Yeah, great day, really great. Can I have a coffee please? Large. Small bit of sugar-free mocha powder in it as well, please? Thank you.'

(Frantic look of confusion) 'Emmm, I'm sorry. Can you repeat that please? A coffee?'

'Yeah, can I have a coffee with sugar-free moch— (Seeing the blank, bewildered look) . . . Actually just a COFFEE, PLAIN COFFEE. Please.' (Grunting and pointing at a picture of a cup of coffee)

'Oh, you do speak English. Coff-eeee, sure thing, no problem. What's your name?' (This is where it gets fun, does my name really have to be on the cup?!)

'Mark.'

(Confused) 'Merrick?'

'Ha, Mark.'

'Eric?'

(Oh, sweet Jesus) 'Nooo. MARK.'

'I'm sorry . . . Omar?'

(You dumb funk) 'Mark. MARK. M-A-R-K.' (Actually, I sound like the dumb funk!)

'Oh, you're silly. Mork! You should've said.'

'Yeah. Should've. Said. That.' (You silly m********* **** **** ****!!!)

Eventually he takes a cup from the counter next to him. Writes Merrick on it. Pours coffee into it. And hands it to me. While I stand there. Trying to figure out who exactly is the dumb one in the encounter.

While I scoured the internet for job leads and sipped on my hard-earned coffee, Layla reminded me about something . . . At times, girls telling me stories can be quite, quite, *quite* boring. About a guy they went on a date with. What a guy did that the girl didn't like. Or didn't do. Stories about guys being normal and just not into a girl as much as she thought. Not as exciting as it sounds. Stories with no real endings or punchlines. Stories where my advice is not actually being sought. 'What would I do? Chill out, don't worry about it.' Stories where the girl wants me to tell her what she wants to hear . . . 'Maybe he does like you. Maybe he was just tired. Maybe?'

What makes these stories so boring, is when I have to sit through various different versions of the same one. Initially, told the real version – the one where the guy kind of didn't give in to their every whim. Followed by listening to the story being told three more times on the phone to various different friends. Each time the girl in question becomes a stronger, more independent, beautiful woman! She is now Beyoncé!!! Actually, it was her who wasn't interested in the guy! Not the other way around. Who cares what I was told earlier. This is actually what happened!!! Finally, a couple of hours later, I am told the new and improved version of the story. Seemingly oblivious to the fact I was told the original, true version earlier on.

Although that is a bit like calling the pot black. Was it not I who earlier fooled myself into thinking I can easily manage to afford the rent? Potato. Tomato. Fool on! And I'm quite sure girls, guys, cats, dogs, cups of coffee, and so on, would find many of my stories boring. If they were repeated over and over. Which is why I've chosen to write them down.

Overall, after a slow, sphincter-squirming start, my day almost edged into the productive zone. Few job leads to follow up on tomorrow. Thanks Craig. According to Google Maps, one Irish bar was a forty-minute walk east of my apartment. Another was a forty-minute walk south. Get to know the area more by walking to these two places. Surely one will take me on. A real Irish person to work in their make-believe Irish bar! My two-day hangover levels started to decrease drastically. Allowing my optimism levels to shoot up. To round off a semi-productive day, Jess told me tonight that she would introduce me to her agent this week. First step on the path to my auditions. Dumb. Bum. On!

Trudging

What a great day! For walking. For job hunting? Ehh, not so much. Decided it would be pointless to just ring up Irish bars, hoping they'd hire me over the phone. Instead, I'd call in and charm them in person. Do a little jig if needed. Smart plan. Only took me an hour to walk to the first bar. Google Maps had lied, told me forty minutes. Must've estimated that I either power-walk or march like a soldier. Flip-flops and heat allowed for neither.

Get down to the pub, Molly Malone's. A Mexican guy is the only person working. Can't understand me. Not a clue what I'm asking him. 'Owner? Manager? Want me to jig?' A few other patrons at the bar find it hilarious that he works in an Irish pub, is wearing a T-shirt saying 'I'm Irish. F**k you' but can't understand my Irish accent. And, in my opinion, not even a thick accent! I actually think he's faking it. Seemed to understand me initially. Until I asked if any jobs were available. Spoke Spanish only after that. *Señor. No.* Keeping all the hours for himself. In the end, the two American dudes who found the whole scenario ridiculous bought me a beer. And then got a bit racist about it: 'This Mexican f**k is working in an Irish bar and can't understand an Irish accent. My Gawd. Stupid Mexican f**ker. You should just take this f**k's job.' OK. Eh. OK? Cheers for the beer, lads, I'll be off.

Worst part about walking for an hour to get somewhere is the fact you have to walk for another hour to get back home. Why not get a taxi, I hear you say? Well, I am sick of paying for cabs already. It's a joke. I can't afford to keep paying over $200 a week on cabs. Especially when I know they are taking me the longest way home (I think, still not familiar enough with the area, 90 percent sure). Is it just me as well, or do cabmen in LA not know where anywhere actually is? Asking me for directions for different streets?! I've no clue. It's the dumb leading the dumb. When I tell them that, for example, I don't know where a certain nightclub is, added to them hearing my accent, they take me on a tour of LA. And there's only one chump who's going to end up paying for it! So, that's why I have decided to use my legs as much as possible. Sick of being ridden.

'Well, why don't you use public transport, you clown,' I hear one last person in the corner say. Unfortunately, LA appears to be unlike every other big city I've been to in the world. Public transport is horrific. Apparently there is an underground. Just nowhere near me, or where I'd want to go. Handy. Only means of public transport I've seen are the buses. Which only seem to carry homeless people or crackheads. Bringing them where, I don't actually know. I tried to find a route or bus that might be able to get me around. Almost broke Google. All the routes appear to be nonsensical. With most buses just going to the ghettos, I think.

Personally, I get a great buzz out of knowing my way around somewhere, and not just feeling like a tourist. My feet will do the walking. Get to know the place. Already I think LA looks like a nightclub. Cool at night. Looks good. Comes to life. Place you want to be. During the day, however, it's dead. Looks like a dump. Smells a bit like puke. Parts are ghastly. Maybe that's why nobody walks anywhere. Homeless people might be hanging out on street corners. Might see people coming in and out of shops. Few others on the street though. Just me and my iPod. Strolling along. Talking to myself. Trying to neutralise my Irish accent a bit for any potential job interviews.

Once I left Molly Malone's, felt a bit deflated. Estimated it would take me about an hour and twenty minutes to walk to the second Irish pub on the list. Now four o'clock in the afternoon. Long walk. Could just go home. Try that bar tomorrow. On the other hand, it would take me along Melrose, through Beverly, up Fairfax, along Highland and into Hollywood. Doing the walk would make me familiar with a sizeable chunk of the area. Still though, what if it's just another Mexican behind the bar? Clever me, I'll ring ahead. What I should've done the first time. *Dring, dring.* Talk to a girl who's not too sure if they're looking for staff. Manager is on at six though. Call in then and speak to him. Actually, she just got a job so thinks they are hiring! Sounds good. Cheers. Walk on!

Two hours later, I finally reach the Cat 'n' Fiddle pub. Two minutes later, I leave the Cat 'n' Fiddle pub…

'Hi, could I speak to the manager please?'

'Yeah, that's me.'

'I rang earlier, just wondering if you're looking for any barmen at the moment?'

'No, sorry, we hired a girl last week.'

'Oh yeah. She said that. Thanks.'

Good work. Good walking. Gave in. Flagged down a cab. Take me home. Gave the cabman my address. He told me I'd be better off walking. Traffic was gridlock heading that way. Mighty work. Back out of the cab. Should only take me twenty minutes to walk it, cabbie reckoned. Wrong. I'd researched it earlier on Google Maps. Forty-three-minute walk. To be exact. Trudging along. Beaten docket. Jobless. Clueless. Knowing one thing for certain: I need a car. Cars cost money. More money than I had budgeted for. Could do with getting a job.

Freddie Cougar

Productive morning. Kind of. Spent a few hours on Craigslist applying for every single job possible. Also posted a few ads in the 'Services' section. Racked my brains for absolutely anything I could offer. Besides my body. And sexual services. Obviously. Not that desperate. Yet.

Translator. German lessons. Irish lessons. Maths lessons. Dialect coach. (Apparently actors pay to talk to people with genuine accents.) Web designer. Soccer coach. Even applied to a few cushy-looking personal-assistant jobs ('duties include grocery shopping, collect dry cleaning, driving, etc'). Had to keep telling myself it was only to keep me ticking over. Not long-term career options. No one cares what you used to do here! Swallow that pride. Just hit apply!

Decided to head up to Starbucks for a coffee. Wasn't in the mood for shouting my name at the server in Coffee Bean. Forgot that coffee is coffee. So is ordering. Starbucks is actually even worse. Far worse. Starting to see how Michael Douglas lost it in *Falling Down*. Something so basic as ordering coffee is somehow made into a frustrating, mind-melting ordeal. From now on, whatever they think I said is going to be my coffee-ordering name. Today, I was good old Merrick.

As an added bonus, they got my order wrong four times. Four funking times! 'Order for Merrick!' I didn't order an iced coffee. I ordered a normal coffee. 'Order for Merrick!' Ehh, I actually said no whipped cream on top. 'Merrick! Merrick!' What's this, tea? Coffee. (Deep breaths.) I ordered coffee. 'Merrick! Coffee. Sugar-free mocha. No cream. No ice.' Oh sweet Jesus. Yeah, no, that is what I ordered. I actually paid for a large one though. You've given me a small one. No it's fine, it'll do, close enough. And then I break down. Fall down. Snap. I assume that will happen in the not-so-distant future anyway.

By way of an apology, they give me all four concoctions to keep. Now laden with a tray of drinks, so tried to hand them out for free to people in the queue. Who didn't know what was going on, and looked at me like I was offering them poison. Whole affair was farcical. And made me think of Michael Douglas some more. Dumped the spare drinks. Went outside to chill out.

While doing anything but enjoying my coffee (Was he just taking the piss out of me? Should I go back in and hurl the coffee at him?! Argghhhh) I noticed a woman next to me looking at me. And yup, laughing at me. Icing on the funking cake. Are you OK? Are you laughing at me? 'Oh my Gawd, that was just too funny. You are too funny.' Thanks. You ape. 'Can I join you? Where are you from? Where's that accent from? So cool!' My accent is from Ireland, but I'm from Wisconsin. 'Oh my Gawd, you're so funny!' Noticed she kept telling me I was funny. As opposed to doing what you do when you actually find something funny. Laugh. Lying to me. In her defence, horrendous jokes.

Although she wasn't lying about really liking my accent. Fascinated by it. Still annoyed. Takes off her sunglasses. Hello. Older than I thought. Hotter than I thought too, though. All in the eyes! Ms Cougar, how are you?! Small-talk time. Asking what I was doing in LA. Asked if I had seen the views from the top of the Hollywood Hills. Did I want to go see them now? Erra shur, why not? My job-hunting is done for the day. Waiting on replies. Views on, Cougar Lady! Nice car by the way. Hood down. Convertible on. Driving up winding roads in a convertible Merc is great fun. Although I think she took me on the least scenic route possible. Every street seemed exactly like the one I lived on. Which she found hilarious. Laughing at all my jokes. Or, to be exact, laughing while I spoke. Never really at the punchlines.

And then. At some point. Her hand ended up slapping my knee. Finally on cue with a punchline! Nudged her back. Making her put her hand back on my knee once more. Dearie me. Tension rising the further we went up the hills. Until we met a sharp fork in the road. Started to daydream a bit. Contemplating was there an alternative reason for this trip, not just the view? Is she going to pull in somewhere? Why did she bring me this secluded way? Should I make my move while she was driving? Wait until we got to the top? What's the protocol here? Hang on. Hup. Looks like her hand is making the move. On my knee. On my thigh. On my . . . oh my. OK. What should I do? When should I do it?! What's she saying? Still yapping. Listen. Sharp fork. Heard what she was saying. Eh, pardon me?

Heard her mention Jackie Chan. Who now trains him? Trains with him? Did I hear that right? As in the martial arts guy Jackie Chan? As in you have a husband? I'm going to go right ahead and assume that your husband is some sort of ju-jitsu expert. Or whatever martial art is popular at the moment. Why did you mention you had a husband? At least wait until after anything might happen. Would've made a great bailout excuse for me as well! Any sexual tension that was there quickly jumped out of the convertible. On my side, at least. Her hand was still. Still. Eh. Where was I?

Seeing as the sexual tension was no longer obscuring my sight, I noticed that she had the lingering look of a crazy woman. Holding my stare for those few seconds too long. Her laugh was less of a laugh as well. Not really a chortle either. More a cackle.

Oh dear God. Seems a tad nutter-ish, now I'm thinking straight. Why are we taking this back route? Fewer witnesses?! Get to the peak, where she wanted to bring me. Spectacular, glorious views. As she kept repeating. Nice views. Great. Couldn't concentrate. Wondering if her husband would have a problem with me sharing these spectacular, glorious views with his wife. Or the whereabouts of her hand.

Thankfully, she believed me when I said I really needed to go food shopping. Better head back. Better head. She was a determined cougar! Finally got going. Arrangements were made on the way home. By her. For us to meet in Starbucks again tomorrow. Her husband would be at work, so it would be something fun for her to do. I smiled. Along. Yes. See you tomorrow. And gave her my fake number. Insisted that I kiss her goodbye the French way. So I gave her two kisses on the cheek. Started to cackle. Staring me down. Haha, ha, ha, no problem. Kiss kiss. Finally unlocked the car doors. Hurriedly skipped out. Freaked that the people walking past the car might know her husband. Quickly dodged into Trader Joe's as she waved goodbye. A random way to spend an hour or two. Be careful of Freddie Cougars!

Into Trader Joe's. Might as well do my weekly food shopping now I'm here. Mighty place. Healthy. Cheap. Tasty. Mighty work, Joseph! While I was mulling over my turkey-slices options, I noticed someone not noticing me as hard as she could . . . the Cat Woman. Didn't recognise her at first without the cats. Great small-talk banter over the turkey options. Got bit sour when I asked how her cats were: 'How's my buddy Pumpkin?' Turns out, Pumpkin died. I knew it. Lying there, looking at me with glazed eyes, on the way out. Cat Woman got a bit emotional talking about it. Eyes started to well up. Not too sure what the protocol is when you're consoling someone over their dead cat. A hug? Too much? Better not, after Freddie Cougar earlier. Kept my distance. Ended up patting her on the shoulder with my turkey slices. She appreciated it. Good old shoulder-tapping.

In fairness to the Cat Woman, she's funny enough. In a slightly weird way. Better-looking than I'd remembered as well. In case you were wondering. Gave me a lift home from the shop. Straight home. Nothing happened. Although she did mention that she might have a friend who could do me a deal on a car. Anything else? Yes indeed, the same friend might also know of people looking for help on movie sets. Nothing major, but could be a way to see how it all works behind the scenes. More importantly, might help to keep my bar tabs flowing. Go on the cats and cougars!

Crazy Town

Yesterday my job-hunting attempts were pretty poor. Undeterred. Today I had interviews. First place was an Asian bar/restaurant/don't-have-a-clue-what-it-was-meant-to-be. Open interviews from twelve to two, a Craigslist find. Showed up for twelve. Maybe half-past. Huge, *huge* queues outside. Group of us told to come back at two. Came back at two. Apparently, over two thousand people had showed up. For two positions! (Turns out they'd gone through the same process the day before.) As a result, they were just taking people's CVs and getting in touch with certain candidates once they'd scoured all of them. Eh, CV? I actually don't think I've even made out a CV in my life. Maybe when I was about fourteen? I thought it was a case of showing up and being interviewed. Fill out one of their forms. Charm them. Like a normal bar interview. In the end, I wrote my name and number on the back of a beer mat. Still waiting to hear back from them. Should be in the bag.

Second open interview, Barney's Beanery. Same bar I ended up in on my first night of pub-hopping. Another setback. Started off well. Until I was asked about my social security number. Good question. I'm hoping to get one of those new one-year visas that are coming out. Waiting to hear back from the company that's processing them. Told me it should be fine. Visa is related to me having a master's degree. Should be no problem. Yeah, technically I don't have a social security number. You'll call me, is it? No, you won't even call me, you'll tell me now . . . No. Cool, thanks.

Third and final bar was an English pub somewhere along Melrose. The manager of Barney's told me they might take me on. Seeing as it's an English pub. And I'm Irish. Decided that that logic was worth the walk down to try at least. The name appealed to me as well . . . The Village Idiot. Melrose is the coolest street I've seen in LA so far – funky, cool, artsy, the vibes were flowing. People were actually on the street as well, seemed to be a bit busy! Plus, the talent was unreal. Maybe this is where I should be living!

My directions had been 'Left on Melrose, walk down about five minutes, you'll see the pub on your left'. Twenty minutes after taking that first left, still no sign. Turned back, still couldn't find it. More directions needed. As it happened, the two girls I asked for directions are also Idiot-bound. Follow, follow, follow on. Seems I walked by the place twice. Even stood outside the bar and wondered if it might be across the road. Minute I walk in, I knew this was not the place I was hoping for. All the staff were wearing uniforms. Even wearing aprons with their uni-forms. Uniforms with aprons are the cornerstone of social secu-rity establishments! Bob Hope I'd be getting a job on the sly here. Might as well join the two girls for a drink.

From previous visits to America, I knew having an Irish accent is an advantage. However, having one in LA is on anoth-er level. OMG, it's like you have a mythical, mystical mouth organ. Is that real? Producing orgasmic lyrical gems for certain people. 'Say it again!' Not a bother. 'Oh my Gawd!' These girls only invited me for a drink to listen to me speak. I know this for a fact. Don't give a flying funk what I actually say. Just as long as I say it. With my accent. Every single one of my horrendous jokes is going down a treat. Noticing, once again, that most of the time they're not really laughing at my punchlines. Just laughing because I say the word 'ye'. Or speak in a hubbula-hub-bula kind of way. Or state the obvious. Say it again, leprechaun boy, jump higher! Seeing as they are kind of very good-looking and a good laugh, I jump higher. Erra shur, why not?

Before I know it, three bottles of wine are gone. Girls are ordering Patron. It's about four in the afternoon. I'm meant to be job-hunting. Knuckling down. Focusing. Not knocking down bottles of booze! One shot of Patron later, and I cross the drink threshold. Can't stop now. Just as we finish that shot, their buddy shows up. Wahey, let's get another shot. After we down that, I recognise their friend. Singer from Crazy Town. In case he'd for-gotten about being in the band, I remind him 'You are Crazy Town! LA is crazy town!!! Let's do another Patron . . . to "Butterfly"!' Suddenly, it's five past four. And I. Am. Drunk.

About nine bells, the two girls and myself stumble out of the bar. They suggest we go along to some beach bar or bikini bar where one of them works. Nay. Too far away. Next time. Party on in my house! Stop off at a liquor store to buy far too much booze. One girl wants to stop off somewhere else en route to buy some Coke. I tell her we have diluted stuff for mixing already. I think I've Pepsi in the house as well? She really wants some Coke. OK, cool, no problem. Don't really cop on to this at all at the time. Did think it was weird waiting outside some-one's house while she went in and got a bottle of Coke. Dumb. And. Drunk. Now I know why she never bought me the packet of Tic-Tacs that I asked her for.

Unfortunately the party was a bit of a non-starter. Jess and Layla were too busy being hypnotised by *American Idol*. Did not appreciate my drunk, fun, *hilarious* ways. Didn't seem to connect with my two new friends either. Girls can be so warm to each other at times, ha. Me not remembering/knowing the girls' names didn't really impress either. I only remembered calling them B&B. Brandi and Brittany? Not impressed. Sober folk. Trying to watch their favourite TV show. Drunk apes. Trying to party. Oil and water.

Funk this, let's party up in my bedroom. We need some music. Laptop on! Wuu! Some party. Although. When you're drunk. And have a few bottles of vodka and whiskey to keep you ticking over. Any party should be good. More importantly, I realised in a moment of clarity, without trying, I somehow ended up with two good-looking women in my bedroom. How the funk did that happen? Wasn't I meant to be job-hunting?! One girl asked if she could use my bathroom. While in there, the other girl and I . . . just had a weird thought. Ever see the movie *Blow*? Great movie. Not sure why that popped into my head. Weird. Anyways. First girl walks back out of my bathroom. Sees us. Talking. Turns around. And then takes a shower? An hour later (fifteen minutes? half an hour?), Blow says she has to head home. Her boyfriend will be wondering where she is. Never mentioned him before. Suspicious. Just let me subtly frisk you first . . . No, looks good. Looks like you haven't robbed me. Eh. OK. You better go meet him so. Good work. And goodbye.

First girl comes out of the shower. Friend has left. She doesn't mind. Realise she's just wearing my towel. Few more drinks. She then proceeds to . . . Another weird thought just came into my head. My favourite colour is blue. Weird. Just popped into my head. Where was I . . . can't remember. Too much vodka and whiskey flowing. Goosed. Not even eleven o'clock. Drunk as skunks. Peaked too soon. Her boozing stamina waned. Dipped. Fell asleep. I was too awake. Went downstairs. Trying to have conversations with sober people. Great hoot. Great party! Fell asleep watching infomercials. Sex. Drugs. Rock and roll!

Except I unfortunately didn't end up actually having sex. And didn't do any drugs. Shots with Crazy Town was a bit rock and roll. A bit. Especially when you're meant to be out hunting down a job. I did well there. Go me. Although at least I did get two . . . I joke. I swear. Duu.

McJob

9.00 Woke up with far too much pep in my step. Bouncing around the place on my way to get some water. Realised I was also bouncing off the walls. Still drunk. Back to bed.

13.00 Think I've managed to sleep through my hangover. Sweated it out. Humidity might've helped. Roasting. And raining. What the funk is going on with the weather in LA?! Like typhoon season. Actually, even worse – like a summer's day in Ireland.

Breakfast and a quick trawl through Craigslist. Think I'm obsessed with finding a job. That I don't want. Just because I can't get close to finding one. One ad showed slight potential. Nightclub PR. Thought my club promotion days were over but I need cheap and cheerful. Should be a shoo-in. Emailed for more info. Quick response. Interview. Today. Two bells. Beverly Hills. Ha, this lead actually looks promising. Threw on my best shirt. Combed my hair. With my hands. Drank a few cans of Red Bull. Good to go.

17.00 Interview over. Strange experience. Got a taxi to their offices in Beverly Hills. Impressive set-up. Well, the building at least. When I arrived I was told I just missed the initial batch of group interviews. Sat around for an hour in the lobby waiting for the second batch. Finally got called to go and wait in another room. A nineteen-year-old dude with a Mohawk had also been waiting around in here for the same length of time. Sound guy. Bonded over our common dislike of waiting. Such a joke, man.

Complete joke. Worried that he should've worn a shirt like I did. Also worried his Mohawk might hold him back. And that he's nineteen. Don't worry buddy, you'll be fine! (If the position was between Moe and myself, I was quietly confident.)

Finally get called in. Introduced to Lola. Interviewer. Seems I've actually been paired up with my new buddy, Moe. Not too sure how they managed to do that. Were they watching us on CCTV? Apparently, we had similar styles and might work well together. I was wearing a shirt. Trying to look respectable. He had a Mohawk, ripped shorts and was holding a skateboard. On looks alone, I couldn't see how we were paired up. Apparently we were also matched based on our personality types. She gathered my personality from a three-sentence email? Was this a dating service? Lola was extremely impressed with both of us up to this point. Emm, how so exactly? The only thing I've said so far has been 'Howdy', while Moe mentioned he was in a hurry. Neither of us had CVs. Neither of us knew anything about the company. Except its name, 5 Star.

My rational side was quickly told to shut up by the rest of me. Lola started to tell us what the job would entail, along with the perks. Promote different nightclubs. On the night of an event we would be expected to mingle with the clientele in the VIP areas. Ensure they were having fun. Started showing us photos of her in different clubs . . . Here's her with Beyoncé and Jay-Z. There's her with some Playboy models. That's where you could be if you get this job. Oh my golly gosh, please let me get this job! Lola then stopped talking for a few seconds. Looking at us. Nodding. Saying there was something about us. She just got a feeling we would both be a good fit. Lo and behold, we were then told we both got the job?! On the spot! Wuu huu! Myself and Moe. Dream team!

Wait. Rational side whispered in my ear. What about payment? We would get paid. Providing. The club is busy. Then we get paid. Per head. All of which sounded reasonable. Normal. Ignoring the rocky start to the interview, this seemed like it was legit. Only immediate problem I saw was that I could count on one hand the number of people I knew in LA. Decided against mentioning this. Lola was busy logging Moe and myself into their online guest list system. We could now add people as we please. That's it. We're done. Sent us on our merry way.

Outside. High-five avec Moe. I hailed a cab. Moe skated off. Both of us delighted. I have a job! Must text everyone in Ireland with the good news. My job is to mingle with VIPs. Like I'm one of them. Aren't I just great?!!

18.20 I am on fire! Might have another job. Text from Cat Woman. She's meeting her friend this evening. Will ask her about the car and the job. Things are coming together nicely!

20.00 Roommates think the PR job is superb. Congrats all round. Just not so great that I only know four people (two roommates and two girls from yesterday). I inform them that I know Cat Woman. And, tell them about Freddie Cougar. That's six. And I do know a few girls from the Valley as well. Nine people. I'm doing well. Maybe if each person brought ten friends to the nightclub, I might be able to make some money. Convince myself this sounds reasonable.

Layla and Jess put a bit of a damper on the Cat Woman scenario as well. Suggest she might have an alternative motive for helping me. Free car? And a job? Asked how old she was. Being honest, no clue. Maybe thirty. Could be older, but looks younger? Was she single? No clue. Who's the friend? No clue.

They're convinced she wants to help me out for one reason only. Tut tut. Suspicious minds.

23.00 Just got a text from Lola. Did I want to go clubbing with her? She could show me the ropes and all that. Not meant to start until tomorrow night, but if I want to go out with her tonight, could be fun. Bring my friends along too: the more the merrier. Long enough day. Fairly tired. Spoof I already had plans. Can't make it. Chill on.

23.10 No reply. Freaked. I might have blown my chances. Was that a test? Should I have been more eager? Might go clubbing with her. Text back that I've changed my mind.

23.30 No reply. Bad reception in the house. Better go outside to make sure.

23.45 Sent the text again. Not sure if the first one actually sent. Forgot I had reports. Text her again saying sorry for re-sending all the texts.

00.10 Just got a reply. 'Something's come up. Can't talk now.' That's it. Bit odd. What do I reply to that? Better say I want to go clubbing still. Act eager. Hope everything else is OK.

00.20 Everything is OK. (Phew). Except she's just had to resign from the company. Family emergency. (Ehhh, pardon?!)

00.40 'On the way home to Texas. No longer with the company.' What the funk?! Reply saying I hope everything is OK, anything I can do, etc. Most importantly, does this affect me in any way?

00.55 Lola just recommended me to the owner of the company for her old job. Gave him my CV. (What C-funking-V?!) Sent me the owner's name and number. Call him tomorrow. She's really upset that we wouldn't get a chance to work together. Yeah, me . . . what, wait?! I'm completely lost. Do I have a job? Did I just get a promotion? Hope your family emergency is not serious. Do I still have a job? Did I ever have a job?

01.00 Text from Cat Woman: 'What are you up to?' Actually have no clue what I'm up to, or what the hell is going on! Gets lost in translation. Her friend wants to meet me. She's interested in letting me have her car for free. Ring her tomorrow. OK. Thanks? Weird day. Or maybe I'm just *waaay* more hung over than I thought. And, as a result, dumber than I thought? Maybe the day is normal. Maybe it's more me.

01.40 Just re-Googled the PR company. 5 Star Promotions. Appears to be real. I can log into the guest list system. Might not be losing my mind. Need sleep. Still no reply from Lola.

02.40 Heard a vibration. Reply. Looks like my job is gone. Great. All the people she hired today are going to be let go. Mighty stuff. Recommended me for her old position though. Ring the owner tomorrow. Lola thinks I'll get it. Super funking news.

Hired. Fired. In under twelve hours. The. Funking. Job.

A Hippie and My Leprechaun

Circles. Roundabouts. Chasing my own tail. What happened to chasing the dream?! Cheap and cheerful job-hunting was making me anything but cheerful. My inability to get such a job leaving me fully sidetracked. Was I not able to do it? Surely I'm making this far harder than it needs to be. Do I even need a job? I'm here to act and write. Surely those avenues will be paying my bills pretty soon. Still have navy money backing me up. At the same time, I am spending money like a crazy pregnant woman. Need something to balance the flow gushing out on a daily basis. With that in mind, I was determined to nail down something definitive today. Informal interview today. Cat Woman's friend. Pye. Who turned out to be a full-on hippie. What could go wrong?!

Spoke to Pye on the phone in the morning. Enjoyed saying 'Hi Pye'. Proposed a deal to me . . . I could use her BMW, in return for doing a few handy jobs around her house. No mention of money. Still, if I could get a BMW in return for a few odd jobs, it'd be better than a kick in the balls. Or having to walk everywhere. My roommates warned me that I was being a bit naive. Seemed to think something else was being implied by handy jobs. Laughed it off. As if. I wish. Probably just needs me to change a few light bulbs. Anything more complicated than that, I might be struggling. Better not think I'm a qualified handyman or anything. Considered buying a tool belt to make myself look more legit. Play it by ear first.

Lived close enough to me, so I walked down to her place at about one o'clock. First impressions when I met her were: 'Not bad. Not bad at all.' Bit older than I thought, mid to late thirties.

(Maybe Cat Woman was older too so?) Seemed cool enough. Also quite spaced-out. And had a lot of airy-fairy mannerisms. Kept saying 'Uuuhhhhuuum' before, during and after I spoke. Don't think she understood/cared what I was saying. Musician. Cartoonist. Hippie. To the core. As she showed me around her house, I made sure to flick every light switch (subtly). All seemed to work fine. Maybe I was needed to paint? Wait, aha. Bulb in the bathroom was blown. I knew it. Legit.

Conversation got around to the handy-jobs-for-car scenario. Call around twice a week. Help her out. Car was mine during the week in return. Hardly ever used it. Just drop it back on Friday evening. Collect again on Monday. All she'd have to do would be to ring the insurance company and put me on her policy. And then. Thunderbirds. Would be go. Sound good to me? Convertible Beamer. In exchange for very little work? Obviously. Sounds very good! What kind of jobs had you in mind? 'We'll see what needs to be done as we go along.' Now. Would I like some lunch? A drink perhaps? Celebrate our new arrangement? Although it wouldn't be official until Monday. Couldn't ring the insurance company until then. We should celebrate still though? Yeah, sure Pye, one drink and a spot of lunch sounds good! By the way, one of the bulbs in your bathroom looks dodge, I'll go take care of that right now!

Arrived back from the light-bulb changing. Lunch was ready. And on the table. Along with a few bottles of wine. Was it not just one drink, no? Few bottles later, and I realise that even though she is the one constantly topping up my glass, I'm the more sober of the two. Or else she is just really out of it all the time. An hour was spent listening to stories about her spiritual trips to India. Where she met her spiritual guru. Who showed her the true meaning of life. Visits her constantly in LA.

Travelling all the way from India. Appearing. Through visions. Where he just shows up as a mirage in front of her. And points her on the right path. I asked if she could get him to show up now. We sat and waited. And waited. He never showed up. Must've been busy.

Felt she was outdoing me with all her gibberish. I had heard too much about her Swamiji. Might as well gibber back. So I told her all about my leprechaun. Growing up on a leprechaun farm. My favourite leprechaun since my childhood, Timmy O'Toole. Missed him dearly. He was kind of like my spiritual leader. Who, in fact, also visited me now and again through visions. Would just show up out of the blue and do a little jig for me. Take off his hat. Tilting it. Pointing me in the right direction. Usually towards the bar. All of which led her to believe that we shared a deep, spiritual connection. Meaning that she believed me. Meaning at this point I started to wonder if the wine was spiked. Definitely laced with some sort of hippie potion.

Being honest, all that was fine. When she went to her room. To change. And came back out wearing a dressing gown. That was fine too. Started to get slightly odder. Asked me if I like to wear leprechaun outfits. Would I wear a leprechaun outfit if she had one? Do I like little people? Did I ever do anything with a leprechaun? Hahahaha, haha, ha, ha. The last question made me worry the most, for some reason. Did she genuinely believe I might've had sex with a leprechaun before? Was I putting the right two and two together here? Double-checked to make sure we were drinking out of the same bottle. I was a bottle ahead. Maybe she's drinking the spiked drink meant for me? Or she's just a nut?

When she asked me if I wanted to go to her room to look at leprechauns on her computer, there were a few reasons why I made an excuse to leave:

Waiting until I'm married. Obviously.

Preferably like to find out *after* anything happens, if the girl is a nut-job. Not beforehand. Preferably.

What if she meant go look at midget porn?

What if she really did mean go look at leprechauns on her computer? And produced a leprechaun outfit for me to wear? And some dude walked out of the closet. Filming it all? What if?!

For all of those reasons, I decided I might want to go home for a bit. Particularly when she returned from her room once more, hiding something behind her back. Guess what I have? Ehh, ha ha, gulp, what? Revealed, a green hat. True, it might've been an innocent St Patrick's day novelty hat. However, what if . . . ?! Too many what-ifs. Stood up. Backed my way towards the door. Told her I had to go home for a while. Think I'm, eh, meant to be meeting someone at my house. Who? Do you know what, I'm not really sure of his name. What were we going to do? Go to my friend's party. Whose party? Again, I'm not too sure whose party it is, just got invited along. Said I'd go though. Robe slightly opening. By Christ, is that the time? Better leave now, need to shower and get ready. I might be back later though. I'll give you a call. Just lay off the leprechaun porn. Or at least wait until I'm as drunk as you are. Bye Pye!

Thankfully, my gibberish threw her off long enough for me to make my escape. Left her there. In her living room. Robe open. Holding a leprechaun hat. With the familiar sound of Indian scat singing wailing out from a speaker somewhere. Kind. Of. Odd. Giddy up out. Hip-hopping home with a pep in my step. Weirdly, I actually wasn't lying to her either. Well, bar the part about coming back to watch midget porn with her. No intention of that. The rest was true though. Bizarrely. I'll let you know how it goes. Must shower on and wash the hippie weirdness off first. Hope Timmy O'Toole shows up at some stage. Must ask him if it was the right call or not to have left Pye high and dry!

Blood, Sweat and . . .

As I said yesterday, I had to leave the hippie (and her drunk, kind-of-odd leprechaun fetishes) to go meet two friends last night. Using 'friends' in the loosest possible way. Particularly as I'd never met one person, and can't remember meeting the other. Looking back at it now, maybe I would've been better off staying with the hippie. Letting her dress me up as a leprechaun probably would've been the safer bet. Unfortunately Timmy O'Toole never appeared in a vision to guide me in the wrong direction. Probably too busy doing a jig back on the leper farm back home. Obviously.

Solid plan was in place. Meet up with a guy who I've never met before. Go to a girl's birthday party who I don't remember meeting before. Guy. Sean. Strong ties. From LA. Has cousins in Cork. His cousin is my buddy. Sean visited Cork. Loved it. Last week my buddy suggested that I should meet up with his cousin who's from LA. Good laugh to go boozing with. Good man to get women. Why not. Saturday? Yeah. I have a party for us! Birthday party. Girl. Rebecca. I was in a club last week. Apparently I met her. She gave me her number. Took my number. Can't really remember. Sent me a text. Invited me to her birthday party. House party. DJ. Kegs. Sounds good. Should be good. Please be good.

Seven bells. Sean comes to my house. Small talk. Informal formalities. I'm kind of drunk after hippie woman's wine potions. Sean's sober. Driving. Time to go party on. Unsure of the address but he knows the general direction. Google Maps fills in the blanks. Chunky drive. Maybe forty-five to fifty minutes. Job. Off we go. Fun car ride! On the way, I'm telling him about the hippie, the leprechaun, reels of gibberish. Sean tells me nothing. Not big into talking, it seems. After twenty-five minutes, I think it's time to just sit and listen to whatever CD is playing. Getting blood out of a turnip. Sean's a great laugh. Nice one, buddy back home.

Eventually we get to the general area of where the party is on. I get Sean to pull up outside a liquor store so I can run in and get a bottle of vodka for the party. Even though I'm after a fair bit of wine and everybody's best friend, I notice that I'm getting weird looks from folk in the liquor store. Dodgy looks. Must be trying to figure out my accent. Think nothing of it. Get back to the car. Sean's not happy. Realised something. What, Sean? Tell me. Talk!!! Oh. We're in gang territory. Bloods, to be exact. Spoof. What? No way. Chill out, man. Wants to know if I'm winding him up. Calm down, it's cool. How do I know Rebecca? Dodge the question. Better off not knowing that I have no clue about her. Not even what she looks like. I tell him it'll be fine when we get to the party. Rebecca's cool. You'll like her, Sean. No way she's in a gang. Catch my reflection in the windscreen. Reminded that I'm wearing a light blue T-shirt. Baby blue to be exact. Is this like me disrespecting the Bloods? Don't think about it. Keep calm. It'll only freak Sean out more. Drive on buddy!

No sign of the intersection I was told to look out for. Phone Rebecca. First time speaking to her on the phone. People here can't understand my accent when I'm talking to them face-to-face. Over the phone is one of the most frustrating things conceivable. For me at least. I assume for the person on the other end as well. Me screaming down the phone as clearly as I can. Being asked in return if I can speak in an American accent. Me shouting in a hybrid kind of accent. Inevitably hanging up.

Resuming texting communication. No different with Rebecca. Although I do manage to pick up that she has got a certain twang. That maybe you might associate with a gang. I choose not to say this to Sean.

Eventually we find the intersection. Crawl down the street, looking for the house number. As we do, a car slowly drives past us. Quite a lot of gang-looking types brimming out of the car. Sean pulls in. Fairly freaked. Tells me there's no way in hell he's getting out of the car. Didn't want to leave me here either. Especially because of my T-shirt. But if I insisted, he was just going to have to drive off. Chill Sean, I'll get Rebecca to come out. Suss things out. I jump out of the car. The car that had drove by us a few minutes earlier has done a U-turn at this stage. Swings back past us. Slows down next to us. Engine starts to rev up. Followed by a hopping-like motion. *Boys in the Hood* style. All wearing red. Me in my baby blue. Oh Jesus. Jump back in the car. Drive, Sean, drive!!!

Never did find out if Rebecca had been winding me up about the party. Or the area. Or if she herself was a Blood. Decided to let it go. Better to cut her loose. At least the fifty-minute drive back with Sean was great fun. Gave us something in common to talk about at least. Got a few words out of Sean. Arrived back in my house for about ten o'clock. Night was spiralling downhill fast. What to do? Bottle of vodka burning a hole in the plastic bag. Up for boozing, Sean? Go to one of the bars up the road. I hear you're a good man for the women! This night shall be saved yet! Sean decides he'll have a drink. Just crash on my couch. Drive home tomorrow. That's the spirit, Sean, there's hope for you yet! Although you could pull, end up with a girl, back to her place. My couch might not even be needed! Finally this gets a smirk from Sean. Cracking. Some laugh.

Myself and Sean head off to one of the bars I've just checked out on Google. Dive bar. Should be good. Please be good. All the cabs are going the opposite direction. No joy. Walk to the bar. Twenty-minute walk. With a fun Sean. Bursting with conversation. Great laugh. Weather cropped up at one stage. Fun walk. En route I'm getting texts from the hippie. She's at a party in her neighbour's house. Her and a bunch of gay men. All meditating. Listening to someone playing the sitar. All going out to the hot tub in a while. Did I want to come?! But only if I brought Timmy! Hmmm. Hot tub. Gay men. Nutter hippie. With a fetish for leprechauns. Or. Dive bar. With Sean. Two-word-answers Sean. Hmmmm . . . Sean got the nod. Well, more the thought of the bar we were going to possibly being good, got the nod. My alternative was to turn around, bid Sean a good night, and go home and booze with my housemates. The dive bar would deliver!

Foolish old me. Bar has a tourist feel to it. And a hint of Irishness. Full of dudes. Along with sound-looking women. Plus for the first twenty minutes a big Italian guy keeps asking me to sell him some speed. He'll pay top dollar. Won't believe me when I tell him (a) I don't do drugs, and (b) I don't sell drugs. Which gets the obvious reply from him . . . Why was I holding out on him?! He has the money. Meet me on the back so in twenty, buddy, I'll hook you up then. Great bar. Not bonding with any women here either. One girl comes up insisting I buy her a drink. Tries to have small talk. Thought she said she was thirty-seven when I asked how old. Gets offended. She's only twenty-five. Not happy. Her friend then joins in. I thought I heard something about just giving birth. Tell her she looks good for having just given birth. She has no children. Neither of them are too happy with me. Sean, anything to contribute? Nothing. Great laugh. Some night so far.

Last call. Two girls are still floating about. Ask if I want to come back to a party with them. Politely decline. They don't think I got what they were implying. I got it. Just don't want any of it. All of which gets more of their wrath. One swings for me. Tries to get a guy in the bar to fight me. All going swimmingly. Myself and Sean make a hasty exit. As we're leaving, the Italian guy starts calling me from down the side alley next to the bar. Doesn't look happy either. Thankfully there are cabs lined up outside. Hop in. Drive off quickly. Leaving behind an angry Italian dude and two large angry country bumpkin women. Probably bonded over their dislike for me. Indirectly, I think I hooked the Italian dude up with a threesome. Lucky him.

Brutal night. Back to my house. Sean is twisted. Can't figure out how so. Jess and Layla are still up. Booze on with them. Finally. Sean starts to talk. Unfortunately. Cheesy chat-up lines dripping off his chin. Cringing. Slurring. I tell him to go to sleep. Crash on my floor if he wants. Need to get rid of him. Girls assume he's my buddy. Not too impressed by him. At all. If he was my buddy, I'd have no problem sticking up for him. Seeing as I just met him, and he's done little to endear himself to me, I don't have the urge to stand up for him. Saying that though, I have done very little to endear myself back. Bloods? Bar-fights? I'm sound.

Sean heads up to my room. I go to the petrol station. Buy a phone card. Ring home. Wish my sister happy birthday. Somehow racking up a chunky cab fare. Night keeps getting better. I like to go the whole hog. Home. Bedroom. Sean's passed out in the corner of my bed. Wrapped in a blanket Jess had given me. I'm twisted drunk. Climb into bed. Strange dude in my bed on the first night? Not a fan. Try to push him onto the floor. Felt a bit bad for doing that. Fell asleep trying to do it again.

Thankfully when I woke up, there was no sign of Sean. Just a wet blanket at the foot of my bed. Why's that wet? Ah, good work Sean. Pissed himself. Also had a barrage of pissed-off messages from Rebecca about not showing up at the party. Plus bizarre texts about Timmy from the hippie. Great work all round. I've great friends here really. Just. Great.

Everybody Needs Good Neighbours

Not a huge fan of Sundays. Never have been. Don't think I ever will be. School. College. Now. Not sure why. Since I've gotten older it's just gotten worse. Particularly Sunday nights. About 3 AM. Awake. Unable to sleep. Hung over. Staring at the ceiling. Waiting. Here it comes. Hello old friend. The Fear. Back again. Irish guilt. Every bad thing I've ever done. Every bad thought I've ever had. Every bad thing that might possibly happen in the future. All flooding into my head at the same time. All feeding on my soul. Great hoot. Tonight it has been covering me pretty bad. Morning wasn't great either though.

Woke up. Blanket. Lovely. Washed. Hung it out my window to dry. Bullish lady in charge of the complex. Took major offence. Claimed it was an unbelievably bad eyesore. Complete spoof. Savage blanket. Bothering no one. She just wanted to pick a fight. Freaked out. Thought she must've somehow known the reason for it being washed and hung out to dry so early. Although it was about twelve o'clock at this stage. So in a normal person's world, not that early at all.

The handbag of a woman calls around. All smiles. All pleasantries. All fake. Starts screaming for it to be taken down. I was a bit taken aback. Calm down woman. Thankfully Jess had my back. Launched into the battleaxe landlady-type figure with gusto. Caused a full-on screaming match. When the hag departed with her tail between her legs, I decided it might be better not to tell Jess the reason why I washed the blanket. Seeing as it was her blanket after all. Claimed I thought it might be nice just to freshen it up. Didn't realise what I would be triggering off.

Arguments continued all day. Embroiled. My peace offering of boiling the kettle was not appreciated. Maybe misunderstood. Don't know the power of a cup of tea here, it seems.

One positive did come out of it. Met a few more of the neighbours. Guy across the way came over saying to ignore her. Turns out he's a writer. Fred. Told me to call over to him some-time during the week. Offered to give me a rundown on the writ-ing business in LA. Sounds promising. Need all the guidance I can get. Especially after running around like a drunk chicken all week. Here to act and write. Not work a job I don't even want to work. Allowing myself to be sidetracked big-time. Which is probably why the Fear showed up. Monkey on my back. Hitting me with a stick. Prodding. Taunting. Teasing. Doubt. Anxiety. Hopeless. Chump. Beat that monkey off!

Introduced to another neighbour of note today as well. Nikki. Who I've been trying to bump into for a while now. Ridiculously good-looking. Perhaps the hottest girl I've seen in LA so far. Something about her. Maybe the fact that she's snubbed me a few times. Turns out she's Australian. And used to be in the television soap *Neighbours*. My neighbour used to be in *Neighbours*. Which is what I repeated to her three times. After she called over to tell us she was on our side against the hand-bag lady. 'So you were in *Neighbours*? My neighbour was a Neighbour? That's so cool.' Smooth. In an attempt to try and save my feeble efforts, I told her not to worry, I never really watched *Neighbours*. More of a *Home and Away* man myself. Smooth. Smoother. Almost too smooth. Go me. Broken ice, at least.

Now lying in bed. Staring at the walls. Beating the monkey off my back. Thinking. Random week. Dumb enough at times. Good laugh though. No joy on the job front. Couple of unex-pected jobs of a different nature. Plenty of nut-jobs. Go LA. Four AM. Time to get rid of the Fear. Easy enough. Sleep on!

Just Like Entourage

Today was meant to be the first day of my acting course. Signed up to do it before I arrived in LA. Paid my deposit. Non-refundable. Only downside of me having to pull out. Not too worried about it though. I think. In the long run I'm saving a nice chunk of money. At least that's what Jess has informed me! When I told her in passing that I was going to be starting acting classes, she stopped me in my tracks. Made me reconsider. Told me why. Finally filled me in on how the whole acting side of things work here.

First. What I thought *might* happen. Arrive in LA. Show up. Do a few acting classes. Go to auditions. Get spotted. Land a few roles. Be on my merry way to the first of many Oscars. Needed to get all this done in three months. As that was as long as my holiday visa lasted. Ninety days to make it. Sounded about right. Very do-able. Very dumb. Very naive. All those adjectives. Did I actually believe that this might be the case? Yes. I actually did. One possibility. Seeing as I'd absolutely no clue. And when I'm not entirely sure about something, I break it down in my head. Nice simple plan. No point in complicating matters with reality. Facts. Or how it all works. Why would I do something as stupid as that?!

Initially decided to go with an acting course at The Acting Corps. Why so? Google. Acting classes in LA. Pretty sure that was the first one to pop up. Also had a reference quote from an actor I recognised, Dwight from *The Office*. Although he didn't actually go to that school himself. His photo and two-line recommendation were still enough to convince me of its merits.

Acting Boot Camp. Four weeks. $999. Hopefully get invited back for the second part. Eight weeks. $1,499. On top. I wouldn't actually have time to finish those twelve weeks of classes. Ninety days and all. Just enough time to get the basics under my belt.

Mentioned this to Jess. She mentioned back that she too was looking to start classes. As soon as possible. We could go to class together. Practise together. Rehearse together. All that stuff. Most importantly, from my point of view, this would mean I had a lift to and from class every day. Acting Corps was in North Hollywood. NoHo. No WeHo. No car. Google Maps. Two options to get to class. Public transport: 1 hour 16 minutes. Walking: 2 hours 29 minutes. Neither was really feasible. Particularly as walking would mean taking a few shortcuts along freeways. Trying out classes with Jess sounded like the better option.

Added to this, her agent had given her a list of acting classes for her to try out first before she committed to one. Another nugget of information I found out: most acting classes can be audited for free. Try them out. See if you like them. For free. And I was about to splash out almost a grand on classes! So if I tried lots of different ones for free, couldn't I kind of get the basics for free? Something worth mulling over. Jess didn't really think about it this way before. More about finding the right class for her. More about finding lots of free classes for me. Told her that's one of the joys of being Irish – the possibility of something being free makes us far more perceptive. Except free hugs. Makes us wary.

Not all good news though. Facts were served cold. Necessities. Apparently. Especially for the likes of me. Starting at the bottom rung. We all have to start somewhere. Headshots.

Photos of your head. People want to know what you look like. Except normal photos won't do. Even if you crop the photo. And it's just a photograph consisting of your head. Won't do. Has to be a headshot. Professional headshots. I've seen a few people's headshots. Majority look horrific. Except if you're a proper model and look natural in front of the camera. Otherwise, you merely look like a smiling cheesy ape. Posing for a camera a foot away from you. Costs a couple of hundred dollars to get them done. Really need these headshots. I'll test that theory. Especially as I dislike photos. A lot. Headshots on the backburner.

SAG? More fun. Screen Actor's Guild. You need a SAG card to be able to act properly. As in get paid properly to act. Be part of the union. You can get this card in one of two ways, it seems. One: do lots of small roles in as many productions as you can. Extras work. Background work. Anything you can get your hands on – and which doesn't require you to have a SAG card. Build up your credits. Maybe three years later (pardon me, *years?*), you might have enough credits to join SAG. To make this even more fun, when you do, it will cost you a few thousand dollars. Pay. Get the card. Join their gang. Now you're allowed to act properly. Whatever that means. Next option please.

Alternatively, you could just get spotted by someone. Director. Producer. Agent. Someone who takes a punt on you. Gets you a big enough role. Then you get all the credits from that one part alone. Allowing you to get your SAG card in one fell swoop. Usually, this only happens if the director/producer/agent takes an interest in you. Probably meaning they want to sleep with you. Probably meaning you will need to sleep with them to get in. Let's not be completely naive about it. Daily occurrence here. Promise of it, at least. Shocking, I know.

Plan A. Chopped. Rearranged. No car. No Acting Corps. Auditing with Jess is on. Basics under the belt. Hit the auditions road. Preferably without the use of headshots. Minus a SAG card. At the same time, plan B will be keeping its eyes open. Just have to hope that there are a few influential female directors/producers/agents who are hot, easily charmed by an Irish accent, and not looking to cast me in a porn movie. All about the plan B really! At least now I have two sure-fire plans. Great day. Productive all the way. Sure.

On that note, I'm off to the gym. Found a good one nearby. Equinox. Week's free pass. Same thing as acting classes. More or less. Feign interest. Pretend you want to join long-term. See what it's like. Handy. Especially when it costs about $200 a month. Pretty penny. Pretty slick gym. Pretty much beautiful-people town. Different calibre. Initially, I thought it was full of posers. Now, I realise that the majority of people in there are just so good-looking that that is actually how they look. Permanently. Abercrombie town. No posing necessary. Except by one ape. Cheek-sucking. Lip-pouting. Getting nowhere with the women. Until a toora-loora slips out. Irish all the way. Ninety days isn't that long at the same time. Gym on!

Acting Up

Finally popped my acting cherry tonight. First acting class. Ever. Skipped a few grades. Ended up in a master's level acting class. Blagged my way in. Googled acting coaches as opposed to acting schools. Found one which looked pretty good. Aaron Speiser's Acting Class. Recommendations flying in from legit people: Will Smith. Gerard Butler. Jennifer Lopez. The Wayan brothers. Well, maybe not all legit actors. But high-profile at least. And made enough movies for me to make the call and get my audit on. Jess wasn't too sure, but I told her it'd be good. Seeing as I would know. What with it being my first-ever class and all.

Made the call: I would like to audit the class. Beginner's or master's? Well, if I'm auditing, I want to do a class with Aaron Speiser himself, please. He only teaches masterclasses? Master all the way. Yes, yes, of course I've done some acting before. Back in Ireland. And, eh, in Germany. Master's on. In like Flynn. Besides, Jess has enough acting classes under her belt to warrant doing the master's. Ergo, it was either me doing the same class or doing none at all. Master's on! I have one in e-business anyway; technically, I was well qualified.

Park up outside the school. Lots of people huddling around in groups outside. Nod, nod, nod, hey, what's up, howdy, hubbu-la. This is pretty cool. Seven bells, head into class. I'm that clueless, I was expecting a classroom kind of set-up. Blackboard. Desk and chairs. Nay. Studio set-up. As in a stage and audience-style seating. Sit down. Wait for it to begin. Eventually, about 7.45, Mr Speiser strolls in. Apologies for being late, he had to deal with some war that broke out on a movie set between an actor he is coaching and the director of the movie. Flew him in to act as peacekeeper. Millions and millions of dollars riding on the movie. Wasting thousands every minute while the filming was halted. And they flew him in to deal with it. Actors, huh? Got to keep them happy. Gerard Butler, you guys know him? Nice guy. Hi everybody, in case you don't already know . . . (pause) . . . I'm Aaron Speiser. Welcome to the master's class.

Everyone else seemed to be slightly annoyed that he was so late. I, on the other hand, was loving the name-dropping and Troy McClure-style opener. Another longer introduction followed. Names were being dropped like there was no tomorrow. 'When I worked with Will . . . Will Smith that is, you guys heard of him? When I worked with Jennifer . . . LL Cool J used to say to me . . . Those Wayan brothers hardly ever listen, or that's what they want you to think! They credit me for all their success . . . ' and so on. I was a thirsty puppy. Tongue wagging. Lapping it up! Drop on, Troy, drop those names! Jesus, these acting classes are a great laugh. Everyone else was nodding along as if they'd heard it all before. Looked at Jess. Not impressed.

In fairness, it was almost nine o'clock at this stage. Besides his own theatrics while recalling various stories, little or no actual acting had taken place. Two students did one scene after he eventually ended his long introduction. Scene study class apparently. (You act it out. He critiques it. You ask your own questions about different parts. He answers. That's the class. Just in case you are as clueless as I am.) Two guys did a scene from a movie. God only knows what movie, but they butchered that scene. Or else it was just a horrendous scene from a boring movie. Hopefully I'll never watch the original. Not great, being honest. Aaron then critiqued them. Well, he would start to give them really good little pointers – 'You gotta sweat the small details more, they're what count . . . which is what I told Will that time we worked on his last movie. Did I tell y'all about that?' – and then carry on with the same story about Will Smith. I could sense a pattern emerging.

At the midway break, Jess and I went to the coffee place next door. Still not too impressed. So I pretended not to be impressed either. Even though I did really enjoy it. But I could see where Jess was coming from. It was all about him. And who he worked with. Or is working with. Plus the actors we saw were pretty poor. As in for a master's class, they were basic. Relaying lines, more or less. Yawning material. One of the actors was pretty funny. Unintentionally. Kept going on about how he knew what he was doing, whenever Aaron would say he needed to improve this, that or the other. Which is what he told the Wayans . . . Actor dude was not a fan of criticism. Kept getting defensive. How he had been classically trained in Florida for six years. In the Observatory. A dramatic pause after he said 'Observatory'. Oh right. Is that good? Eventually, when he said it one time too many, Aaron replied: 'So you've been trained to be shit? Just make the change.' Shut the dude up fairly lively.

Finished up our coffee. Jess wants to go home. Had enough of Aaron talking about Aaron. Merrick thinking about Merrick, I convince her to stay. Most productive thing I've done since I got here. No way am I leaving halfway! Back to class. More of the same. Students acting out scenes. Aaron giving nuggets of info and advice. Hidden amongst a sea of his name-dropping. Eleven bells came along. Class. Over. All in all. A mighty four hours.

Just as we were leaving, Jess and I were told that Aaron wanted to see us in his office. Say hi. See what we thought. About

Aaron. Sounds good. In we go. Mr Speiser, how's it going, who's this Aaron you were referring to the whole time? Gave us a spiel. Talked us through what Aaron does. Asked us our credentials. Jess rattles off a few of hers. Aaron seemed impressed. My turn. Eh . . . Told him all about my training in the Laboratory back in Ireland. Plus the theatre classes I did in Germany. Waffling. Oddly he was impressed by the Laboratory training. As if he had heard of it. Good man. I didn't intend on saying any of that gib-berish, but I am an ape. And, unless he was acting, it would appear he is too. Act on!

Free Jim!

Seeing as yesterday had been so good – first acting class and all – the plan was to equal if not better it today. Went well. Highly productive. Emails for part-time work online. Food shopping. And I went to the gym. I outdo myself at times. At least the gym made me fool myself that it wasn't a fully wasted day. Kind of good to get that sorted a bit more. Yet another monkey which was up on my back. Badgering away. Back in the day, I was not a fan of the gym. Now, groupie. For me it's a bit like Mass. Even if I just go and not do much, it makes me feel better about myself. Physically there. Mentally meandering off elsewhere. Dumb. Yet effective. I like to fool a fool.

When I first got here, my trusted sidekick GM showed me a few gyms within walking distance. Nice gyms. Really nice. Expensive gyms. Really expensive. Needed to figure something out. After forking out too much money on rent I can't really afford, saving money is paramount. Plus, they tie you to a two-year contract, which are meant to be even harder than a full nelson to get out of. Great offer lads, cheers! Thankfully, I have found a way to get them for free. Short-term anyways. Maybe long-term too, but I'll come back to that.

First gym I went to was Crunch. Spoofed on about how great it was to move to LA, really like it, settle down here, long-term stay, looking for the right gym to join for life. This gym is just magnificent, really spectacular, they don't make them like this in Ireland, my God this place is amazing, what a gym! Spoof on. Reel them in. Pull back . . . Although I hear that other place down the street is good too. What's that? A free pass for a week so I could check out this gym and get a feel for the place? Why thank you, free pass on!

Not 100 percent free. In return, I give them permission to annoy me to the max. Fill out a form: name, email, address, number etc. I'd advise saving the phone number for whichever gym it may be. Straightaway. So you know who's calling you. So you know who you must dodge. As they call you straightaway. Minute your foot leaves their door: 'Hey Merrick, this is Jaymes with a "Jay" from the gym, we just met. How was your first visit? Would you like to join? We have a great deal on today, only for you.' You can literally swivel. Look back in the window. See them on the phone to you. 'Hey Jim, how are ya boyo! We did literally just met. I can still feel your sweaty palm from shaking hands goodbye. I can hear you speaking to me through the window.' To which Jaymes gives you a big wave. Full of WeHo enthusiasm.

First time around, I immediately cursed myself for not just giving them a wrong number. Although in the end, perhaps I subconsciously knew what I was doing. See, I've being doing the rounds with the different gyms. I am a gym whure. First Crunch. Then Equinox. Free passes over. Time to look for the next one on the list. GM delivered 24 Hour Fitness. My walk was getting longer, but still fine. Still free. Last night was my first night going. And my last. Still a bit rattled. Maybe if I'd known what I was getting myself into, I might've been more prepared. Instead, I skipped merrily into a gay orgy. Not copping on what all the rainbow flags outside would mean. Instead thinking of how a flag like that would be good for Timmy O'Toole. In I went. Front desk, friendly vibe. Really friendly. Sign in. Guy handed me a pen to write with. Left his hand on my hand. As I signed. That was a bit odd. Headed to the changing room. Full of guys. How did I not cop on?!

Equinox and Crunch had similar clientele. Really hot women. Few dudes. And lots of gay dudes. Both places made me realise I'm better off avoiding eye contact at times, so didn't really notice much out of the norm in 24. Initially. Walking around like a lost puppy in the weights room was nothing new. Never sure of what's where in a new gym. Did think it was kind of weird that there was an old guy standing in the middle of the room, just staring as you walked by. Old guy in jeans. Too short for him. Wearing a headband. Jeans. Headband. And. That was it. No top. So, yeah, that was kind of weird. Triggered suspicions.

As did the dude wearing a wig. The one that kept falling off when he lifted weights. He was also wearing purple spandex pants. So he too was a bit odd. Suspicion rose a wee bit more. Everyone seemed to know each other as well. Staring at each other. Shrugging their eyebrows. Smiling. Not happy smiles. Something creepy about their smiles. Decided I should check out the other weights room. Might be a better call. Continued on. Hoping to see a machine I was familiar with. Just do a quick few exercises, say a few prayers, get communion, then quickly be on my merry way. Just make sure to avoid eye contact with the weirdo with no top. Who seems to be following me.

Aha. I know that machine over there! That'll do nicely. That machine there. Behind those two guys. Who are now leaning against it. Now kissing up against it. Now almost fully getting it on. OK. I'll check back later perhaps. Maybe over at the other end of the room, there's a machine for me . . . Some guy telling another guy that he will 'bite it off if you do that again'. Not sure exactly what he meant. Hang on, that guy over there seems to recognise me. Trying to get my attention. Keeps waving. Eyeing me up and down. Keeps saying 'Hi'. Nodding his head towards the steam room. Hang on buddy, I must get my weights session in first!

Eventually I found a bench and free weights. Which was grand. Until two guys started using the bench next to me. Kind of had a Right Said Fred look. Started to simulate stuff next to me. Joking, in fairness. I think. But still. I decided I'd just go home. Do a few press-ups in my room. Walking home, it all sank in. Dazed. Piecing it all together. Wondering did that classify as a gay experience? His hand had been on mine for a long time. Where was his other hand?! Was I just part of an orgy? How would I break the news to my parents?! Arrived home. Must've looked shell-shocked. The girls asked what was wrong. Told them where I'd been. They screamed – with delight. 'What?! We never knew!!! We have a gay roommate! We thought you were straight!'

At least they were happy for me. Until I told them I wasn't actually gay. Dubious looks. Filled me in. That 24 Hour Fitness, specifically that one, is a full-on gay gym. Only gay guys go there. Work out. Get it on. Oh right. Crunch and Equinox just had a lot of gay men who went there. Not gay. Full anyways. Sussed out a bit more from the girls. Is it normal that I'm getting so many calls plaguing me to join the other two gyms? It was. They're hounds. OK. Is it normal that the guy from Crunch keeps leaving me messages with his personal cell number? Call him anytime. For anything. He's here to help. Did I know there's a great new bar opened up on Sunset. I'd love it. We should *so* go. Is that kind of message normal? It's not. OK. Now I get it. I won't even tell you what Chad in Equinox has been saying so.

Rattled all night. Where would I gym?! Needed Mass. Today I decided to take advantage of the situation. Another missed call from Jim in Crunch. Had a quick shot of whiskey. Rang him back. 'Howdy Jim, Merrick here. Did you see *Queer Eye for the Straight Guy* last night? Oh, it's not on any more. Anyways I thought about it and I figured I do want to join for the two years. Yes, that is great news. Only thing is I might have to go back to Ireland for a week soon. I'll join when I get back. Anything you can do for me until then? You'll put me on the system until I leave? Sorted? Cheers Jim! Yeah, it *is* a fabulous day. What am I up to? Do I have plans? Emm, oh no, my battery is about to di– ' Goodbye.

Diet Coke Head

Overall, happy with where I'm living. As gay as Christmas, safe as houses, and plenty of hot women to balance it out. Overall, happy with the girls I'm living with. Most of the time. Maybe just not every night. I thought I was a night owl. They put me to shame. Up until at least four or five, almost every night of the week. Buddies over all the time. Dudes. Drinking. Smoking. Playing Guitar Hero. Talking about Scientology. By the by, found out they are all Scientologists. Not that it matters or anything. But that might explain why they all love *American Idol* so much perhaps. Cult-like. In it's own way. Maybe just not as funked up. Maybe. Anyways, I sound like an old biddy, but still, that late, every night? Starting to get to me. Plus, they can be really loud. Jesus, I *am* a biddy. Still, the lack of sleeping is killing me.

Added to this, I've random dudes coming into my room every night. 'Sorry man, the other bathroom is taken, do you mind?' Only half-four on a Monday night, of course I don't mind. To cap it all off, most annoying of all, when I went downstairs last night to politely ask them to shut the funk up, I bite the bait. Offered a drink. Ended up boozing. A lot. Whiskey was flowing. Which is why today I was so ridiculously hung over. And late to my acting class. At least I went though. Bugs have bitten. Scouring for as many free classes as I can. Class today was my first daytime one. Night owl and all. Think I might stick to the evening classes. Numerous reasons.

Daytime. Jess had no interest. Decided to get a taxi on my own. Not too happy. Cut those corners! Stood on my street. Flagging arm out. Obviously. Not one cab would stop. Mighty.

Walk on. Half-jogged. Hung over. Thirty-minute walk. In the heat. Bad call. Seriously. It was roasting. Sweating like a whure. Realising that I made a terrible call. Complete schoolboy! Wore a blue T-shirt. Not good. Sweating even more once I realised what I'd done. A vicious circle of dumbness. At least the air conditioning in the studio would cool me down. Stop me from looking like a sweating freak. Thank God for A/C.

Arrive. Late. Everyone seems to be doing warm-up exercises. Standing on chairs. All looking giddy. Happy to be alive. Oh no. Not those kind of apes. Hang on, I'll worry about them in a minute. First. Sweet Lord. This small studio is pretty funking hot. In fact, even worse than outside. Where are the windows? Where is the steady hum of the air con?! Beads were forming and multiplying. Getting worse. What's that on my forehead? Sweet Jesus, this is like a sauna! Sweat. Dripping. Lady in charge picks the perfect moment to introduce herself. Lizzie. Trying to shake my hand. Sweat oozing out. Dodging handshakes. Instead just waving back at her. Like an idiot. Mopping myself off as inconspicuously as I could. Jack and Diet Coke oozing out of me. Tasting it on my lips. Started to get the impression that the airy-fairy-kind-of-odd teacher thought I was a bit of a weirdo myself. Standing there. As if I just got out of the shower. Waving at her. Licking my lips. I could see why. Excused myself for the bathroom. Tissues. Towelling. Drying off as best I could. Acceptable. Ready to start class!

Straightaway my suspicions were confirmed. People in the class. Hyper. Constantly changing their accents while speaking. Half-talking, half-singing while chatting amongst themselves. Disillusioned. Annoying. Those kind of people. Pantomime. Cruise-ship people. Fun folk. While I was standing there trying to regulate my breathing, hangover and perspiration issues,

Lizzie sprang a surprise on me. Would I like to try out a scene? Yeah, sure, no problem, next time sounds good. Oh, now? Did not think I would be doing a scene. Thought I was merely going to observe. Unprepared. No real way of saying no, though. OK, I'm in. Lizzie looks like she want to give me a hug. I give her a quick 'Yay' instead.

Perspiration kicks up a notch. When I see who I'm paired with, goes up another one. Keep acting out scenes on their own. From movies in their heads perhaps. Full-on nutters. Wuu. We're given five minutes to prepare a scene. Which I assume is from a brutal straight-to-DVD movie. Three characters: two prostitutes and a cokehead. I throw it out there to see if I can play one of the prostitutes but get the cokehead role instead. Handed the script. See I've very few lines. Mostly actions in the background. Come into the apartment, find my bag of coke, act jittery, get irritated that I can't find a dollar bill to roll up, get pissed off with the girls over the argument they're having, and then say my big line. Not too bad. Suits me fine.

Up onto stage we go. Must have been slightly elevated, as the sweat starts bucketing down some more. Sauna. Hangover. First-ever go. Remember my few lines. Sweat. Dripping. Nerves perhaps. Although, once 'Action' is called, and a few seconds go by, all is forgotten. Some buzz. Especially as I realise that I've the cokehead role down to a tee – cold sweats, jittery from it being my initial role, not remembering where they said the bag of coke would be. (I keep looking under the wrong part of the couch.) To the trained-yet-clueless eye, it appears as though I can act. Or so the teacher keeps telling me.

Scene progresses. The two prostitutes say the majority of the lines. I hear one that I noted beforehand. Coming up. Here we go! And I finish the scene with my 'Shut up and find me a f**king dollar, you stupid f**king whore!' Giddy up! Dirty whures! Get up them steps. Venom in my response. Maybe taking out my sleepless frustrations at the same time. Therapy on! Lizzie gives me great credit. 'We should really observe how Merrick instantly transformed into the character. Sign of a real pro!' Ha, why thank you. Half-jokingly asks if I'm a cokehead. And tells me that the weird voice I used to say my lines was really great. Pardon? Oh, my accent? Thanks. All in all, though, well worth going to the class. Over the first of many humps! Scene over. Time to observe and take notes for the rest of the class. These annoying people are all actually fairly crap. Boring scenes. Way too hot. Keep nodding off. Oh, looks like I'm getting an important call. Just go outside to take it. Back in two minutes, Lizzie. Off home I went. Acted my way out of it!

Bought a Bucket

Craig and his endless lists. Love him. Hate him. Unsure. Greatest website ever. Biggest waste of time. Full of gems. Riddled with scams. Paradox beyond belief. Now part of my morning routine. Wake up. Breakfast. Hi Craig. Look for a job. Fool myself that I'm being productive. Lunch. Check to see if I got any responses from the ads I emailed. Past few days have been slightly different. Now quite apparent to me that LA is horrendous to get around by foot. You need a car. Tried to fool myself otherwise. But. You kind of do. Shop where I buy protein powder. Five-minute drive. Or a forty-five-minute walk. You kind of do.

However, seeing as I don't know how long I'll actually be here, I'd no intention of splashing out on a motor. Too busy splashing around elsewhere. That was, until I saw a pick-up truck that looked cool. More importantly, cheap. Pick-up. Cool. Cheap. Hooked. Rang the number last night. Today, the guy rings me about eleven o'clock. Says he's at my abode. Here so I can have a look at it. Go outside to my street and wait for him to show up. Noticed that the Mexican painters are blocking the parking entrance to my building once again. Actually, no, that's my potential bucket. I knew from the photos that it wasn't the prettiest of buckets. I knew this. However, those photos must've been airbrushed. Or else the bucket is very photogenic. Might've been a nighttime shoot? Maybe I was drunk looking at the pictures? Whichever it is, now that I see it properly, in the daylight, I realise that it is pretty, pretty, *pretty* ugly. Duck. It.

Assumed it was white. ('White Pick-up for Sale!') Seeing it in person, it is actually several lovely shades of white. Yellowy white. Creamy white. Not so much white-white. Hand-painted at least, which is a good thing? I could literally see the brush strokes. A guy gets out of the truck when he sees me. Reminds me of The Dude from *The Big Lebowksi*. Scruffy long hair. Beard. Even wearing a cardigan and hair clip. Starts to walk over to me. Well not really walk. More waddle. Oddest walk I've ever seen. Making me forget about the bucket and its seven shades of white. And that it looks like shi— How's it going? Introduces himself 'Heeey duuude'. He is the Dude. Dude on, dude.

Before I go any further, I should mention two things: cars don't turn me on. Don't know much about their inner workings. Watch *Top Gear* and all, but more for the banter. If I fill up the water for the wipers without doing damage, I feel like a mechanic. During my college days (and a bit after) I was fortunate enough to get free cars from Ford. Managing director of Ford Ireland was one of my soccer coaches. Mighty man! Hooked me up. Shiny brand new Ford, every second week. All I had to do was collect the car. Drive away. Ran low on petrol. Drop it back. Get a new car. (Buy Ford!)

Parked outside my house was a Porsche, an Escalade and a Phantom. All in my eye-line, as I saw the truck. False sense of grandeur, howdy. Absolutely *no* intention whatsoever of buying this truck. Bob Hope.

Anyways, the Dude starts to tell me absolutely everything about the truck (ironically, a Ford F350). And I mean everything. Fuses, sparks, carburettors (thank you, spell-check), starters, belts, tubes, pistons, horses, cows (seriously, he told me he once used the truck to move a cow for someone). Kept going. Bangs, whirls, nets and pops. Going on and on. Pointlessly. Oblivious that I've no clue what he's going on about. And that all I've been wondering was . . . What was with the waddle? Weird. His legs look fine. Is he drunk? Smells drunk. Does he have a duck curve? Hang on, he's showing me something. After a lengthy period of me staring at God only knows what in the engine, I tell him that it all sounds well and good. Out of courtesy, I agree when he says we should take it for a spin around the block. He did drive an hour to get here. Couldn't just shoo him away so soon. Could I? Come on we go for a spin so, dude.

Informs me that the driver's door doesn't always work. Must open the window or get in on the passenger side. Convenient. Inside is even worse/funnier. Dash all torn. Windshield is cracked I see. Nice of him to clean it a bit before showing it to me as well. Peanut butter jars. Piles of Coke bottles. Few broken brooms in the back. Along with a weird-looking cooler of some kind. Plus numerous other delightful items, including a sprawling fishnet. Sit in and straightaway I notice the horrific smell. Thankfully, that turns out to be his feet and not the truck. No A/C. Nail in the coffin. Nice smelly sweat-box. None of this mentioned in the ad. I wonder why.

The Dude revs up the bucket. Smiling at me in delight. Yay. Off we go. Cruising around WeHo. Getting dodgy looks from the guys walking their poodles. Waves from the Mexican gardeners. Truck runs fine. Drives. Good to know. Pull back up outside my house. I jump out. The Dude is beaming. Probably seeing as I did mention on the night before that if it ran OK, I'd probably buy it. Which was before I saw it. Not knowing it wasn't a white swan. Instead a haggard old beast. Blind date. False impressions. Not the same girl as in the photo! Now, how do I break the news? Tell him I must have a quick think. Back in two minutes. Go back into my house. Drink a glass of water. Pretend to think about it.

Layla comes downstairs. Asks me why I'm just standing in the middle of the kitchen. I'm pretending to think. Asks what's in my drink. Quickly fill her in. Killing time before I go back out. She thinks maybe I should buy it. I think she just wants me to chauffeur her around the place. Lists out a few points to me. Cheap. Yeah, but it's a horrible-looking Bucket! So what! Handy to have as back-up. Could drive to acting class. Good point. Seeds of doubt. Maybe. Emm. Funk. Decide I'll quickly ring my friend's dad. Who is a car salesman. What did he think of this offer? Asking for his advice. On a car he's never seen. At the time it made sense. He's not sure but sounds like it could be OK. Cheap. Runs OK? Go for it. Didn't really mention the ridiculous amount I was paying for rent. Without having a job. Even if the truck was about half a month's rent, it could just be more money pointlessly gushing out. Never mentioned any of that to him. So he might not have got why I suddenly said that I actually definitely won't go for it. Definitely not. Thanks for the advice though! And then he hung up on me.

Back out to the Dude. Broke the bad news. Blamed it on the lack of A/C. Tried to make a leprechaun joke out of it. Did not go down well. At all. In fact, it made him cry. Started to tell me how he needed the money badly. Must get a hip operation. Won't be able to get into or out of the truck after the operation. Will be out of work for a while after it. Told another guy who rang that morning that I was almost 100 percent buying it. Now it might be too late to get the other guy to buy it. So that's why! His hip. Made me feel bad for thinking he was a waddler. His sob story guilt-tripped me. Maybe it was his haggling. Because out of nowhere, I was offering him a few hundred dollars for it. Within a few seconds I was shaking on double my original offer. Tears. Guilt-tripped. Now owned a truck. That I did not want. What was I doing?!

Never before have I immediately regretted something so quickly. When he mentioned that I said I'd drop him home if I bought it, I regretted it even more. He lived an hour away. Worst decision I've made in a long while! Time to go for a drive. Great. On the upside, I think I may have got a handy job from it. Turns out the Dude is a caddy. I used to caddy when I was younger. The Dude rang the boss, said I would be good to go next week. Perfect timing, seeing as I now have transport to get out there! Few good days of caddying and the Bucket will have paid for itself. Thinking that the Dude was sound for hooking that up, I got suckered into going for food with him. Listening to his stories about women. This really hot girl he saw in a bar. That was it. He saw a hot girl. Didn't speak to her. Took him about thirty-five minutes to tell me that story. While eating a sandwich in the Bucket. With the smell of his feet wafting around. Great fun.

I must say though, driving home on the freeway was a great feeling. The Bucket is a beast! Windows down. The radio, which I believe is stuck on one station, was pumping out some Akon song. Brutal song. Singing along. Belting it out! Truck runs. I now have transport. Who cares if it's horrendous looking?! What's inside is what matters! And eh, inside the Bucket would be me! Five hours later I finally got back to my abode. And found out how bad parking is in LA. Could only find a spot about twenty-five minutes from my house. Fine long walk back home after I parked up. Plenty of time for me to think about whether it was a good call or not. Oh Jesus. Time to go drown my sorrows. Maybe the Bucket will look better when I'm drunk!

Transformer

Woke up with the eyes of terror. Where am I? Afraid to move. Afraid to breathe. Until I took a long enough look around whatever room I was in. And figured out I was in my own bed. Fully clothed. Not a good sign. But seemingly unscathed. All good. Stood up. Tried to take off my jeans. Fell against the wall five feet away. Bounced off the wall. Onto my suitcase. Top of it buckled. Fell into my suitcase. Not so good after all.

Kicked me into gear. Did the quick check. Phone, wallet, passport, iPod: check. Not sure why I checked for my iPod. Anyways. No phone. Balls. Flashback number one. Invited to an after-party by a girl I met before. Invited along to the Blue Moon. I was too drunk to understand the name of the place. Might not have been the Blue Moon. Or else I got it right and the cab man couldn't understand my accent. Either way, I ended up highly frustrated. And threw my phone out the window. Window of the moving cab. Dumb. Still feeling drunk. Only one concern. Must buy a new phone. Immediately. Hung-over brain works in mysterious ways.

Open my laptop. Try to Google the nearest phone shop. Can't connect to the internet. Ugh. So hung over. What am I doing wrong? Go downstairs. Still no connection. Plonk down on the couch. Confused. Turn on the TV. Soccer might cure me. TV isn't working. Blank. What? Why? Is it my dumbness or is my world merely falling apart. Need some water. Head to the kitchen. Confused. Note on the kitchen table. 'Forgot to pay the cable bill. Internet and TV cut off. Sorry :-)' I pay all this rent, and the girls don't pay the bills on time. A smiley face, gloating at me?! Sweet Jesus. So goosed. Then. Remember. Bought a Bucket yesterday. Which is parked a good few blocks away. And needs to be moved. An hour ago. Seeing as it's in a tow-zone of some sort. Sprint time. Hung over. Wearing flip-flops. Horrendous.

Due to my lack of water, and the sheer heat, by the time I get to the Bucket I am close to passing out. At least it wasn't towed. Although would that have been such a bad thing? Almost snap the key in half when I try to open the door. Slightly cracked. Forgot I had to go in the passenger side. Stupid Bucket. Get in. Dangerously dizzy. Nearly pass out. Hot outside. Sauna inside. Gasping for air. Disgusted as I look around. Last night I was kind of pleased that I had a mode of transport. Not a bad pull. Could do worse. Cold light of day. Horrible-looking. Woke up next to a transformer. Disgusted with myself for what I'd done.

Time to do the drive of shame. Start her up. Nada. Not even a rev. Although I was barely paying attention. Too busy thinking about my phone. Not that I even really liked that phone. Barely got reception in my house. Still though, all my American numbers were in it. Each and every contact I had made. What a disaster. What am I doing again, oh yeah . . . By now I must've tried to start the Bucket four or five times. Won't start. My mind is elsewhere again already. Thinking about the numbers I lost from yesterday alone . . . Caddy master who I was to ring about a job; Bouncer who I met at the club who told me he would get me on guestlists of good place, just text him in advance; that hot Spanish girl who was an act . . . Finally the Bucket feebly kicks into life.

Pull off. Drive on. Realise I'm going the wrong way. Away from home. Do a U-turn. Unfortunately, a third of the way through the U, the Bucket cuts out. Fully. Turn the key, nothing. The Bucket is a big beast too. Blocking my side of the street. And most of the other side that I was turning into. Traffic now building up either side. People who drives cars in LA are highly strung. Must not be having enough sex. Majority are on edge. Beeping starts. Followed by honking. And cursing. The Bucket revs up. I turn a few steps more. The Bucket dies. Now I'm faced across the street. Like a police barrier. Blocking all routes. People are getting out of their cars either side of me. Shouting. For some reason I shout back that it's not my car. Belongs to my friend. Only moving it for him! Calm down. I appear to be ashamed of the Bucket. Harsh.

Key. Turn. Nothing. By now my head is on the steering wheel. Eyes closed. Thinking only about my phone. Getting a flashback from the night before. Singing a song on Hollywood Boulevard with a Swedish version of Boy George. Going back to a party with his Swedish friend. Annika. Anna. Having to leave the party as I was too drunk. Weird party too. Drug-den buzz. Good music though. Getting her number. Which was in my phone. The phone I threw out of the cab window. Felt like this flashback lasted for ages. Rudely interrupted by some guy angrily banging the bonnet of the Bucket. Snapped me out of it. And kicked the Bucket into gear. Revved up. Finally. Took off. Leaving the sexually frustrated people behind. Although my frustrations were high too. Found a parking spot on my street. Ran into my house. Got my laptop. Beeline to the closest coffee shop. Wireless. Internet. Craigslist. Ad up. For sale. Pick-up truck. $1,000 o.n.o. Try and get a bit extra if I can. Cover the added cost. New phone and all.

Headed off to closest phone shop I found on GM. Stumbling down Santa Monica like a weirdo. Shorts.

Mismatching flip-flops. Same top from last night. The one with the Red Bull stain down the front. An hour later, still hadn't reached my destination. Meant to be only a twenty-minute walk. Needed help. Into a bar for directions. Rage. Think it must've been a gay bar. Seeing as the guy who gave me directions was the manager, who was dancing on the bar, in short shorts. Pointed me in the right direction. With a thrust of his hips. Straight across the street. I'd been walking up and down the wrong side of the (wide) street the whole time. Mighty work. Cross the street. Into the store. Can I buy a phone, please? Just sold the last pre-paid phone they had in stock. You're lying? They weren't. Trudged home. Phone-less. Time to give up. Frustrating day. Done and dumb.

Made some food at home. Perked me up a bit. Made me remember that I was meant to be playing soccer. Downtown. Forgot about that. Guy saw my ad on Craigslist offering soccer coaching. Rang yesterday to see if I'd be interested in playing with a team. Game on today. Seeing as I had the Bucket to take me there, I said I'd definitely play. In the long run, I wanted to play with the team. Short-term, I just wanted to go to bed. Hide from my hangover. Time to cancel. Balls. No phone. No number. No way to call the guy. Funk. Decided to bite the bullet. Test the Bucket out one last time. Changed. Back out again. Thankfully, it seems that the Bucket and I have one thing in common at least. Night owls. Some difference in her when the daylight was gone. Only took two attempts to get going. The Bucket was warming up!

My brain was working slightly better at this stage. Knocked on my neighbour's door. Days of a cup of milk are over. Any chance I could borrow your wireless internet password please and *danke*? Back online. Back to having a second life. Got directions to the pitch. Off I went. Ripping through the streets of LA. Beast of a Bucket once it got going. Bonded with the Bucket en route. Allowed me to see more of LA in that one drive than I had previously in the entire time I'd been here. My brain also started to work. Remembered the name of the golf club. And the name of the caddy master. Could just ring the golf club. Ask for the caddy master. Once I bought a new phone. One problem solved. Almost. Good work.

Arrive at the pitch. Well worth the risk of trying out the Bucket. Savage set-up. Floodlit pitch. In the heart of downtown LA. Surrounded by skyscrapers. Savage. Find the English guy who rang me, Dave. Getting introduced to everyone on the team. Few Americans. Few English. Couple of eastern Europeans. And now, a token Irish guy. Oddly, I hear a version of my name being called out: 'Maaaaaark'. Followed by 'drunk Irish guy'. Thinking it was a generic name, thought nothing of it. Hear it again. Turn around. Look down . . . the bouncer from last night. Same guy who said he'd hook me up with guest list *et al*! Over by the fence, tying up his laces. What the funk? In a city as big as LA! Fills in a few blanks for me. Gives me a loan of boots. (Only realised then that I had none.) Ready. To. Shine!

Played well. Really well. Usually do when it's the first game with a new group. Usually also happens when I'm hung over. Plus. The other team weren't the greatest. Dave (or going by his fussball-pitch name, Copelando) calls me over after the game. Impressed. Asks if I'd be interesting in playing five-a-side with him and his buddies during the week. Let me check my busy schedule. Looks like I'm free. Sounds good. Where? Beverly Hills. On Mulholland Drive. Copelando lives in his friend's house. Who has a pitch in his back garden. As you do. What kind of friend has a full-on AstroTurf in his back garden?! Casually mentions his friend's name. Oh right. That makes sense now. Pretty funking savage. Decide to act cool about it until I get home.

The Bucket kicks into life straightaway on the way home. Windows down. Akon pumping out of the one speaker. Two girls pull up next to me in traffic. Howdy. 'Oh my god I love that song, what station is it on?' Eh, 101.4 KGB All Night Long. My favourite spoof station. 'Oh my god I love your truck, so retro, is that the Loooove Truck?' Just as I was going to say, no, it's the Bucket, the lights went green. Better off. Didn't really care if the girls were being sarcastic or not. All I know is that I drove off loving the Love Truck! Bucket by day, Love Truck at night. Go on, the Love Truck! Who cares if I lost my phone. Rebuilding my contacts already. Even better, when I got home I found $50 in the jeans I wore last night. Wuu huu. Safe to say my night was far better than my hung-over day. All about battling through the hangover! And who is the buddy that has a football pitch in his back garden . . . Robbie Williams. Go on the Bucket!!!

Waddling Fat Duck

Registration in college used to be a head-wreck. Now, looking back, not so bad. Not so bad at all. Especially compared to my trip to the DMV today. Where I headed to register the Bucket. Seeing as we bonded so well the other night, I decided maybe things could work out between us after all. During the day we'd just give each other space. Share quality time at night, when we would both be at our best. That was the plan. First things first, make the Bucket legal. Apparently I had a two-week grace period after buying it, but I decided to get it over and done with. Surprisingly organised by me. Register. Move on. Back to what I came to LA to do. Whatever that was again. Need to focus. Life keeps getting in the way.

As it was such a nice day, plus the fact I didn't want to risk the Bucket during daytime hours, I decided to walk to the DMV office. Let the Bucket have a lie-in. Google Maps informs me it's about a twenty-six-minute walk away, give or take a minute. iPod in. Walk on. About twenty minutes into the walk, I realise something. Lately my shorts or jeans have been laden down with my wallet, iPod, phone, notebook, chewing gum, Tic Tacs, keys, I could go on . . . just too many essential non-essentials. My belts don't seem to work. Most of the time my pants are falling down while I walk. Which is why I left a few things at home today. One being my wallet. Funk. Balls. Ape. One thing I needed. Idiot. Decided to plough on. Almost at the DMV. Find out what I needed to register it and get an estimate for the price. Kind of productive. If you're an idiot. Better to be looking at it than for it!

Get to the DMV office at about 4.58. Closes at 5. About fifty people still queuing. Get my ticket. Number 591. Number 541 being served next. Fifty was a good estimate by me. Sit down. And wait. And wait. Time to think. Wonder how much this would cost. The Dude had told me that it would cost very little. About $40. Maximum $40, actually. Now that I think about it, I remember he gave me his solemn word that it would cost me a maximum of $40 to register the truck. Swore on his mother's grave, in fact. 'MAXIMUM, maaaan. Tops. At the very most, $40 to transfer it to your name.' His exact words. Should have maybe questioned why he kept repeating this at the time. However, I was oblivious. Beyond belief. Now realise I should've maybe pondered a few more of the situations. Contract we signed. Back of a piece of notepad paper. Transaction. Occurred at the back of a church car park. Too many things for me to look back on and question. Not enough time to go through them all. Forward is the only way!

Finally get called up. Whip out my pink registration slip. Tell the lady I forgot my wallet. She doesn't care. What do I want? Could you just check how much I have to pay to register it, please? She checks the computer. And tells me eighteen sixty-seven. Jesus. That's brilliant. Only $18.67? Unreal cheap! Naivety washes over me. Must've beamed across my face, as the lady then says: 'No. That's eighteen hundred and sixty-seven dollars, not eighteen dollars . . . . ' Eh, what? That dirty fat fu— Sorry, not you. The guy who sold it to me. Are you sure?! Could you check again please? Double. Triple. Actually, hang on . . . (I knew there was a mistake!) . . . Another $50 fine from last week on it. Price just went up a bit more. Declined her next offer to check one last time. Couldn't take it getting any worse.

Apparently the truck hadn't been registered since 2001.

Owed penalties on it. Plus fines. Tickets. The works. Balls. Although when I was walking home, I wasn't too pissed off. Probably an innocent mistake. Probably. Somehow. Even if my gut did give me diarrhoea in an attempt to tell from the start that something was up with the whole affair. Always go with the gut. Now I just had more hassle with it. I'm sure it's all by accident though. Mistake of some sort by the Duck. Not like he would do it on purpose, surely. It'll be fine.

So, like I said, initially, didn't really bother me. Shrugged my shoulders. It'll all be sorted. And then. A song came on my iPod. 'Battles' by Atlas. If you're not familiar with it, I highly recommend it. Unreal to pump you up for going to the gym or before a night out. Not so good when you're slowly realising you were actually definitely made a fool of. Even more than you thought. Now that I think of it, why did we go behind a church in a back parking lot to exchange the cash? Pink slip? Didn't even have his name on it. Proof of purchase? A handwritten illegible note. Carfax report? $35. Ehh, I'll just take his word that what he's saying is true. What was I thinking? Mugged! Clueless. Naive. Ape. Dirty, fat, waddling duck!

At this stage I'm no longer walking. Now power-walking home. Swinging my arms. Turning up the volume of the song. Blaring. Fuelling my own rage. Marching to the beat. I'll get that b*****d somehow. Dirty f**k. How could I be so dumb!?! Nothing worse than the feeling you've been mugged and made a fool of. Power. Walk. On. Takes fourteen minutes to stride home. Raging. Remember his number was in the ad! Check Craigslist. Still up. Borrow Jess's phone. Ring the prick. Take a few deep breaths. Calm down. Maybe it was a misunderstanding. Yeah. Maybe. Rings twice. That's not a normal ringtone. Message. Delightful . . . 'Sorry, this number is no longer in service.' Oh Jesus. Message is repeated in Spanish for me, as if to rub it in. Calm down. Obviously dialled the wrong number. Punch in the digits again. Dial . . . 'Este número . . . ' You dirty f**ker!!! Arrrgghhh!!!! Prick!!! Nice cherry on top. I now have to buy a new phone for Jess as well. Seem to have developed a phone-throwing habit.

Write On!

Whole point of me coming to LA. Pursue acting and writing. I think. So far, mundane tasks such as visa issues, finding a job, buying a bucket, all that fun stuff, are making it hard to concentrate on these two things. Along with having fun every now and again. Obviously. These little everyday occurrences are constantly distracting me though. Setting myself up. What happened to hitting the ground running? Smooth sailing?! I didn't read anything about juggling in the contract when I signed up for this mission. In fairness I didn't have any acting classes scheduled for yesterday or today. However, I was planning on writing all day yesterday. Writing what, exactly? Not too sure.

Today, I was focused. Determined. It would be a writing day. Nothing could get in my way. Thankfully, as it turned out, I was only going across the courtyard. Only a fountain blocking my route there. Easily navigate around that. As I mentioned before, a writer lives in the house directly across from me. Fred. As he described himself to me: 'A big fat gay man. Who writes.' Funny old Fred. Reminds me of the character in *Jake and the Fat Man*. Not Jake. Obviously. Not fully sure what he's written, but the girls tell me a few feature films. Working on a reality show that's being developed. Anyways, he called over earlier looking for a cup of milk. No worries, Fred. In exchange, he offered some advice.

Fred asked me what my writing background was, briefly. So I briefly told him. I've written two pilot episodes. Nutshell! You did say be brief. Told me keep those sitcom episodes on the back burner. They could be the stuff to get the big break in a few years. Said he would read over them if I was interested. Let me know what he thought. No problem. Cheers Fred! Quickly warned me I needed to be more wary. Copyright everything. Then let him see it. Fred was delivering gems already. So Fred, how does one break into the writing world? Especially coming from another world.

One way in the door would be as a writer's assistant. Lowest rung. A start. Way to do this is by writing an episode of an existing show. Write a spec script. Send it to the right people. Read it. If they like, you could be offered a position as a writer's assistant. Which means you get to sit around the writer's table. After a while, start to throw out your own ideas. If your ideas are liked, you might get bumped up. And pretty soon you're a writer on *The Office*. (It was on TV at the time.) Fred knew of plenty of writers who broke in this way. Beaten path. Some even ended up playing parts on the shows.

Fred suggested that I should think about writing a spec script for *The Office*. Then asked if I'd ever read one of their scripts. I have. Brilliant. Really well written. Laugh out loud while reading it. The reason a spec script works so well is that you can visualise the characters in your head already. So you are playing out the scene. Making it funnier. My approach – my own fabricated story – made it harder for the reader to get an idea or know who the character might be. Unless their imagination is perfectly in sync with mine. Doubtful. Highly. Harder to imagine. Still, not impossible.

Let's call a spade a shovel all the same. I presume if you produce a beast of a script, it's a different story about needing a spec script to get your foot in. Maybe it's about who you show it to. However, until I produce that beast, writing an episode of *The Office* or some other show seems like a good way in. Good to know at least. Making today kind of productive. Learnt plenty about writing. Found out what to do at least, even if Google probably could've told me that if I'd asked the right questions. Now all I need is for an episode of *The Office* to pop into my head. Should be easy. Just have to get that dirty waddling b*****d out of there first.

Ehh . . . Happy Birthday!

Opportunity cost. Tonight. Do I. Go to another acting class. Or else go to some party with Jess. Or. Instead. Go play soccer. Emmm. Soccer on. My logic was that parties seem to be every night. Acting class . . . ehhh . . . I don't want to take too much on board too quickly. Need to soak in what I've learnt so far. Hopefully missing it won't cost me an Oscar. I'll catch up the next time. I swear. And in fairness, the venue for soccer was pretty unique. A pitch is a pitch, but this pitch was slightly greener. It's not every day of the week that a global pop star invites you up to his house to play ball. Unique old offer. The man is global! Plus, I'm sure Robbie was dying to hear how I had 'Strong' and 'No Regrets' on repeat on foreign exchange in Germany when I was in fourth year. Dying to hear.

Before playing *le foot*, I had one errand to run in the morning. Just the one. Unfortunately, it involved the Bucket. So that errand did not really run. Barely limped. Need to make a choice about the Bucket. Sell it. Or sell it faster. Until then, I need to make sure it'll get me from A to B, reliably. Thus far, it's been hit-and-miss. For my own peace of mind I also wanted to find out if I bought a complete dud. Or just a bucket of junk that would cost me triple the amount I first thought. Time to bring her to a garage. Mechanic could suss it all out for me. Change the oil. Change the wiper fluid. Should do the trick. Smooth over her builder's crack.

Like a fair few women, the Bucket and daylight do not get on so well. Looking worse every day. Her rusty fake tan spreading like a disease. At least it doesn't smell like curry. Just a lingering smell of my old buddy's feet instead. Oddly, I'd take that over a fake-tan curry smell. Too many clingy memories. Anyways, this morning I noticed there was something on the windscreen. Perhaps the waddling duck had called around. I wasn't in, so he left his new number for me! Lots of numbers on this paper. Words. 'Facing the wrong direction'. Parking ticket?! Close to the curb. Permit is showing. Not obstructing anything. On a two-way street. Just faced the wrong way? Great rule. Well worth the $43 fine. Looks like the registration fees and fines will soon tip over the $2,000 mark. Go on the Bucket.

Another bad thing about the daylight driving. People can see me in the Bucket. Churning the key. Grimacing. Six times before any spark. Head shamefully hanging each time. Spark. Strangely, condensation appeared on the windscreen. Thought that was pretty weird. What with the weather being so nice and all. Not even turning on the heater got rid of it. Soon after, I woke up. Realised it was smoke from the engine. Go on the Bucket. Jess recommended an auto-repair place to go to, Pink's Autos. Big bright pink place on Melrose. Can't miss it. Didn't miss it. Except it was the wrong big bright pink place. Turns out there are *two* big bright pink auto-repair shops. Find the right one the second time around. Guy comes out. Tells me he'll look at it, no problem. Just not until the morning. Can I leave it in overnight? Funk. Did not plan for that. Quick think.

Quite clearly something needed to be fixed. Or replaced. Or smashed open and beaten down. I'm not sure which. On the other hand, if I did leave it there overnight, I wouldn't be able to get up to Mulholland Drive for the game of soccer. Five-a-side. In you-know-whose. What to do? If it was anyone else, *anyone* – say, Gary, Mark, Jason or Howard – I would have left it at the garage. Seeing as it was an invite to play soccer in Robbie

Williams' back garden, I decided to take the risk. Fortune favours the brave! (Or is it the foolish?) Told the mechanic I'd be back bright and early tomorrow. The Bucket would be sleeping with me. Go on the Bucket!

Revved her up. Smoke starts bellowing out. Dodge. Ah, it'll be grand. Not wanting to risk driving home in one spurt, I made as many pit stops as I could. Bought football boots. Got something to eat. Walked around the Beverly Center. Eventually made it home. Chilled out. Spent far too long deciding what jersey would be best suited for the game. Went with the blue one. Decide it'd be the one to make a good first impression. Ended up wearing a T-shirt I usually reserve for nights out. Great work by me. Basically, I was now trying to impress a dude. And his buddies. A group of dudes. Living in WeHo must be rubbing off on me. T-shirt picked. Time for a quick cup of tea. Checked the time. Did a quick GM search for directions to the house. See the distance from my house. Check the time. Balls. Probably going to be late. Funk.

Sun has set. Only two churns to get the Bucket going. Managed to hook up my iPod to the radio as well. Sorry Akon, I've had enough. Threw on a mighty song. 'Bob' by Drive-by Truckers. Off I went. Cruising down through Beverly Hills. Which was pretty cool initially. Oh look at me, look what I can do! All by myself, kind of feeling. Until I had to take a few right turns. Up narrow roads. Winding. Steep. The Bucket still tipping away but not happy with me. Clouds trying to escape out of the engine without me noticing. Smoke signals getting worse. Begging for me to reconsider the drive. The further I go, the steeper the roads get. Bucket feels dodge.

Driving along shrouded with uncertainty is not the greatest feeling. Constant fear that you will break down in the middle of nowhere. Even if I broke down in the middle of somewhere in LA, I wouldn't know what to do. For one dumb moment it gave me a bit of a buzz. Living on the edge! Can we make it . . . yes we can! All that complete stupidity. Quickly beaten away by the very uncomfortable feeling of not knowing what's going to happen for the rest of the journey. Keeping you on edge. Not being able to control if you fall off. Never have I been so happy to arrive at such mundane venues like a garage or a shop, as I have in the Bucket. Or. Miraculously. Making it to a pitch on Mulholland Drive!

Pulled into the driveway of the address I was given. Steep enough driveway. Get out. Start walking around like a lost puppy. See a cluster of cars, most similar to mine . . . Mustangs, vintage Cadillacs, sparkling new Mercs . . . the Bucket blended right in. Kind of realise I probably should be parking where they were. As opposed to blocking the driveway. Plus I might've been facing the wrong way. Start up the Bucket again to move it quickly. Boom. Massive cloud of smoke bellows out. Not now Bucket, not now . . . Won't start. No life at all. Just smoke. Pouring out of her. Crying like a hysterical girl. Oh sweet Jesus. C'mon! Nada. Balls. What to do?! Funk, it's already 7.04. Told to be there at seven on the dot. Balls, balls and more funking balls! Keep turning the key in hope of a spark, a vroom, a sign. *Anything* but the horrific noise it's now making!

Suddenly it starts to freewheel down the driveway. Backwards. Without me releasing the handbrake. Panic kicks in. Oh my funk! I reverse into a bush. Hit the curb. Bucket stops rolling. Jump out. Panic some more. Sprint up to the house. Away from the murder scene. Bucket can be dealt with later. Don't want to miss out now I made it this far. Running up the steep hill. Wearing flip-flops. Clip-clopping like a demented horse. Get to the front gate. Locked. I can see the floodlights of the pitch. I can hear the voices of the people. How do I get in? Sounds like they're about to start. How the funk do I get in?! One asks where that Irish guy is . . . I shout out a feeble 'I'm here! Heeey. How do I get in?' No reply.

Only one option. That I can see. Has to be done. Go through the bushes. Don't look that thick. Should be fine. Head down. Go! Running through a bush. Arms held out in front. Eyes closed. Muffled yelps (*arrrrgh*). Eventually I get through. Emerge on the other side. Hear a nice loud rip. Favourite going-out T-shirt is ruined. Look up. And immediately see the entrance on the other side of the pitch. In fact, there are two. Ah, that's great. Good work out of me again. Quickly forgotten. Pitch. Is. Savage. Sitting above the house down below. One of the houses, it seems. Swimming pool next to it. Overlooking all of LA. Unreal views. Unreal backdrop. Savage. Greatest five-a-side pitch in the world. That *I've* played on, anyways.

Copelando sees me. Shouts over, telling me which way I'm playing. Oh, yeah, cool, I made it fine, thanks for asking. Start pretending to stretch. Pretend to be cool. Glancing around to see how many famous people are here. Pretending to be cool some more. Maybe I should've paid more attention to the match. Which had kicked off. And not been gazing out at the views as much. Thinking: 'I'm playing soccer, in Robbie Williams' house, on the top of the Hollywood Hills, overlooking all of LA. How did this happen again?' Maybe if I'd been paying attention to what was going on around me, I could've dodged a football square in the face. With what was maybe the first kick of the match. Maybe. Bang. Balls. Bollocks. Stumbling backwards to the ground. Eyes watering. Mouth spitting out blood. Seeing floaters. Getting helped up by the guy who had kicked it. Trying to focus on who was helping me up. Seeing. Splurting out: 'Don't worry about it Robbie, great meeting you, man!'

Then I wiped the tears from my eyes. And saw that it actually wasn't Robbie. Just a guy who kind of looked like him. His chef, I think. Eh, no worries bud, game on! Ha, good first impression by me. I'd like to tell you then how Robbie did come straight over after that. Introduced me to everyone. Gave me a high-five for coming up to play. Asked if I could sing, interested in doing a duet with him, etc etc. However. That didn't happen. As he wasn't even there. I don't think he's even in the country. Bit of a letdown. To say the least. I did get to meet his dog at least. Who jumped out of the pool and soaked me. So that was nice.

Good game in the end. Went on for about two hours. Managed to line up a back-up lift home. Just in case. Feared the worst for the Bucket. Thank God I did. Although being stranded up there for the night might not have been the worst thing. Not even a whimper out of the Bucket afterwards. Gonzo. Embarrassing me in front of everyone. Popped the hood. Not sure why. Just looked at the engine. Hummed. Hawed. Looked at it some more. Tried to start it up again. No joy. When asked if I had AAA, I laughed. Followed by mumbling out a bit of gibberish. Not much I could do really. Only option was to just leave it there. Pity I didn't break down in the slums or get carjacked. Could've just left the keys in the ignition. Early birthday present for Rob instead. Small thank-you for the game of ball. Nice touch by me really. Might go back in the next few days. Give it one last try. Otherwise. I shall be throwing the keys over the side of Mulholland Drive. Get rid of the junk. Pretend it never happened. Good birthday present all the same. Pumped to see what Rob gets me for mine!

Sign What? Sweat Where?

Mighty morning! Woke up. Present for me on my bed. A T-shirt. Whoever gave me that knows me too well. Check who it's from . . . Bill Clinton! Bill gave me a T-shirt? Well, kind of. Not really. Not at all. He gave it to Jess last night. Who was chatting with him at his fund-raiser party. Asked if she could take one of the T-shirts to give to me. See, kind of. Go on the Jess! Cheers to Bill. Then. I checked my phone. Text. From Robbie Williams! What the what? 'Footie again tonight? Good game last night.' Well, not exactly from Robbie. His buddy. All the same, to my delusional eye, it would appear I am in the clique. Delusion on! I knew my tricks and flicks would come in handy one day. So, obviously, after all that, it was a mighty morning. How could it not be? I can be quite easily entertained at times. Now I had a choice to make. Rob's for soccer? Or Aaron's for acting? Decided to go for a stroll. Mull. Up to Coffee Bean I go.

Thus far, my trips to the Bean have been pretty interesting. Random selection of people. Last week I think Perez Hilton tried to chat me up while I was pocketing a few extra Splendas. Or else he was giving out to me. Couldn't read his tone. Hard to say. Chatted with an actor who I recognised from an episode or two of *Friends*. Telling me how much he still struggles. I would've thought otherwise. You were on *Friends*! Wrong. Another day I spoke to a rather voluptuous girl. Can't remember how I ended up talking to her. A lot of that conversation seems to have escaped my memory. I do know she's in porn. Apparently. That's what she told me at least. Some random guy did come up while we were chatting and asked for a photo with her though. Got the impression she was making big bucks from porn. Took her number. Not for me. Purely to give to my *Friends* buddy. Struggling and all!

One guy stood out from the rest. Good old Amadeus. Long curly hair. Rotting teeth. Dressed in purple pajamas. Mid-forties. Thick New York accent, kind of reminded me of Gene Wilder. (*Willy Wonka!* was my first impression.) Initially I thought he was a homeless guy. Whose feather I picked up and handed back to him. After he dropped it by my foot. In return he spoke to me for a good hour about the origins of hemp. Rambling on about hemp and a book about the emperor wearing no clothes, and Amsterdam, and Jack Herer, and his friend putting up money for hemp, and his mystical Irish friends who pre-dated Ancient Greece, and when he was young and he just kept going on. Putting Abe Simpson to shame. Rambles of a new magnitude. I thought I was bad. Amadeus then moved on to the origins of the chain I was wearing. Apparently, he knew that the chain had been in my family for generations. (It hasn't.) And was worth a lot of, *lot of* money. (It's not.) All the time, speaking in a Welsh/Jamaican accent. Thinking it was an Irish one. All a bit odd. All a good laugh. Pinch of salt. Harmless crazy dude.

Although. He did then start to tell me stories about guys from The Who and Led Zeppelin. As if they were his friends. Which threw me off a bit. Especially as they sounded legit. Names adding up. Interesting stories. Caught my attention. I have been told that in LA the only difference between being crazy and being eccentric is a million dollars. Amadeus was definitely the crazy side. I thought. Until he started lashing out $100 bills to the server. Half-expecting him to ask me for some change when I offered him a coffee. Nay. Amadeus had it covered. Big thick wad of hundreds. Tipped a couple of hundred.

While wearing purple pyjamas. Waving a feather. And dancing around my table. Making me realise that LA is odd. Very odd. Not that I needed much reminding. But. Normal life, this is not. Normal logic does not apply. Then again, if I wanted normal, I could've stayed at home

Alas, none of my interesting acquaintances were beaning it up today. Just that loving couple. Little Asian chap. Big black fellow. Who kept telling me how they both loved basketball. Asking if I might be able to get them courtside. Which I started to think was code for something. Then asked if they could take a photo with me. Sure? Asked for my autograph. Eh, pardon? Realised it was mistaken identity. Still, gave them my autograph. Must've seen that it did not say Kobe. Just Merrick. Giving me a look of complete disappointment. Told them I don't play for the Lakers. I thought ye just wanted to be buddies with me lads, I'm still the same person! Felt bad for letting them down. At least they didn't mistake me for Amadeus, I suppose. Although he's probably in a better situation than I am. Financially anyways, it seems. Spur. Mind made up. Tonight. Soccer, no. Acting, on. Need to get on the road to my big break. Seeing as all I've really done up to this point is move here. Time to wrap up my Oscar! Then I too could wear purple pyjamas.

Needed to confirm the class. *Dring dring.* Howdy. Merrick here. Think I might sign up long-term. Although one more class to audit would help. Just to see if it's the one I'm going to go with. Just to make sure. As Aaron was the best teacher I'd been to so far. Shur didn't he say so himself! One more class for free would probably sway my decision. Before I committed. Which I would do next week . . . And on I went. Amadeus style. Until my gibberish worked. Free. Giddy up them steps! Unfortunately, Jess wasn't up for it. Disappointing. Not just because of the lift or anything. More that I'm a fan of hanging out with Jess. And the lift. Taxi on.

Class starts late. Suits me. When Aaron does arrive, he opens with the same: 'Sorry I'm late, sorry, sorry . . . reason being, not to brag, just the truth . . . saved a multi-million-dollar movie from folding . . . not saying it to impress you but . . . millions of dollars would have been lost if I didn't make a few calls. Sorted out the whole mess. What can I say? I'm a firefighter. I'm not saying it to brag. That's just how it is. I saved a lot of people's lives by saving that movie. Life-saver.'

Lets out a deep breath. Shrugs his shoulders apologetically. Showing immense modesty. Should we all be clapping? Finally he finishes with: 'And by the way, I have a huge, massive . . . ' Which is when I started clapping and cheering him on. Well, maybe he didn't say the last line. And I didn't clap. But that is actually a watered-down version of the great work he's doing. Weird enough seeing someone physically take his hand and pat himself on the back, while speaking. Odd. Maybe he had the hic-cups.

I will give the man credit though. When he pauses, stops talking about himself and teaches, he is pretty, *pretty* good. Might be basic stuff but he highlights gems in the scene studies. My eyes are untrained too though. Seems good . . . Don't anticipate the lines . . . Pick a role suited for you . . . Drop your inhibitions. One thing that stuck in my head was this: if you're serious about making it in this business, you should know that your relation-ships will suffer. As in the couple kind. Probably friends as well. That's the sacrifice. This is not a normal way of life. He's defi-nitely right about that! Have to be strong-willed. If you're seri-ous about it. Know this now. Decide if you're still willing to take the risk.

Finally, after opening his pants for a while and flopping it out on the table for another half an hour, Aaron finished on a good point at the end. Sweat the small details. Acting-wise. Writing-wise. They're what really count. His knowledge of the small details was impressive. Although now I think he might be a cross-dresser. Extensive knowledge about what it feels like to wear high heels all day. Maybe that's why he insisted on being the man in class. Anyways, all about sweating the small details. Which got me thinking on the way home. Walking back. Through the barren streets of LA. Not so much sweating about acting or writing though. Instead. Cold sweating. About life. Mighty. Doubt. How are you?

Fear Not!

Sweating. Small. Details. Cold. Sweating. Buckets. Had a few drinks when I got home last night. Listened to chilled mixes on my iTunes. Hangover mixes. Slow. Deep. Haunting. Repeat. Ever think you're messing up your chance at life? Too much thinking. Mixed with drinking. Not a good combination. All leading to the return. Hello buddy, you're back I see. Fear. Soul herpes. With you for life, it seems. This time, showing up with his buddy, Doubt. Oh Jesus, I think I'm funked. Not funked as in funked. Not like someone who has a mortgage, lost their job, and has a family to support. Not that kind. More that I don't really know what I'm doing – here, in LA, with my life – except that I'm spending every penny I have doing it. Calm down. I'll be fine. Just have one more glass of whiskey. Listen to one more Sigur song. Funk. Doubt. Get out!

All along I didn't really think about it not working out. Not worrying about the possibility of ending up in LA with no money, no job and no visa. Sting used to be an illegal alien and he turned out OK. Plus, I can always go back home to . . . ? None of my friends were telling me good things. Life does not seem to be fun there at the minute. Would I even get a job at this stage back in Ireland? Doing what? Back to what I was doing? If I had to go home. The thought of being broke at home. Moving back in with my parents. Like the chump that I am. Balls. I did not budget for this. Or think this through. B*****ks. Doubt. You're dominating me! No light in my dumb tunnel. Cue dizziness and cold sweats. Cheers for the advice, Aaron. Small buckets of sweaty details oozing out of me now.

Subconsciously I've been ignoring the fact that I don't have a bottomless pit of money. While at the same time, shovelling my money into a furnace. Avoiding the facts, by not looking at my Irish bank balance. Buy now, pay later. Which is perhaps why the fact that I spent thousands of dollars this week took a while to sink in. Even after I checked my balance. Due to delayed reaction in my online banking. Still looks good! Pretending not to know that it wouldn't show up for a few days. Lying to myself. Like an ape. Until today. When it showed up. Wiping far too much off my balance in one fell swoop. Reality head-butting me in the face. Too big a chunk of my dwindling gun-funded pennies was just horsed into the furnace, spent on a bed that I can't afford, and a broken-down Bucket. Shrewd. To think I took an investment class for four years. If you ever need investment advice, give me a call. 1800-IM-AN-APE.

Adding fuel to the Fear, I've now gathered that fulfilling my dreams and ambitions is not going to be a quick fix. No magic wand. Where's Simon and *American Idol* when you need him. Pity I only like to sing when drunk. And naked. Would they let me on the show like that? Nay. My goals lie elsewhere. Might take a tad longer than the three-month time-frame I'd given myself. Which has had me thinking, for a change. On a separate note. I wonder what Mexico might be like at this time of year? Might check it out. Just for a few days. See if I can get a cheap deal. However, if I was going to go down for a look, I'd need to do it soon. Not leave it to the very last minute. Might look suspicious. That could be a call. Slump off. Plan on.

Action needed . . . Bucket, I love you. But I can't stand the sight of you. Reminding me of the bad choices I've made in my life. Time we part ways. Try and get some cash back for it. Anything. To put my mind at ease, if nothing else. Show to myself I'm not a complete ape. Just half an ape. Contacted a junkyard. Made me an offer . . . $180. Ha. Plus, they'd come and tow it. Time to wash my hands. Could've offered me a biscuit and I would've probably said yes. Jess tried to stop me. Don't do it. She saw the bond we shared. Plus, she thought I'd get a better deal. Nay. Sorry, has to be done. Didn't tell her my internal dilemma. That I couldn't see the light. Bottle up that darkness! Accepted the offer. Someone from the junkyard would come by tomorrow and take it away. Sounds good. Although in my dizzy, panicked state, I forgot to ask Robbie if he'd mind me taking it back. Hope he doesn't mind. I'll get him something else.

Settled my mind a bit. Girls tried to settle me by luring me to the party they were having downstairs. Consisting of them and a lot of rocker dudes. Sipping on cans and smoking. Usually I would be well up for it. Not tonight though. Chilled in my room. Chatted with my buddy back in Ireland instead. Good old Facebook chat. She gave me some encouragement. At least I think she intended it to be. Only have a few weeks left, make the most of it. Don't want to come home with nothing to show for it. Told her I wouldn't be coming home empty-handed. I bought a good few T-shirts and jackets my first week here. Weak joke. Conversation kind of freaked me out. Wish she had urged me to do more to stay for as long as I can. And the T-shirts made me think that that money would be handy now too. Oh Jesus. What am I doing?! Lying in bed. Staring at the ceiling. Covered in Fear once more. Bleakness all round.

Personally, I think a night makes far more of a difference than a day does. Not the greatest sleep. First time I eventually nodded off, Layla and Jess woke me up by bursting in and jumping into bed with me. I thought I was being attacked physically by the Fear. Didn't have a clue what was going on. Worst things have kept me awake at five in the morning in fairness though. Fell back to sleep. Woke up this morning. Fully aware of my current situation. And it felt great. Not great as in how it would feel if something good was to happen. But great as in some sort of burden had been lifted off my shoulders. I think it was the burden of fooling myself. Far better to know and accept that you're in a bit of a predicament, than just hope and think that you're not. Time to change things.

First things first. Voicemail. Junkyard guy. Postponing until Monday. Who's the chump now?! Grab my laptop. Ad up on Craigslist. Laying out in exact details the story with the truck – how I bought it under false pretenses, got screwed, and does anyone want to take it off my hands? Ten minutes later. Phones ring. Mexican dude. Asking how much for the Bucket. Make me an offer. I'm looking to get rid of it ASAP. '$1,000?' Eh, pardon me? Double-check to make sure he's read all the ad. You've seen what's owing on registration? And that it's a Bucket? He has. Still interested. Says he'll come check it out. In the next hour I get three similar offers. Eh, OK, call around during the week to see it, lads. I tried to sell the Bucket last week. Zero offers. Maybe something down to me using words like 'lovable', 'quirky' and 'reliable'. Faced facts. Told the truth. Out of nowhere, karma was back on my side!

Someone turned on a torch. Light came shining back. Stopped freaking myself out. Worrying about what might happen. Waste of time. Came up with a plan. A rough one at least. Sell the truck. Fly to Mexico for cheap. Come back. Get another three-month visa. Keep the dream alive. Hopefully win the green-card lottery. Win the normal lottery. Be plucked out of obscurity for a movie role. And write an episode for *The Office*. If I could do all that, I'd be sorted. If not, at least I tried. I might sleep better tonight as well knowing I'm f**ked. For once, it actually is a good thing to know. Time has come to do something about it! Time to go swinging. Fighting Irish!

Hands Off My Sex Pistol

The Bucket must've had a make-over. Or recorded a hit. Something. All of a sudden, she is *en vogue*. An overnight sensation! Offers flooding in. Emails, texts, phone calls, voicemails. People are chomping at the bit to get their slice of her. Most of them seem to be Mexican. Perhaps the Bucket is a sex symbol down there. As her trusted agent, I inform them all the same thing. First come, first served. As long as the Bucket likes her new suitor, obviously. Whatever my plans for the morning were meant to be, they get flung out the window. Looks like today could be the day the Bucket flies the coop!

Time for breakfast. Oddly, I've been having to drink my porridge lately. Spoons go missing on a regular basis in my house. Yet another mysterious thing in LA, which I cannot understand. Where. Are all. The spoons?!! Drink my porridge. Cup of tea while I wait. And then get hit by the tidal wave. An onslaught. Spoof phone calls. Bluffers. Time-wasters. Ridiculous lies. 'I'm one street away.' OK. 'Now I'm outside your house.' You're not. 'I am outside your house, sir.' Don't lie to me. And so on. For five more minutes. Until he hung up. Just before me. Dick. Phone rings again. Different Mexican guy. 'I am in San Diego. Will you drive to me? I might buy it. I have cash. $50.' Click. '*Señor*, I am here. Where are you? Can you wave your hand so I can see?' Wave. Wave. I am waving. 'Keep waving, I cannot see.' Prick. Continued on with at least ten more people. Sitting around in false hope. Giving out the benefit of the doubt. Like a fool. Dumb. Muppet. Muppets. Three hours well spent.

At least the next three made up for it. Headed up to Rob's

house for some soccer. Pretended not to know who owned the Bucket when asked by Zen, the guy who gave me a lift to the game. The English vs. the French, it seemed. Except the French had a famous Italian singer. Apparently. No clue who he was, to be honest. And the English had an idiot Irish guy, who spends his day waving at no one. I'm sure they all heard of me. Eclectic mix of DJs, musicians, actors, successful people and the likes. Plus me. Even a Sex Pistol was playing, Jonesy. Sex Pistol? LA. Is. Random! Good game of fussball. Sweated buckets. Savage heat. World's greatest five-a-side pitch! Although I probably enjoyed afterwards even more. Listening to the stories. Everyday stories guys tell each other. Except it's an LA-day version.

Jay's friend did that to Michelle's buddy? Who? As in the movie dude? Isn't she an actress as well? Who slept with that big fat sweaty guy to get her break? Cameron who? Really? She's mad for it? So is Rose? Heather? Helena? Kristen did what? No way, with who? Christina? Oh, with him. No way. And you used to date both of those girls? *You* did? No way. All in all, impressive post-match banter. Probably arms and legs added onto the stories, but at the time I didn't care. Interesting to hear. At least now I know who I have to sleep with to get my break. And then a plane crashed into the pitch. The end.

Dumb morning. Random day. Night followed suit. Went out. Got drunk. Met a girl. Who happened to be Mexican. My one line of Spanish worked out well. Went to her place. Tequila. Some more. Socks full. Bit of Irish dancing. Continued on to a bit of . . . Duu. She started speaking Spanish midstream. Started off hot enough. I was drunk though. Thought I heard the word Bucket. I was really drunk though. Asked her. The word Bucket came out of my mouth. In some context. She thought I called her a bucket. Looked like a bucket? Either way, whatever I said, it did not go down well. Tried to punch me. As in fist-clenched would've-knocked-me-out kind of punch. Missed. Tried to kick me. In my sex pistol. While my clothes were on the ground. Would've been that bit sorer. Missed. Realised she was an angry woman. So I had to run away. Ran for dear life. Minus a pair of socks. And one runner. Random. Dumb. Fun. Duu!

The Cable Guy

Woke up. Went outside. Saw a guy in a turban. Big long beard. He waved. I waved back. Turned around. And went back inside my house. Back to up bed. Woke up twenty minutes later. Phone ringing once more. Back outside. Guy in the turban was still there. He shouted out to me. Which is when I realised that was him. That was the guy I'd been speaking to on the phone. I thought I was looking for a surfer jock guy! Which is what he sounded like. Hey bro. Duuude. Felt bad for profiling. Anyways, he wants to buy the Bucket. Very keen. He is Roy. Asks me to take him to the Bucket. Jesus, he seems legit. I mean, he's actually here. Not just pretending to be on the phone. Let's go to the Bucket!

En route we stop off at the petrol station. I pick up some Tic Tacs. Roy fills up a small tank of petrol. Just in case that was the problem with the Bucket. Don't be so silly. Tic-tac? Takes about twenty minutes to get there. Great small talk all the way. He's laughing at everything that comes out of my mouth. Before it even really comes out. Odd. Told him I spoke German. Thought it was the funniest thing he'd ever heard. Hmmm. Odd. Keeps telling me that I'm funny. And informing me that I'm Irish. And that we should go get drunk together. Hmmm. Odd. Maybe if he stopped interrupting all my funny interesting jokes, I might've believed him. Tested him. Purposely made up a joke. That made no sense. What do you call a man holding a stick? A tree! Laughed like there was no tomorrow.

Get to the Bucket. Sunshine sparkling down on it. Making it look horrendous. Must've been out last night. Decrepit-looking.

Looks more hung over than I do. In. Key. Turn. Churn. Nothing. Roy suggests the petrol. Begrudgingly I fill her up. Not even a flicker. No life at all. I'm ready to start smashing. Between it being so early and everything, my tolerance was low. Then started to remember last night. That girl last night was hot enough! Why did I call her a bucket?! Tolerance grew lower. Wanted to abuse the Bucket. Not that I could actually smash the big beast of a machine or anything. Definitely the most head-wrecking thing I've ever bought though. Wasting time and money on the whure. Roy interrupts my mutterings. Shows me that the petrol I just put in was now leaking out. Must be a hole in the tank. Leaking tank? And a broken gas gauge? I hadn't a hope in hell!

Resigned failure. Plonk down on the curb. No more. Sick to death of everything related to the truck. Don't care about selling it. Don't care about putting more petrol in. Don't care if I've wasted all this time and money on it, for nothing. Roy, please, just take me home. Please, Roy, please. Roy throws his arm around my shoulder. Consoles me. It'll be all OK. Don't worry. One more tank will do the trick. Felt his beard too close to me. Creeped me out. However, I no longer had the energy to argue any more. Whatever you think, Roy. You're driving. To the closest petrol station. Which is the one we went to en route. A two-minute drive away from my house. Half-tempted to just walk home. Didn't have the energy. I was sapped even more from that drive. Twenty minutes there. You're so funny. You're Irish. Twenty-five back with traffic. You love to be drunk. You are Irish. You don't say, Roy. Tell me again, please.

One more tank will do the trick. Obviously. It doesn't. Never going to be as easy as that. Roy, please take me home, I've had enough. Now almost two hours since he picked me up. On the way home it all gets a bit weird. Well, weirder. Roy changes the topic of small talk. Away from me. Which was nice. Asks who I am living with. Looks like it's a nice place. I stupidly tell him I live with two girls. And that it *is* a nice place. Oh man, the four of us should go out together tonight. Or I should come to yours and we should drink with them, see what happens. Could he come in and see it, see them? Emmm, no. Get to my street. Again he asks if he can come in? Just to wash his hands and face. And meet my roommates, perhaps. All that does sound appealing Roy, but I can't, I'm afraid. I throw him twenty dollars for petrol. He examines the note. Notices I made him stop at a different building. Asks me why I did that? Starts to get annoyed. Slow hard blinks. Did we not have a good day together? Oh Jesus. Time to go. Car is still rolling slowly down my street but I decide to jump out. Tell him he can't come in. Definitely can't. We have the painters in. Painting the whole place. Looks awful. Wouldn't want guests around. Another time. Goodbye Roy. I said *goodbye*!

Stopped the car. Staring at me. I thought initially it was a look of dejection. Now I'm beginning to think it was the look of a psychotic person. 'I know where you live.' Great. The minute I got in my door, texts and emails started to roll in. Can he just have the truck for free? Can he take all the parts he wants off it? Can he call over for a beer? What am I doing right now? Did I get his voicemail? Can we be friends? Roy, you are a big bucket of nuts. Please funk off! Decided to lay low for the night. Hide out. Just in case. Jess decided to chill for the night as well. Took my mind off the Bucket. Off Roy. Off my poor lost runner from last night. Brought me to Yogurtland for frozen yogurt. Roy still had me very suspicious though. Fat-free, sugar-free, carb-free, and it tastes good? Come on Jess, I'm not an idiot. Which is what I was saying to her, as she suddenly stopped at a red light. And I ended up spilling both our containers. All over her leather seats. All over the floor. All over myself. Ahem. *Not an idiot?*

Spanglish, Sí? Eh? No? Sí

Sunday starts off with a call from a Mexican guy looking to buy the truck. Buddy, you know what, you actually don't. I've given up on it, no longer interested in selling it. 'No, *señor*, I want buy truck.' No my good man, you don't, trust me. I'm even dumber in the morning. Convinced him to let it go. No longer something I was going to worry about. Out of sight, out of mind. Gotta go, *señor*, I've another call coming through. Robbie Williams. Well, my buddy who lives in his house. What's that now? I have to move the Bucket. Blocking the driveway. What happened to out of sight?!!! OK, I'll call you back. *Dring dring* . . . Hey *señor*! Yeah, maybe you *should* buy that truck. I was lying, it *is* a thing of beauty! Time to give it one last try. Be outside mine in ten!

Cautiously venture outside, give a quick look for the cable guy in the bushes. All clear. Looks good. See two little Mexican chaps waving at me. Figure out quite quickly that they can speak almost no English. One guy can say 'I want buy truck' along with the number three. And I think the other guy can just look at me grumpily. Kind of has a look as if he wouldn't mind shooting me, for some reason. Usually, Mexicans are the only people who understand me. And I get on quite well with them. However, it seems these guys speak little English. And are not a fan of me. My Spanish consists of 'Que, sí, noo, Rauuuuuul' and some chat-up line which I don't even think makes sense any more. Whatever. Business deal. Jump into their pick-up truck. Off we go. In silence. Me breaking it up now and again with the odd sentence here and there. Odd sentence. As in I keep repeating the

Spanish chat-up line. Back on the road to the Bucket. Feels good!

Something odd happens then. Arrive at the Bucket. I get into the Bucket. I turn the key. And the Bucket starts up perfectly. What did I do? Am I am miracle worker?! Not a clue what happened. All I know is that the Love Truck is back! The two Mexican guys have no clue what I'm on about when I proclaim this to them. The guy who looks like he wants to shoot me, jumps into the passenger seat. Looks like we're heading back to my house. The Bucket is coming home. Prodigal son returns! Just like that. Smooth sailing all the way. Parking spot right outside my place. Go on the funking Bucket!!! For the next few minutes the grumpy dude checks the engine out while I have a good free-flowing conversation with Raul. So do you want to buy the truck? '*Si* . . . Three.' OK, pardon, three which? Three hundred? 'Noo, three.' OK, three what? 'Eh.' *Si?* 'Eh?' Pardon? What what? What the funk? I don't know what you're saying. And why does the grumpy dude hate me so much?!! Tell him stop clenching his fists!!!

For some unknown reason, I try to speak German to him. Nothing. Long shot. Irish perhaps? A phrase or two of French? My Spanish chat-up line one last time? The line which makes zero sense? Maybe that's why you want to punch me? I'll give it one last go, shur. Nada? None of the above work. Round and round we go. In the end, I tell him I'll take $300 for it. Cut my losses. I think that's what he has offered anyways. All I get back is 'Ehh? No. Three.' That's what I said, $300! This time, they've had enough. Look me up and down. Complete disgust. What did I do chaps? Please fill me in. But they don't. They just walk away from me. Back into their truck. Drive off. Just like that. Not saying a word. I called after them. I waved. They kept on going. Haggling was over.

Being honest, if he had waited for one more minute of haggling, I would have said '*Sí*, ehh, here' and just given him the keys. Take it off my hands for free. And . . . now that I think about it, free . . . OK three . . . yes three . . . no free . . . sound a lot alike. Balls. Come back, Raul, she's yours!

Obsessive and Clingy,
I'm on the Rebound . . .

Obsessions are never healthy. Quite clearly, I have one. A Bucket. I admit this. I admit it, in the hope that I can now move on. I just need to get rid of it. Her. It. All of this has been going on for too long. My brain won't settle until I do. Unhealthy relationship. I might keep losing runners and calling women buckets during sex if I don't sort it out. Wrecking my head. And I also realise it's absolutely wrecking some of my neighbours' heads. One neighbour yesterday released an orgasmic 'pheeeeewww' when I told her it was for sale. Ape. Hot ape though, in fairness. I've realised as well that everything else has been put on hold while I've been trying to sell it. For the past few days, there has been no job-hunting, no visa-sussing, no acting classes, no boozing, no going out, no gallivanting, no nothing. I've had no life, all because of my obsession with the Bucket. No more. Cutting her loose. Getting my life back on track . . . Enough is enough!

At least, that was the plan. Lasted all morning. Until I got a phone call from Silverstre. Yet another Mexican guy. Silvestre. *Señor*, I wants to buys the Buckets. Today. $400 cash. In hand. Preferably mine. On his way. Half an hour. Max. Not sure why, but yet again, I kind of believed him. I must just be dumb. Although he did go into a lot of detail as to why he needed it. Carry his horse around. Presume he meant transport, but who's sweating the details. Well, actually, me is who. Seeing as two hours later there was still no sign of Silvestre, nor his horse. Sweet Lord above. Once again, a dumb ape!

At this stage, my agitation had built up a nice head of steam. Needed to calm myself down. By having a yogurt. As you do. As it's a great relaxant? Go to the fridge. All my yogurts are gone. Three left this morning. See that Layla is sitting at the dining-room table. Eating one of my yogurts. Two empty cartons next to her. My yogurts! What the funk?! 'Sorry (fake smile), I'll buy some more today.' No. You won't. That is what you always claim while you're eating my food. It's only a yogurt, I'm told. Layla claims not to have eaten them all. Well, I don't see anyone else here. And you're always eating my yogurts. And it's always only one. And I could really do with a yogurt right about now. And you never have any yogurts of your own. And after a while it starts. To drive. Me. FUNKING NUTS. I JUST WANT A YOGURT!!!

Worthwhile argument to get into. Apologies. Awkward smile. Leave the room. Time to cool down. (Although between you and I still think I'm right.) As I'm cooling, my phone starts ringing. If this is Silvestre and his horse . . . no . . . 'Mike'. Who the funk is Mike? And how is he saved on my phone? Was he a weird gym buddy I met? The dude who owned the house in the Hills who took a fancy to me? Swedish Boy George? Was he . . . clickity click, drop of the penny . . . the Dude, that fat waddling bastard. Sweet Jesus, almost dropped the phone with the surge of rage that flooded through me! Go to your happy place. Go to Yogurtland.

Took a deep breath. Calmed myself down a bit. I'll see what he has to spoof to me at least. Wait until he finishes apologising. Then launch into him. Clicked the green button . . . 'I am going to f**king hunt you down and kill you, maaaan. You don't know who you're messing with.' What? Wait, what? What. The. Funk?! A stream of threats then pours out. He's going to kill me. Stab me. Sue me. F**k me. Forgot to say 'Up' there, Mike. I better watch my back. He knows where I live. I better take his name off my ads on Craigslist. Better not call him a con man. Tough man and all that I am, I included in my ad on Craigslist trying to sell the Bucket that if anyone knew the fat waddling prick, tell him I wanted a word. Someone must've told him. Coinciding with his phone working again. So now, somehow, he was the one threatening to kill me? How the holy funk did this swing around?!!!

'That s**t is derogatory and blasphemous, motherf***er. Take those ads down. And are you calling me a duck?!' Idiot. You don't even know what word you're trying to spit out. I presume you meant defamatory, fat duck? I spit back. Great comeback by me. What am I saying?! I try to launch into a proper retaliation. Keeps cutting me off. Please shut up for two seconds.

Does it again. You used to be the Dude, you fat miserable cu– again?!! Rage spills over. Finally. Effing. Blinding. Swearing. Cursing. I won't lie, it takes a bit to get me going. Yogurts seemed to start me. He topped me off: 'Come up. Kill me. I'll get you first, you effing prick, we'll be waiting, you fat f**king b*****d, wasting my time, you f**king langer!!!' And so on and so forth. At the time I thought it was a good rant. However, typing it out now, eh, vicious. Felt good at least. Pity he probably didn't get what a langer was. Not sure who I was referring to when I said 'we' either. Pity as well that I think he hung up a few words into my rant.

Bit of a pity as well that I finished it all off by throwing my phone through the living-room window. Didn't smash the window. Just ripped open the safety-net yoke covering it. Burst through. Kept going. Hitting the right shin. Of the handbag lady. Who happened to be snooping around outside. Probably sue me for that. She and the Duck should team up. Unfortunately, not really the worst part. I didn't realise that Layla and Jess were at the door watching all of this. Along with Jess's mother next to them. Who I had forgotten was visiting this week. Great way to introduce myself to her. Usually like to make a good impression with the mums as well. Making matters worse, she then apologised for eating one of my yogurts earlier. They'd all had one. One each. Layla didn't devour them on her own. The girls said I was nice like that, wouldn't mind them taking it. Made me feel super. So, eh, nice flight here? Great.

No harm done in the end. Invite me along to Chateau Marmont for a drink. I needed one. Good old laugh. Cameron Diaz happened to be sitting next to us as well. Not looking great to be honest. Although, after what I heard the other day, I might have a chance! I think I may have been slightly distracted by the whole bucket affair for a while up there. Seeing as her friend tried to spark up a conversation. And I just said howdy. And that was it. Shook her hand goodbye. Girls looked at me strangely. Even Jess's mum asked what was wrong with me. Sorry. Still under the Bucket's smell. Spell. Dumb. Bucket is over. Time to break free. If I sell it, I sell it. If not, at least it's been eventful, a passionate affair.

At least the rant and the boozes afterwards did me the world of good. Time to move on. Forget about fools who claim they want to buy the truck. Forget about fools threatening to kill me over the phone. Forget about who has been the real fool in all of this fiasco! No more time-wasting. From now on I'm going to stick to not being smooth when girls come up saying hi, while being surprised at how Cameron Diaz doesn't look as good as I thought she would. All of which is quite clearly *far* more productive!

Lads' Night Out

Kind of gutted. Might no longer be able to use the line 'Oh, my friend, he's in the bathroom' to explain who I'm out with on my solo nights out. Seeing as it looks like my friend might actually be in the bathroom. Woah. Would be weird. Up until this point I've been more or less heading out on my own. Like a weirdo. Until. Two offers last night. Two?! Look at me go. Popular ape. Karaoke with Layla and Jess. Or head out with the lads from soccer in Robbie's house. Spoilt for choice. Re de de. What to do, where to go? Lads' night out. Welcome change. Even if I am living in Boys Town. Banter on. Could always fall back on karaoke if needs be. Boozing with the lads first, meet the girls later. Never left me down before.

Text Copelando. In. Flynn. What's the plan? He'll swing by my abode. Pick me up. Running late though. No worries. Suits me. Few cheap boozes at home first. Fairly pumped by the time Copelando arrives . . . C'mon the lads!!! Cope, where are we off to?! Les Deux. Rock night. Meeting the lads in there. Sounds good to me. Pull up outside the door. Crowd outside is rock and roll. Funky as funk. Mohawks, top hats, get-ups, get-downs, the lot. Cool as funk. Looks good to me. Just as we're going in, Copelando tells me: 'I faawking hate this place, mate. Bunch of w**kers.' Which I thought was a bit odd. As he suggested the place. I must be shallow though. Walk in. Music is savage. With a load of hot funky women. Buckets of gems everywhere. Great call out of Copelando! Rock on!

Someone doesn't agree . . . 'I faawking hate this place. Look at the state of her . . . Don't fancy yours much, love.' Ooook.

What are we drinking boss? 'Naw mate, I don't drink much . . . Don't like yours much either, love!' Oh right. Bit odd. Especially as she was funking hot. Eh, want to go find the lads or what? 'Yeah, not sure who's here really, one guy who used to play might be in here, I think he's DJing.' Oh right. Are the lads even out? 'Not sure mate . . . Don't fancy yours much either, love. Bunch of W**KERS!!!' I'm completely lost at this stage. 'The lads' don't seem to be out. More worryingly, Copelando appears to be the angriest man alive. Hates this place with a passion (no clue why). I think he's engaged, so it's not another gay scenario. I need a drink. I'll be back in a minute boss! Decide I'll still get two, could be another long weird night.

Head back out to Copelando. As I walk back up to him, he tells me, loudly, surrounded by people: 'I'm not a racist, but . . . ' Always a good sign. Starts to list off people he doesn't like. Includes this bar in that list. Doesn't seem to fancy hers much either. 'Who wears those w**ker V-neck T-shirts?' he shouts at a guy walking by. (I was wearing one the exact same that day, ha.) 'This music is s**t.' (It's rocking.) 'Purple Haze' comes on. Crowd gives a cheer. Cheers the guy next to me, clinkity clink buddy! See who it is. Dave Navarro. Standing next to me. Clinking me. Mighty place! Look to my other side . . . 'Put something good on MATE!!!' Sweet Jesus, this is going well. Is this a sequel to *This Is England*?!

Pretend to get a text, must make a call, back in a minute boss. Leave Copelando and go for a little stroll on my own. Listen to the band playing inside. While chatting to a few hot groupies. Top o' the morning. Who am I here with? Eh, my buddy, he's in the bathroom. Exchange numbers. See then that buddy is calling me to come outside. Copelando. Not Dave. Head back out. Walk into a complaint about a guy who asked him for a light. 'What the f**k do I look like, mate, a smoker?' Good point. Agree with him this place is crap. Lost cause here. (I got that girl's number. I was easily swayed now.) All right so, Dave, I know somewhere else. Come on, we'll go to karaoke instead. First time I see Dave smile all night. Beaming that he gets to leave. The place he brought me to. Oook. Time for a song.

Perhaps I should have guessed. Didn't even consider it. Pretty obvious now though. Karaoke in Hollywood is on a different level. Like comparing an NFL team with an American football team in Ireland. People weren't mumbling into the mike, eyes trained on the screen, guessing a few words, in the hope that everyone else will sing the chorus and save them looking terrible. Instead, I walked in to find an old Chinese dude rapping with an R Kelly-style guy. Both savage. I found it hilarious how good they were. I'm pretty sure they were sober too. I think the majority of them were – which made it even stranger. No inhibitions whatsoever! Probably hoping for the tiny chance that there might be someone in the bar who could give them their big break. Based on an *outstanding* karaoke performance. Better plan than mine, at least.

Not that everyone was great. Obviously there were a few idiots who thought they were better than they were: cheesy boy-band-style apes. Two guys ripped open their shirts, while singing 'End of the Road'. Being serious. One guy had nice man boobs in fairness to him. Seriously. Oddly, I think he was sober as well. Even the girl doing the MC was like Christina Aguilera. Kept singing between people coming up. Hot. But had a boyfriend. (So do I. We should double-date . . . Didn't work.) Two girls rapped some nineties rap song. Savage. Cream of the crop was a Frank Sinatra-style crooner. About sixty, slick, groomed, smarmy, way too good for that bar. Serenading the crowd.

Walking around the bar while singing. Reaching the highest of high notes effortlessly. Belting out passion with ease. Even managing to get in a little jig with me while singing the last verse. Brilliant! All this on a random Monday night?!

Myself and Copelando went looking for the girls. Girlitos, booze on?! Booze on! Up the front, plus one. Some old dude I'd never seen before. Gerry. Suited up. Bit creepy. Maybe it was his age. Dishing out the drink to the girls. Which is maybe why they kept laughing at all his crap jokes. Couldn't understand it. Until the girls mentioned what he did while he went to get another round . . . movie producer. Produced the movie Jess was just in. Few good movies under his belt. Recently did one with the likes of Ashton, Emilio, Shia . . . a lot. Movie producer, you say? Interesting. Here he comes. Back down with a round of shots. Told another brutal joke. Which for some reason seemed far funnier now. Ha ha Gerry, ha ha ha ha. You're funny, Ger! Almost flirting with the man. Collect those contacts, sell that soul!

Few shots later, I needed a pit stop. While in the bathroom, I'm 97 percent sure that Justin Timberlake was at the stall next to me. Hollywood after all. Couldn't turn and stare. At the stall and all. Asked him was he going to sing? No, not tonight. Told me to go up though, was I Irish?! I am man, are you . . . actually I am going to go sing, those shots are kicking in! Good talk buddy. Back to the table. Come on, let's do a song, Gerry! Gerry is pushed up by the girls. Up we go. Singing 'She Drives Me Crazy' by the Fine Young Cannibals. Music kicked in. I belt out the first line. Shit. Wrong song. Apologies Ger, stay up man, we'll figure this out! Thankfully Jess comes up and saves us. Me. Oh yeah, 'Tiny Dancer', hold me closer Gerry! Dancer!

Waved down at Justin to come up. He declined. Don't think

Copelando was a fan of the song either. Seeing as he left half-way through. Great song! Great night in the end. Gerry even asked if he could add me on Facebook, ha. Gerry, you can spacebook the funk out of me! Unfortunately I had to cut Gerry loose after that. No after-party for me, Ger, I've other plans I'm afraid . . . Rock chickaruu, how are you? Les Duu!

A Messy Break-up

Not too sure where to start. Emotionally drained. Long day. Break-ups and goodbyes are hard to do. Got little sleep. No, not rock-chick-related. Well, maybe a little. More that I had to share a pillow with her cat. Which was fun. I lost our battle. Kind of won the war. Couldn't hack sharing the pillow. Home to my own bed. Too soon after that, my phone started buzzing next to my ear. Forgot to put it on silent. Answered without looking at it. 'Hey, my friend, I'm calling about the horse, *sí*.' The horse? What did I do last night?!! Hang on, I know that voice . . . Silvestre? 'Yes, I am Silvestre, do you still have the horse, my friend?' No, but I have the truck. What happened to the other day? You never showed! *'Que?* The truck? . . . The truck! Sorry sir, I'll call back.' Hangs up. Back to sleep. Funk you, Silvestre. Reminding me about the bloody Bucket so early. I moved on last night!

Woken up again by the buzz of my phone. Seriously, why is silent not working?! Hello . . . Some guy is outside my house. Saw the ad. Wants to buy the Bucket. Sure you are. Good luck. Champions League is on so I tell him I'll be right out. Get up. Sit down. Watch the match. Tired. Hung over. Not in the mood to go back out waving at no one again. Except the same guy rings again five minutes later, asking can he get into the truck and have a look. What colour is it? 'Several hand-painted shades of off-white.' What kind of brush is in the back? 'A broken one.' Actually, there *is* someone outside. Out I go. T-shirt and boxers. Not expecting it to be legit still. A guy is bouncing around the truck. Hyper Californian dude. Almost getting turned on by how bad a shape the Bucket is in. So old. Complete crap. And yet, he loved her. Could see the beast underneath it all. I got his vibe. He too was into sturdy older women. He saw that the Bucket was a former beauty queen!

Turns out he's a mechanic. Loves fixing old cars. He'll take it. Without even driving it or turning the engine on. I'm highly hung over. Highly dumb. Nowhere near being with it. Let's take a test drive around the block first, buddy. Why I didn't just agree to sell it, I don't know. Finally starts after five attempts. His enthusiasm wears off a bit. Balls, why didn't I just take his money and run? Take off down my street. After barely a hundred yards, the Bucket runs out of gas. Breaks down midstream. I'm goosed, very hung over, and feel all that frustration coming back. Randomly start to put it into neutral, park, drive, reverse, while freewheeling down the street. Killing the transmission. (I've learned a bit more about trucks now!) Finally he makes me stop. Laughing at me. Asks if I had too much Bud. I have, buddy. Too goosed to drive. Out of petrol too, it seems. He can try if he likes. Gives me a knowing look: 'I knew you were a stoner, man. We have the best bud in Cali! I have to buy this thing now! Helping each other out, maaan.' I thought he meant booze but this misunderstanding works. The deal is back on!

Somehow he gets us to the petrol station in first gear. All the way the Bucket making noises like a cat being raped. I can see that he has fallen in love with the Bucket. Almost giddy with excitement over this battered truck with no petrol. Offers me $326 for the Bucket. Ha, all this turmoil for such vast sums of money! Snap his hand off. Even give him $6 back for gas to get him home. Deal done. Done and dumb. Tell him I'll walk home. Don't want to get into the Bucket again now it's off my hands. Clean break. No afters. Walk home. Which is when it all kicks in . . . I'll never see the Bucket again.

Broke up with my Bucket. End of an era. Tried to convince myself I did the right thing by selling her. Bad influence on my emotional well-being. Money was needed. The Bucket would forgive me. Sure we had bad times. We had some great ones too though! The highs. The lows. All that jazz. Romanticising it all! That was it though, the affair was over, time to move on with my life. Plenty more Buckets on Craigslist for me to waste my money on! I'll miss her though. I texted her a few times to see if things were cool. No reply. Probably off having fun with her new man. Hard to think of her with someone else. Tried my best to make things work. Just wasn't to be. I'm better off single and walking. Best holiday romance I've ever had though. I miss her! What have I done?! Come back . . . ah, Bucket.

Aw Yeh

Moving on with my life. Found a new acting class today. Really close by. Sorted. Audit as many classes as I want. For free. Aw yeh. I think the girl at the desk had a huge thing for an Irish accent. I could've asked her for a kidney and she might've ripped it out there and then. Go on the accent!

Got an email from the navy as well. Appears one more gun manual needs translating. Am I interested? I'd say I funking am to be honest. Bite off that hand! Not a huge pile of money. Better than no money. Better than a kick in the balls! Aw yeh. The flicker of whatever dream it is that I am supposed to be chasing flickers on!

That is all. Aw. Yeh.

You Are Ricky Bobby!!!

Wednesday. Two options. Stay in. Go out. Should stay in. Quiet night. Chill. Sounds like Ireland. Out I go. Being told that a well-known Page 3 model was coming out with us did help sway my decision. Even if it was Copelando who told me. Gamble on. Left my house. Off to My House. Current new hot spot in LA. Place to be. Huge queues outside. Massive. Full of chiselled, vacant-looking guys. And unbelievably hot, vacant-looking girls. Good few funky heads as well. Queue alone looked like a good spot.

Zen. Buddy, from soccer. DJ. Promoter. Handy. Very. Skips us through the queue. VIP. We are dancing! Literally. DJ AM is playing. Savage music. Club looks savage. Surprisingly, looks like a house. Oh right, because of the name . . . Clever designers. Pretty slick all round. Best part of the club? The women. By a country mile. Ridiculous. In a ridiculously great way. Zen brings over one of many bottles of vodka to our table. Zen is a dancer! Now just for the Page 3 . . . She's not coming? That's a pity. No worries though, Copelando. Especially as our cocktail waitress is probably hotter. Wuu huu. Booze on! Anyone else happy to be here, no? Too busy. Looking cool. Not yet ready to embrace my *wuu*s so early in the night.

Copelando was less wound up, it seems. Appeared to be less 'c**ts' here. Plus a few more of the lads from soccer showed up. Good man, Copelando. Not too bad as a wingman either. Although the first number I got was from a dude. Sound English guy. Chatting about a documentary I saw recently. About the African Cup of Nations. Seemed like he was well into football.

Asked me to text him the name of the documentary if I remembered the next day. Turns out he wrote and produced the first few *Goal* movies. Which could be handy. For me. What with me thinking I could be an actor and thinking I can play soccer. Handy. C'mon the lead role in *Goal 4*!!!

Zen came over to say drinks at our table were sorted all night. Work away. Zen, you are the man! Filled up my glass. Went for a stroll. Worked away. Chatting. Mingling. Floating like an ape. Amongst celebs. At least that's what they told me. Asking did I not know who they were? When I might ask them their name. Hello hot yet whurish-looking Asian girl. No, I'm not aware. Who? Bai what? Ling? As in ding-a-ling? Yet another brutal joke. Yet another person saying it was funny. As opposed to actually laughing. Look, I'm not really bothered who you are. I just think you're hot. And I'm drunk. Sure, I would like to go outside with you, where it's quieter. Where we could get to know each other better. Where . . . I could buy a bottle of champagne for us to drink? As in, I buy it? Can we not just get to know each other better in here? No. OK. Wait here so. Back in two seconds. Any champagne in particular? On I go.

Two girls stop me and ask will I take a photo of them. Yes indeed, ye hot women. Accidentally take a photo of myself. Blinded by the lights. Girls laugh. I open my mouth. Out pops my accent. Girls shriek. Half-thinking of setting up an Irish hotline. Just call up and listen to a leprechaun speak. I'd clean up. Anyways, 'Oh my Gawd, where are you from . . . ' conversation. Invited to come meet their friends. Group of guys and girls. Ladies. Turn up my accent a notch. Lads. Tip my hat. Get chatting to a guy in a cool hat. Asks me am I a fan? Yeah man, great club! Fan of your hat too, I like that feather . . . No, of his music? What music? Sing me a song. They laugh. I'm lost. One of the girls tell me he's in a band, Shwayze. Oh right. Who? Actually, I think I know one of their songs . . . Isn't Shwayze black though? You're white. Long hair. Oh, you're his DJ . . . Cisco. Oh right, is Shwayze about? No. Man, you are Shwayze, don't mind what people say. I love your music, big fan of your hat, all about the feather! Are you a fan of mine?! And I don't think he was, at all.

Girls found it all funny at least. Or else they were laughing at me and my hubbula way of speaking. Introduce me to their other buddy. In the hoodie. Cool guy. Looking cool. Bobby. Only when I hear the name do I remember who he is . . . the dude from *The Hills*. Bob-be, jamming Bob . . . Man, you should go to Ireland, Bobby, the women love you there. You are global!! Bobby. You are Ricky Bobby, I am Ricky Bobby, let's have some more vodka, Ricky Bobby! Couldn't stop saying Bobby. And vodka might be the reason I kind of forgot that his name or alias is Justin Bobby. Not Ricky Bobby from *Talladega Nights*. I know that now. At the time, I just kept calling him Ricky Bobby this, Ricky Bobby that. Then Ricky. Richie. Rich. Dick. Richard. Even Little John at one stage. (Little Richard?)

However, seeing as Ricky and Shwayze were calling me Merrick and Omar from the word go, we were even in my book. Boozed on. I prefer to turn a blind eye to negative vibes that were potentially being thrown at me. Great chats with the lads. Full. Of. Fun. I swear. People started flocking over. The lads were good for something after all. Girls. How's it going? Ye all look the same, but ye're all *mighty*-looking, Jenny Erics all the way! What do I do? How do you do? Oh, seriously, what do I do? Well, if we're being serious . . . do you really want to know? Hopefully, duu, wuu. I'm joking, chill. Oh, you *are* chilled. You had the same idea? Good. Cheers everyone, toast to tonight, the future's green! To the Irish! Everyone was my new best friend.

Some dude started singing a song with me at one stage. What song, no clue. I was lost. Which is when I realised he was an actor from the TV show *Lost*. Ha, I found you man! Booze on!

C'mon we stay for after-hours, lads! Feels like I'm back at home!!! Just slightly more bizarre! Ah shur, here comes DJ AM to join us! Lads, ye are all my new best friends. Just so ye know. Seriously. Feeling's mutual, right? Cheers bouncers! To us . . . pardon . . . what's that now? No after-hours for me? Are you sure? OK. I've to be up early in the morning anyways. Next time maybe? Maybe not next time either. OK, cool. Just let me get either of these girls' number and I'll be on my way. Girls, hey girls, I think I have to go, what are your names again . . . Kamie and Tamie? No way? I thought ye were asking me about my mum the whole time. OK, bouncer, calm down, I'm leaving! I love you Shwayze! You are Ricky Bobby . . . see ye next week lads!

Quiet nights can wait for Ireland. Drunken ape nights all the way for the time being. Now I just have to decide whether to text Kamie or Tamie. Remembering who was who might be handy first. More importantly, I must text *Goal*, as well. Can't find the documentary anywhere online. Thought I had the DVD of it myself, but must be back in Ireland. Maybe I could get it posted over? Or I could just buy the DVD off Amazon for him. Too much, too soon? Speaking of which, I must give Gerry a Facebook before I forget. Touch base. See how he's doing. Find out if he has a movie role in mind. Yet play it cool. Must phrase the text and that email just right. Finding the right words is tough at times. Don't want these guys to be just random dudes I met out one night. Would love it to be more than that. Wait, what? Hang on now to funk.

Once again, I'm more concerned with impressing the men

that I meet out and about than I am the women. Good work. Look, time to ask yourself the question that everyone needs to ask themselves at some point in their lives . . . Are you gay? It's OK if you are. You know that, right? I do. OK so. Are you? Emm. Hum. Haw. No. I'm not. Fine, work away so. As you were . . . Although. Maybe I should text Gerry and Goal, like I would Kamie and Tamie. Play it cool. Reel them in. Food for thought. Just to double-check if I'm gay or not, I'll ask Kamie when she calls over in a while. Or Tamie. The blonde girl. If only they were producers or directors. I know what I need. Women in power. Hot, influential, ambitious women. My new type.

Full of . . .

Let's get one thing quite clear. I am not smooth. Not in the slightest. Particularly when I try. Just in case you thought that I think I am. Lot of thinking. Must've had Sigur Rós on for too long today. Anyways, here is proof of how I know. Woke up. Downstairs. Cup of tea. Happened to see. My hot neighbour outside. Playing with her dog. Hey little doggy, hey. Sun was shining. Neighbour was sparkling. Sweet Lord. Ho hup, I think I better go dump the bins. Say hello while I'm out there. Giddy up, looks like the bins are empty. Better chug down the milk and dump that one empty carton. Giddy up!

Scuttled out the door. Nearly slipped on something. Nearly fell onto her. Should've fell onto her. Howdy Nikki, toora-loora, top o' the morning, mighty day. All that smooth jazz. Forgot she's an Aussie. My accent is powerless. Begrudgingly smiles a weak hello-get-away-from-me-as-I-don't-recognise-you-and-therefore-I-doubt-you-can-help-my-career-or-support-me-financially kind of smile. Know them well. Plough on regardless. Off to dump rubbish again. Rubbish, huh? Bins, huh? Never-ending, huh? Why do I keep saying huh, huh? Throw my eyes to heaven. Tut. Nudge her elbow as if we shared a joke. Now she's looking at me as if I'm deformed. Did I mention I'm really good at small talk?

Dump the carton. Nikki's still outside my house as I get back. Surprising. Start playing with her dog. Warms her up. Asks me do I have any dogs myself? Before I answer, I realise there is a smell coming from somewhere. Me. My flip-flop. Ask her to balance me a second. Before she can get away, my hand is on her shoulder. Lift up my flip-flop. Oh right, I stood in shit. Show her my flip-flop. Show her the shit. Roommates' dogs must be sick again. Either stood in puke. Or diarrhoea. Smell it. Diarrhoea. Tut. Those dogs. Throw my eyes to heaven. Nudge her elbow. She pulls back. Walks away. While I was in the middle of my next sentence. Asking her if she wanted to come in and see the dog's puke stains. Weird. Usually that line is a banker to seal the deal.

Talking about rubbish. Talking about shit. Quite smooth. Should really have told her what happened the morning before. Toilet was blocked. Some dude at a party. Cheers, muppet. Plastic bag. Elbow deep. Unblocked. She would probably have liked that story. Let that slip. Balls. Thankfully, at least I know there's always someone who's worse. Way worse. Seeing as this person called over to my house today. My 'buddy' Timothy. Buddy: few years back, I spent a summer in Santa Cruz. Timothy visited one of the guys I was with. Stayed for ten days. That's how I know him. Also from Cork. Went to the same school as I did. Year below. Only started going to the same school the year after I finished. Nod a hello if we saw each other out. Obviously, that should make us tight buddies here. Obviously. Yup.

Apparently, Timmy is flying. Lives in Hollywood as well. Modelling. Acting. Movies. Pipeline. On the way up. Living the dream! Get on to Timmy, he'll be able to point you in the right direction. Cool, cheers, Timmy, I'm in Hollywood, where are you? Oh. Really? You live in Santa Barbara. Is that not two hours away from LA? How are the movies coming along? Oh right. You're going to be in them. Are you just making money off smaller roles now? How's the modelling going? Oh. Right. You work in Walmart? Gardening section. Nobody really told me that at home. Oh, you spoofed to everyone about how you were getting on? Good work. That would be the . . . smart thing to do, somehow?

Anyways, Timmy called around. Initially he was in Hollywood for an audition. Big movie. Which movie? Actually, just auditioning for a producer. Audition go well? Actually, it was cancelled last-minute. Timmy, was there even an audition? Are you a little bit of a spoof? Shucks. OK, there was no audition. Picking someone up from LAX. Good work, Timmy! Apparently there will be an audition next week though. Seeing as he knows a guy. Who lives with an actress. Who knows a dog. Who has diarrhoea. Who can hook him up with a movie role. Which is actually what he told someone back home, after he had called over to see me. Go on, Timmy! Both of us out in LA, living the dream, talking non-stop about shit!

Who's Your Paddy?!

As of late, I've been trying to buckle down a tad and not gallivant as much. However, seeing as yesterday was a national holiday, I decided to take a little break for myself. Well, national holiday back in Ireland. The day the snakes were banished. Parade time. Go on St P! Big old day for me! Seeing as my main talent thus far in Hollywood seems to be that I'm Irish. Shine, Paddy, shine! Who is your Paddy?! Celebrations. Which went well. Ish. Kind of. Not at all. At all, at all.

Decided I'd go to the gym before a big old boozing session. Greeted by a sea of green – balloons, streamers, banners, flags, hot pants, sweatbands, shamrocks painted on faces, green grass, green everything. Transformed into the Emerald Isle. I was the only one in there not wearing a green T-shirt. Not to worry. People knew I was Irish. Somehow. A real-life Irish man-leprechaun. Which was actually said to me. I assume Jim said something to someone. Guys coming up asking if I was real. Really Irish. Say something. Oh my Gawd! An Irish man-leprechaun on St Patrick's Day. Do a little Riverdance for me. Can I get a photo with you? My friend too? Eh, OK? In the bathroom. Slightly/highly gay gym. Posing for photos. With the guys. All shouting 'Who's Your Paddy?!' Looking back at it, it was funny enough. Except when one guy kept telling me he'd love to be my daddy. Oook. Thanks for telling me that, sixty-year-old man. A step too far.

Headed out with Jess that night. Korean bar. Paddy's night. As you do. Place is owned by a good few famous heads. Which Jess casually listed out to me en route. Being honest, the appeal is starting to wear off. Famous people are a dime a dozen here. Every corner. All I cared about was that my Irish appeal would give me celeb status. Wore my brightest green T-shirt. Ready to whip out a few leprechaun stories. Met a few of Layla's friends. Delighted to meet a genuine Irish person. Hi Mr Rapper/Actor dude, yeah I am Irish, yeah that is so cool, yeah I will do a shot of Jameson with you. Hey Mr Actor/DJ dude, yeah, Jameson on. Don't actually drink that myself back in Ireland, but when in Rome . . . Hey dude, hey guy, hi guys, dudes, guys, men. Hey girls! Top o' the . . . pardon? No, I'm not putting on my accent. I am Irish. I swear. You've been to Ireland? Where? That's where I'm from! Seriously. No, I'm not lying. I am Irish!

Went well. Not one girl believed I was Irish. Don't deny me my one trick! Even started showing people my passport. Chump. Look, proof! Yeah, we don't believe that's you in the photo. Loser. It's an old photo! Believe me, I'm Irish!!! All right, fine, don't believe me. I'll be over there getting drunk if you girls change your minds. Those guys will be me buying drinks. Anyone want to come join me? No? OK. I won't be your Paddy so. Green dream was over. (Somehow the logic that tonight I might get the Holy Grail, for being Irish? I'm that dumb. I had it *that* built up. Previous nights out did give me some shred of logic to fall back on. Still. Always destined to fail.)

At least the barman was excited that I was Irish. Seeing as he was also Irish. Just like me. Part, anyways. Part-Hungarian, Bulgarian, Welsh, Scottish and American too, I think. Made me think I'm actually part Viking. Got me drunk for free, at least. Happy days. Irish. Hollywood. Paddy's Day. Impresses the guys. Drives the girls away. Happy Paddy's Day.

Mandatory Mandate

Kind of an odd week. Different to the norm. Less running around like a headless chicken. Balanced out by less eventful nights out. Free week of acting classes in a different place around the corner. Free gym still going strong. Weekly soccer in Robbie Williams'. Doing a bit of writing between all this. Oh, and I went on a few unintentional dates. With men. Man-dates. Which were great. Just great.

First one had a mandatory air to it. I've been dodging it for as long as I can. Timmy. Constantly wanting to go out. Wants to check out a night in Hollywood. I thought you lived in Hollywood, Tim? Main issue I had with that offer . . . well, I had a few issues. Our connection was a mutual friend. No longer even talk to that friend much. People drift, and all that. Spoke to Timmy few times in a two-week period. I have more of a connection with my current postman. However, we're both Irish. Both from Cork. Both in Hollywood. Well, county of LA. Therefore presumed we should automatically be best friends? Even though I wouldn't hang out with him at home. Forced into an arranged friendship. Do it! You must. Why? Because he's Irish!

Anyways, decided my thoughts were a bit harsh. Timmy isn't that bad. Give him a chance. I'm just being ape. Timmy, let me know when you're up for going out. Holla holla. So Timmy called up. A girl he knew was having an album-release party. Actually, I think he was with her before. Party was on in a ritzy nightclub. We're on the list. Good man, Timmy! Hello bouncers. Pardon me? No Timmy on the list? No album launch on here tonight. Oh right. Good man, Timmy. Good man yourself. Ended up going to the club next door, which was well past its sell-by date. Horrendous. Timmy tried to hook me up with a girl who kind of looked like a goat. Stuck with her naying in my ear. While Timmy went dancing. Unbuttoned his shirt while grooving on the dance floor. Don't do what I think you're going to do, Tim. Don't take off your shirt and flex your muscles to that girl. Unless you're joking. Not even if you *are* joking. Don't, Timmy . . . And then Timmy took off his shirt. Flexed. And I went home. Good luck to Timmy.

Second date, with a man, was stumbled into. Chatting to a guy in acting class. Swiss dude. Good laugh. Well, he laughed at all my jokes. Asked where I went out at night. Anywhere boss, follow my nose. He needed to go out more, must come along the next time. Yeah, cool, we should go for a few boozes sometime. Thought nothing of it. Next class, asked if I wanted to go to the bar around the corner afterwards. Erra shur, I'll have one. Bar. Ordered. Sat down. Small talk. Minimal. Awkward vibe. Not sure why. Maybe we should've stayed standing. Started to wonder if Jean-Paul was actually gay. Didn't even think of that. Assumed he wasn't. We chatted about women in the class. Maybe he swung both ways? Was I unwittingly leading him on? Subtly threw it out there. Are you . . . Not that it would be bad obviously, I just . . . He wasn't gay. Why, was I? No. I'm not gay. And that whole thing made the vibe even more awkward. Obviously. Great fun. Good work. And good night to you too.

Final man-date was last night. Down in Barney's. Guy I play soccer with. Gave me a few lifts up to Rob's house. Howard. Chowder. Not sure why I started calling him that. Meant to be heading out with Copelando and Chowder. Headed down to Barney's. Get in. See Chowder. No sign of Dave. Cancelled.

Women issues of some sort. Just the two of us. Swiss flashbacks. Will I just dodge? Stayed. Pint. Chatted about soccer. More pints. Chatted about women in LA. More pints. Chatted about how we should've done this before! Jesus, man, why hadn't we thought about this before?! New wingman. Come on, let's get a few shots, Chowder! I know, I know, this is a great night! High-five Chowder!!! New wingman. Both of us gushing to each other about our new budding friendship. Surprised we didn't bloody kiss at the end, ha! Two apes.

All of these dates have made me realise something of note at least. New city. New life. New friends are needed. Hit or miss in the dating world. One in three isn't too bad. All about holding out for the right man to come along. Actually, hang on, just got a text . . . oh Lordy, it's from Chowder. Eek! What am I doing tonight?! Ahh, what should I say?!!

Ted! Do What to Who?

Unfortunately, my days of mocking myself for solo clubbing are over. Unless I now do it purely out of choice. Friday night, the texts were flying in. Dose. Five texts. From five different people! Woah. Calm down. Look at me go. Popular ape. In the end I dodged them all, and headed to Teddy's with Jess. Haven't seen Layla in a few days. Gallivanting, no doubt. Anyways, not too sure why I haven't accepted Jess's offer before to go to Teddys. Heard it was a good spot. Bar in the Roosevelt Hotel. Hollywood Boulevard. Bang. Middle. Historic place. All that. Great spot to mingle with celebrities. Or with me now. Whichever you prefer.

Arrive. Queue. Grumpy yet hot-looking people. All about who you know, guys, come on, get with it! Guy in charge at the door loves Jess. In love with her. Told her again that night. Pleasantries. Parting of the red velvet sea. In we go. Skipping through. On a gibber side note, would countries avoid being invaded if they just threw up a velvet rope around the borders? No. They wouldn't. Great side point by me. Danced into the VIP section. Wuu. People look to see who we are. Some wave at Jess. Others wonder who I am. Wouldn't ye like to know? That I am not who you think I might be! Small enough place. Dark, old-fashioned kind of décor. Bar to the right. Tables to the left. Dance floor straight ahead. Tables on the far side.

Waltzing through, I notice a few proper celebrities. Whatever that means. High up the alphabet chart. People people of all ages would know of. I did well not whipping my camera out like a tourist. Left. Right. Centre. J.T., was that you at karaoke?

Remember me, no? Dance-off later. Get ready for my jigging! Macy! Love the new hairstyle! What happened to your career though?! Paris? Is that you? Drink perha— oh no, it's not you, don't want to talk to you so. Actually I do. As you are hot. I'll be back! Jess heads for the tables at the far side. Head off for a wander on my own. Sussing time. Actually. First. Booze time.

My credit card is a student credit card. Has a limit of €400. Must be up around the €397 mark. However, it does have one curved side to it. Which makes people think over here that it is a special card. As I am a special person. As in a VIP perhaps. Special is right, but maybe not what they're thinking. Calmly wait to see if it is accepted for the drink I ordered. Smile. Keep cool. Don't run away. She's coming back. Dancing! All clear. Casually look at the receipt. Like I don't care. Only $25. For the one drink. I care. Only $25?! Almost spit a mouthful out. Until I realise there's no way I'm wasting a penny or a drop.

Try to calculate roughly how much it'll cost me to get drunk at those prices. Two girls misconstrue my quizzical, annoyed, deflated look for a mysterious, brooding look. Sidle up next to me at the bar. Tell me: 'You look very mysterious. Brooding. We love it!' OK, thank you. Fake eyelashes fluttering non-stop. Think one had a slight twitch. Constantly fluttering. Like a demented, drunk butterfly. Next few moments were spent posing. Sucking cheeks. Puppy looks. I joined in. Probably me who started it all off, ha. And then . . . and then the usual conversation developed.

I've noticed a familiar trend. No wasting of time with pointless words such as *hi, hello* or *duu*. How do you do? Never asked. Instead . . . 'What do you do?' Something basic like . . . How are you? Don't be silly, instead . . . 'Who are you?' Ah, not too bad, thanks for asking. Yourself? Accent washes over them. They go again 'Who are you?' Oh, my bad, I'm Mark. 'Merrick?' MARK. 'Eric?' No, MARK! 'Omar?' Sweet funking Jesus, this is painful. Lucky you're so hot. OK, girls, just like Starbucks – MARK. Nothing. MAAARRRK. Still nothing. M. A. R. K.? M-A-R-K! 'Oh, Mork, why didn't you just say that?! You're silly!' And they're looking at me like I'm a bit slow. Special kind of person.

Somewhere along the line, they gather I've an accent. Ergo, I must be rich and famous. Basing this on the fact that I can overhear them saying this to each other. Presumptuous is the mother of who again? 'Mork, what?' Hubbula. I lose one girl at this point. Turns away texting on her iPhone. Blonde girl is hotter anyways. 'Where are you fraom?' Ireland, whereabou– 'Oh my Gawd I'm Irish too!' Sure . . . 'I aaaamm. I'm half-Irish.' Oh yeah, which half, top or bottom? 'Which half? OMG. I don't even know that! Am I stupid for not knowing?' No. Not stupid for that part. 'My Mom is Russian. I'm told I look like her. So, bottom half?' Yeah, thought that. See, you're not stupid. No. Definitely not.

Brunette rejoins us. 'I can't find you on Google. What's your name again? Are you an artist?' I see now that she's typed 'Morkus' into Google search. What the funk?! Wandering time. Don't want to disappoint them with the truth . . . I've no clue as to what I'm doing really. Almost homeless and sporadically unemployed. Still interested? Less they know, the better. Go for the old mysterious approach. Can't really say why I'm in LA. I do love to paint though. Bit of an artist. Anyways, Justin is calling me over, must head off. Sense that they're losing me. See if I'll give them a scrap at least. 'Are you going to buy us a drink before you leave?' Sure. Be right back, girls. Wait here for me, OK? Wait for me, by the bar. And I'll go over there, away from the bar, and get ye drinks. 'OK Mork!'

Back on my merry way. Giving them credit, they were hot. And quite keen. And very ditzy. Wander on. Bit of ice whacks me in the head. Look up. Jess. Blaming the person next to her . . . who's that . . . no way, is it . . . Prince! As in Prince? Sweet Lord. Jess calls me over. Prince doesn't wave when I say hi. In fairness, he was at the other table. Same couch though, Prince, come on, give me a look at least! Jess invites me to tuck in. To the table covered in various bottles of liquor. All free. (Guy at the door! Good work, Guy.) Maybe I'll be drunk after all. Maybe I'll burst into a version of 'Purple Rain' with Prince. Maybe this will be the greatest night ever! Should've worn my raspberry beret! (Mental note: Buy a raspberry beret!)

Booze starts to flow. At one stage I try to high-five Prince like we're old buddies. Leaves me hanging. Drunk. I don't care. (I cared.) Place is ridiculously cool. Or at least that's what the look on everyone's face is implying. In fact, it's so cool that when I remind one girl that she can't smoke inside, just as she's about to light up, she laughs me off . . . 'We can do what we want here.' Wuu huu! Wait, me too? Yeah? Wuu! Drink up. Guy comes over. Fake-smiles at me. Another guy comes over. Jess's ex. Not even a fake smile. Four of us. Time for me to go wander some more.

See another bar outside. Non-VIP. Looks like more of a laugh. Tempted to head out. DJ throws on a Lykke Li remix. Actually. Stay. Dance on! Partially dancing. Mostly mingling. Small dance floor. Do about six laps. Appears to be three kinds of women here. Model. Actress. Or really hot girl looking to sleep with a celebrity. Not a bad mix. All have an immense thirst for Coca-Cola. Pepsi must be freaked. Few offer me some Coke. Vast majority ask me for some. Tell some of them I only have Diet. ('Is that the good stuff?') Or else hand them my Kleenex handy pack. For their cold. Both responses are met with confused looks. Bewilderment. In my drunken head, my jokes are hilarious. Joy of being drunk. Another Kings of Leon remix kicks in. Time for me to go off dancing again!

Mid-song, dancing like a drunken ape, I get a tap on the shoulder. Blonde girl, swing those Ruski hips! Try to make her pirouette. Half-heartedly does it. So I do a majestic swivel. Almost fall over. Pirouette, you ape! Drink-fuelled, she looks hotter than before. Informs me: 'I know you're a movie actor.' You couldn't know that. As I'm not. 'Stop lying.' I'm not. I'm drunk. I'll lie if you want me to? 'You're that Irish actor! I've seen your movies.' OK. You caught me. I tried. Trying to keep a low profile. 'I knew it!' Just too clever! All she wanted was a green light. Asked if I had seen outside yet. I hadn't. Come on, let's go check it out. Out we went. I went left. Towards the bar and pool area. Got yanked back right. Towards the lobby. And bathrooms area. I thought we were going to the . . . oh right. And then . . . I remembered what the girl told me earlier . . . We can do what we want here!

Duu. Duu. And a duu. *At least* five minutes later, we go back inside. Stallion! Ha. See Jess waving me over. Grabs my hand. We must leave. OK. Ruski girl lets go of my other hand. Look of disbelief. Followed by a coy smile and a 'call me'. Sure I will. Seeing as there was no exchange of numbers. Good work. Jess was dodging Guy. Who had confessed his love once again. Better if we left. Club was over soon anyways. High-five Prince? Even a nod in my direction? No. OK. Cool. Gone. Repeatedly asking Jess on the way home why I never went with her before? A mighty night! Nice décor in the bathrooms too, I must say. Duu!

Did You Know . . . ?

Every Monday since I arrived in LA, I've meant to be introduced to Jess's agent. Her commercial agent. Commercials. Money. Buckets. Sign me up. This Monday, sorry about last week! Every. Single. Monday. That's been going well. Can't remember the reason why it was called off again today. Not sure why I keep thinking it will happen. Although Jess did give me one good story in return for giving me the run-around. How Brad Pitt got his agent. Apparently. She turned him down at first. Not impressed by his resumé. Photos. Reel. Etc. (Photos? Really? What hope do I have?!) No thanks. What did he do? Persevered. Showed up every day at her office. Bearing gifts. Cakes, flowers, mix tapes, home-made stuff. Eventually, she said yes. Found him the role which was his big break. Talent. Good looks. Ability to bake. One way to get your foot in the door. The custard is setting on my trifle as we speak!

Another thing which has been going on behind the scenes is that my neighbour Fred, the writer, has been reading over some of my material. Stories, scripts, ramblings. Called over today. Likes my writing. Likes the style. Although that is me taking 'raw' and 'rough' as good things. Good in most all other areas. I think. Moving on. Fred now wants to know, what's my plan? Eh, what plan? You need a plan. Then you need ten more. Try everything. Act. Write. Do stand-up! Get yourself out there. Network. Work hard. Yet make it look effortless. Always someone funnier. Better-looking. More talented. You'll just have to work harder than them. Not give up. Keep at it. Keep going until one of the plans starts to show progress. Foot in the door. Everything you need or could be doing, do it! Overnight sensation in Hollywood = ten years' hard work. Or was it the seven-year struggle? One of those phrases. What about my ninety-day plan?! Fred gave me a big thumbs-up. And shook his head. While laughing. Oh right.

All the same, all that coming from someone in the business, was great to hear. Gave me direction. Focus. Whole concept of what I'm trying to do no longer feels as alien now. Has been a bit E.T. Just need to work harder. Although they've yet to taste my trifle! Fred's advice and words of wisdom did make me realise something. Which has been touched on in acting class a few times. Fairly obvious. I've been oblivious. Must start small. Any little break at all. Better than nothing. Don't just land your own sitcom. Get the lead role in the movie that you'd love to star in. Small things lead to bigger things. Baby steps! More exposure, bit by bit, slowly but surely. Next week, I shall be going nude! I joke. Won't be going down the porn route. Not just yet. I joke. Ha ha. Ha. Not yet. Ha.

Speaking of baby steps, a flutter came of out my closet today. I've been asked to write an article for an Irish newspaper. Life in LA. I can do that. No problem. I live in LA. Well-qualified. Write on. I was also asked to do an interview for an Irish magazine. Two-page spread. On . . . life in LA. My main talent, it seems, is . . . location! Which is also why I was asked to be on an Irish radio show tonight. Talk about life here. What it's really like, and all that jazz. So I knew that I had been asked on. Just not when. As they never replied to confirm. So the interview was kind of sprung on me. Last thing on my mind. And that might explain why I was chugging down cans at a party when they happened to ring. Just getting ready to get into a hot-tub. With a few girls whom myself and Chowder had met in Barney's earlier in the night. Chugging cans. *Dring.* Howdy. Oh Jesus. Drunk as a skunk on Irish radio. Rambling out a few tales. Not slurring. I think.

Seemed to start off well. Ramble on. Asked me about the area I lived in. Told him. WeHooo. Asked me if I was gay. No. I've asked myself that question. Comfortable enough with the answer. Are *you* gay? Think it ruffled his feathers. Suddenly started to hear something which I'd forgotten about. Certain tone from an Irish person. 'Sounds like you're having fun.' Yeah, it's a good life. Highs and lows. Struggling every day at the same time. 'Yeah, well doesn't sound too tough. All sounds unbelievable.' Which part? Where the aliens showed up? Or where I grew a second head? That part was bizarre, indeed. 'Sounds like you're having too much fun. Are you lying about what's happening?' Yes. You ape. All lies. Can't be having fun if you're not. Go on the cynicism. Good old Irish sentiment. Can't do something that you wish you were doing. Or wish you had tried to do. Before you became a sarcastic, cynical radio presenter. 'Mark, are they really Norwegian girls in the background? I find this all rather hard to believe.' Actually, no, they're not. They're Swedish. If you want me to lie for your sake, I'll say they're Mongolian. Would that make you feel better? Ape.

Mixed reactions after the radio interview. Texts, messages, Facebook and so on. Family and friends saying it was funny, good work. Mumbled a bit. At least no one copped on to what I had just being doing a few seconds before going on air. All in all, though, went well. Few randomers as well gave thumbs-up, which gave me a boost I wasn't expecting. Go on the randomers! Prefrenders (pretend friends) said the same, along with the added parts . . . Ah, fair play to you, coochy coochy coo. Seriously though, they must have nothing better to be doing if they're talking to you. When are you going to cop on anyways? Your visa is running out soon, isn't it? Have to come home. Stop fooling yourself. Come home and get a job. I know a guy in a bank who could hook you up. Can't be running around LA like that. Ah, best of luck though. Fair play. Just give up though.

One demographic in particular seemed really annoyed. People in their thirties. Most digs thrown from that corner. Must be the 'What could've been' age. Dose. Not sure. Second-guessing. I do know that whatever it is I'm doing, it seems to have irked and annoyed a few people. Apologies? At least it's given me more of a spark to annoy them some more. Thanks for fuelling the fire of whatever dream it is I'm chasing! Go on the doubters, cynics and begrudgers! All jokes aside, definitely not ready to go back to Ireland yet. Sounds like they're having too much fun. Wouldn't want to ruin the party. Now. I just need a plan.

I'm on a Plane

Last night. Was a drunk night. Karaoke. Again. Forgot what song I was meant to sing. Again. Jess had to help me out. Ended up doing a duet with Jess. Party back in our place. Jess brought back a drove of people. Rocking night. Can't really remember the wee hours. Woke up. Rolled over. Someone next to me. Oh right. Got up. Showered. Girl got up. Went into her own room. I went downstairs. Found Layla passed out on the couch. Ciao ciao Lay Diddy Lay, I will be seeing you in a week or so. Hopefully. That's the plan at least. Please God. Please. God. Please. Where's Jess? Eh, her own room now, I think. Must bounce, cab on! Plan is on. Keep the adventure going. Visa run to Mexico. In. Out. Trout's. Mouth. Back to LA. That is the plan. Sweet Lord please let me get back in. Come on the plan! Innocuous little trip. Head down. Low profile. Say nothing. Detox for the week. Fred had me given me assignments. Do some writing down there as well. Good plan. On the way to LAX, the cabman informs me of something that I was completely unaware of. Spring break. On this week. Oh right. Coincidence. Handy. Brilliant. Main thing is the plan works. Obviously. Just a nice little added bonus out of the blue.

Pleasant trip to the airport. Followed by a run-in with airport security. Probably my fault. Security guard was not a fan of me. Metal detector. *Beep beep. Beep beep.* Please step to the side, sir. Please raise your hands. Loose baggy shorts. Belt off. Might fall down if I let go. Robocop didn't care. Thought I was getting hostile. Sir, please raise your arms for me now. My shorts are going to fall down. Just so you know. Sir, are you getting hostile with me? . . . Security issue on row five, hostile passenger. Jesus, calm down, it's just my shorts are going to fall down. Fine. Arms up. Shorts down. Standing with my bright orange boxers for the whole of LAX to see. Innocuous. Low-profile. Started off well.

Got me a bit paranoid, in a hung-over way. Need to work on my cover story. Just in case anyone asks. Just in case they're undercover immigration. Paranoia. Better safe than sorry! Either going with the line I'm heading there to do a bit of writing. Which, technically, is almost true. Even if it just involves me sending postcards home to my grandparents. Or else, I'll just tell them the truth. Just on a little holiday for myself. Why is it I'm traveling alone? Eh, as I am a priest. Well, actually, a trainee priest. And this is my last holiday before I'm ordained. Spring break, then priesthood. Makes sense. Honesty is the best policy!

After all that. All that. Right now. I am on a plane. Sitting in the bathroom. Where I've been since I've been allowed to leave my seat. Seeing that the older, gruff Mexican chap I was sitting next to seemed to release his bowels the minute the plane took off. Even gave me an insidious smile. He knew what he was doing. Plane was full. Bathroom had the only seat not taken. Smells better at least. Great journey so far. Trying to kill time by attempting to write some stand-up material. Plane just went through a bit of turbulence. Gave me a shot of clarity. Maybe clarity is the wrong word. Jolt of awareness. This is a weird scenario. Sitting in a toilet in the sky, on the way to Mexico, trying to make up gibberish for stand-up. This is now my life? Kind of odd. Momentary bit of turbulence. All smoothed over by a knock on the bathroom door. Air stewardess. Offering me a warm Mexican beer. Clarity, ciao ciao. Come on the Mee-hee-ko!

Sprung Broke

Parties. Hot women. Free-flowing booze. Crazy parties. Savage clubs. Time of my life. Spring break. Eh . . . yeah. Almost exactly like that. Almost. Land. Clap. Dodgy pilots. Bus. Hotel. All-inclusive. Split into two areas. Grand. And Club. Grand is slightly nicer. Club is slightly cheaper. My package had me in Club. It'll be grand, Club on! Straight to breakfast. Sit down. Wait for all the hoards of college girls to trundle in, some dude to give me a beer bong and the music to blare up. Just like MTV. Pretty soon my *Spring Break* would be under way! And here they come! Oh sweet Lord. This is amazing. Have I died and gone to heaven? Well, maybe the waiting room before heaven. Hoards of old people. Really old. OAPs. False teeth and cardigans. Along with a few people in their thirties and forties. All sharing a common garment. Muubuu. Homer Simpson-style. OAP home. Fat camp. Mighty. Wuu. Spring break? Sprung broke.

Hotel was nice at least. Hung around the pool for a while. Drinking a few watery vodkas. Chatting with my new older friends. Books. Life. Cardigans. Apparently it gets chilly in the evenings. According to my new buddies, Ned and Sue. Ned offered me a loan of one of his cardigans if I was stuck. Even asked if I wanted to join their game of bridge that evening. Sound people. Go on the old folks! Odd encounter with two German dudes. Both looked like Gary Glitter. Sunglasses. Weird goatees. Red baseball hats. Matching red muubuus. Matching red thongs. Thought they were twins. Actually a couple. Overheard them talking about me. Saying I needed a haircut. Didn't know about my past life as a translator. Told them it was a wig. That'll teach them to mock me to my face. I think I said wig, anyways. Bit rusty *auf Deutsch*. Which is why I think they gave me a strange look. And then invited me around to their hotel room later, if I had no plans. Never mentioned what game of cards they were playing. Told them Ned and Sue had already asked. Strange smirks on their faces. Not sure now if I did say wig. Decided that it was a good time to go check out the Grand part of the hotel. See ye Glits, *auf auf*.

Apparently there were younger folk over in le Grand section. Moseyed my way over. C'mon the other pool, c'mon the hoards of women, c'mon the less-watered-down drinks! C'mon the . . . Tom Cruise wannabes. And bored women. Majority of dudes were small, pumped-up, finger-pointing, gun-pointing, high-fiving, cringe-worthy, rooting-tooting apes. With none of Tom's good movie lines. Some wore bandannas. Others went with too-tight-for-their-heads Speedo sunglasses. Seemed to be mostly couples. Girlfriends all looked fairly bored. Looked a bit different from how MTV had led me to believe as well. Music was pumping at least. Cher's classic 'Do You Believe in Life After Love'. On loop. Every third song. Over. And. Over. All day. Aw yeh, this is what it's all about!

Anyone I spoke to there was only interested in asking who I was with. Telling the truth seemed to make a few of them dubious about me. Why on your own? Well, if I was to wait around all my life for other people to join me, I'd do very little. OK. I'm going to go back over here to my friends. Bye. Weirdo on his own vibe. Ha, must start saying Andy and Colin Todd from now on if anyone asks. Aka, on my todd. Just a more confusing, less wary way of not lying. Which is why I said Andy was feeling sick and Colin had sunstroke when I went along to the night out the hotel had set up. Downtown. With the Toms. The Glits. No

Harry. Although there was a little Canadian dude called Barry. Bandanna Barry. On to the bus. Head for the club. Some place called Zoo. Hoped it was Zuu. It was Zoo. No duu. Walk in. Cher. Again? Come on to funk! I no longer believe in love! Springs are breaking!

Bandanna Barry, aka the Canuck, comes over to me by the bar. Fairly drunk. Bandanna still nicely on. Pink Speedo glasses resting on top of his head. 'Are you Irish, eh?' I am, boss. 'I was just talking to another English person over there. We should all do shots, eh?' Are you Canadian? I was just talking to another American person over there, shots sound good though! Onwards to the shots bar we go. Little Canuck starts to pound back the tequila. Impressive going. After a few, I'm looking for a breather. Not a fan of tequila. Dodge. Wander off for a stroll. See a girl I saw at the pool earlier. Nay too shabby. I could tell there was a glint in her eye from the pool. Bored, but I still saw a bit of glinting. Although where was that dude she was with? Looks like she's on her own. I'll ask her.

Howdy. Where are you from? Hollywood? No way! Eh, where's your boyfriend? He's sick. Must have same bug as Andy. He's not your boyfriend? Must be a family holiday! Canuck swans in at the perfect time with another round of tequila. Wahey, not her boyfriend! Go on the Cher! Burst into my 'Anyone see Timmy the rabbit?' dance. Hard dance to resist. Lures her in. *Dancing*! Coming back to the hotel? Yes? Wuu huu . . . oh yeah, forgot you're staying here anyways. Anyone up for some watery vodka? Party on in my room. Back we go. And do a bit of . . . do a bit of nothing. Well, not nothing, but nothing of note. Alas, it was not to be. You want to know the time? Pardon. That time? 4.30. What month is it? Spring? I think. Time? Month? Oh, right. I don't get what you're telling me. Oh, right. No, I actually still don't have a clue. Those tequilas have kicked in. Just say it. Don't whisper. Oh. Right. Balls. No can duu. That is a pity. Mentions we could meet up back in Hollywood. Gives me her number. Checking out in the morning. Up early. Better head back to her room now. Call her when I get back to Hollywood. Grabs her clothes. Scuttles off. Ciao ciao. All in all, though, not a bad start to my last holiday before I'm ordained. Sprung broke might not be so bad after all.

Forgive Me, Father

Hung over. Highly. Sun. Blinding. Sunglasses. On. Head. Throbbing. Head. Down. Breakfast. Badly needed. Money's-worth and all. At least that's why I think I woke up before eleven to go down to the buffet. Struggling with the coffee machine. Noticed Hollywood girl. And her brother. Walking alongside the pool. Bellboy in front with their bags. Weird. Thought they would've checked out already. Weirder. They seem to be holding hands. Perhaps he's just making sure she doesn't fall into the pool. Hmm. Now walking with their hands around each other's waists. Interesting. Brother and sister. Look more like a couple. But she said . . . Not my boyfriend. *Must* be brother. What else is there . . . Oh Jesus.

Now making toast at this stage. Two and two are coming together. Finally. Sweats. Must be the heat. Must be the hang-over. You did nothing wrong here. You are the victim. Just keep telling yourself that. Keeping walking straight, brother and sis-ter. Follow the bellboy. She does. He doesn't. Oh great. Heads for the buffet. Beeline. My direction. Oh holy funk. Did I men-tion he's a beast? Oh Jesus. Play it cool. You're the victim. Play it cool! Wait for the toast. Beast is now getting coffee next to me. Ha-huh. For some reason I mumble out a laugh at a joke no one has told. Playing it cool. Subtly throw a glance at his left hand. Just to make sure. And yes, of course you are . . . wearing a wed-ding ring. Oh Jesus.

No punches thrown yet. Presume he might not know about his WIFE being unable to resist my rabbit dance move. Oh Jesus. Come on toast. Hurry the funk up. Come on . . . TOAST

THE STALE BREAD FASTER!!!!! Manage to stay cool. Did jump slightly when the toaster popped. Gave him a nervous chuckle. Gives me a dirty look. Brings two coffees out to the reception. One for him. One for the missus. Who is looking quite hot this morning in fairness to her. Hands her the coffee. Kisses him on the lips. Maybe they're just an affectionate brother and sister? Maybe not.

Checked out. Thank funk. Could've been awkward. Could've been detrimental to my health if they hung around much longer. Might have to break my promise. Looks like I won't be calling her when I get back to Hollywood. Probably not. Just a quick text to make sure she got home OK? Hope it wasn't their honeymoon. Sweet Lord, I'll never be ordained at this rate. Forgive me, Father!!!

Naked Wrestling with the Cleaning Maid

Past few days have been, emm . . . fun? Great hotel. Claims to be all-inclusive. To me, that kind of implies you can eat and drink what, when and where you want. Not the case. More a totalitarian all-inclusive. Eat what when and where we tell you to. Which is why I ended up going to watch an Abba tribute band. Only place I could get dinner. The 'where' part was cool, in fairness. Down on the beach. All lit up. Stage at one end. Food buffet on one side. Sand and sea on the other side. Lots of tables in the middle. Cordoned off. Rope. Ribbons. Just lovely. Table reserved for Merrick. Follow me, *señor*. Nice big round table. Very big. Wedding style. Dinner for one. Plus nine empty seats. Cheers bud. Next to the stage. Nice spotlight shining down. Brightening up my table. And illuminating the shadow of my head across the dance floor, as people jived to 'Dancing Queen'. Wuu.

At least the Glitters asked if they could join me. Work away, lads. Gibber in German. Funny old meal. Until they asked if I wanted to join them for a party. Again. In their room. Anyone else? Nay, I'll leave ye at it lads. Went to the shop. Bought a six-pack. Onwards to Subway. Ordered a roll. (All-inclusive worked out well!) While my sub was being rustled up, I went to the bathroom for a quick pit stop. Open. Door. Close. Lock. Light. No light. Unlock. Clickity click. Round and round. Lock broken. Ah, super. Bang bang bang. Not a murmur. Ah, even better. Bang BANG BANG HELLO, HELLOOOO . . . nothing. Mighty. Sit in the sink. Nothing I can do. Well, I could. Can of Bud Light, how are you? Might as well throw in a few of these lime Tic Tacs

I bought, Mexico it up. Three cans later. Employee knocks on the door. *Señor*, do you still want your sub? Yes. I'd love it. If I ever get out. Three more cans later. After much discussion. The manager finally kicks the door down. Out I go. Free at last. Along with free subs for life. If I ever go back. Silver lining all the way. Wuu.

Last night was my last night. Few drinks with Ned, Sue and their gang before they went to bed. After that, about nine bells, the Glits came over to wish me off. Cheers lads. Booze on. Into the night. Barry Bandanna came over to see if I was going out. Canuck on. Out again with the hotel crew. Canuck ploughing the tequilas into me once more. Some man for the booze. Beast of a man, tequila-wise. About seven healthy ones in a row in the club. Some boy, as it turns out. Found out he was sixteen. What the funk?! Sixteen?! You're phutting me shoo shame! Letsh go dan sing! Blurry dancing. An English girl. Come straight out with what? We couldn't do much what? What time . . . does the club close? I don't know what you're on about. Fill me in . . . Oh. For funk's sake. Canuck, you're back! One more shot, why not!? And then the Canuck put me in a cab. As I was a tad funked. Cheers Canuck! Sound man. Boy.

Woke up this morning. Shrouded. Surrounded. Fear of God. Body on the bed. Legs not. Somehow slept kneeling down. Must've been praying for my sins. Woken by a piercing noise. Hotel phone *dring*ing next to my face. Ignored it. Looked for the essentials. Phone. Wallet. Passport. iPod. Laptop. Camera. Clothes. Runners. Hair. All still here. So why the Fear? *Dring. DRING!* Hellyeauggh. Ugggh. *Señor*, you need to check out. Ughh huhhh. Spotted something poking out from under the door. Credit card. Good sign. Fear. Time for a shower. Wash the Fear away. Unfortunately, it's an eco-friendly shower. Water barely dribbling out. Conserve that water, you brutal whure! Get out. Goosed. Fear, still here!?! Spins. Dodge. Nearly fall over. Need to sit down. Head thumping. Sounds like a knocking. Actually. Look up. Open door. Cleaning lady. Looking down at me. Sitting. On the toilet. Hunched. Naked. Towel on my head.

Now normally, I'd have offered her a cup of tea. Or a dance, if she was hot and under forty. Neither. Not even close. Too hung over to speak. Cave man. Grunting. Ughing. Towel on my head. No other towel. Too tired, too dumb to cop on. Stand up. Birthday suit. Towel. Grab. Waist. Falls. Floor. No towel whatsoever. Barely raise a smile at her. Naked. Hung over. Dumb. Expecting a look of some sort. Apologetic. Embarrassed. Intrigued. Nay. Disgusted. Shouts 'You must leave. I must clean. Now! Leave!' Eh, pardon me? What? Wait. I need to leave?! *You* just walked in on *me*. Naked. *My* hotel room. Emphasising all over the place. In my head. All I could manage to say was a limp 'Ugggghhh'. Yeti-style. Responds in the normal way I would expect. Pushes me. Pushes again. Shoves me. Against the bed. Tripping over my suitcase. Towel I had put back on, now falls off. Naked, again. Stumbling against the bed. Covering my front. Flashing her my tan lines at the back. Cupping myself. Forgetting to break my fall. Bouncing off the bed. Onto the ground. What the funk?!

Jump up. Turn around. Wrestle stance. Slightly hunched. Facing each other. Deadlock. Screams at me to get out. What?! What's wrong with you?! Brain kicks up a notch. Should I half-nelson her? Body slam? Whose move is it? Probably mine. Seeing as I'm naked. Grab the towel. Wrap it. Put my hands up. Palms out. Submission. You win. Crazy woman. I give up. Barks back at me. Five minutes. Dry. Dress. Pack. Leave. *Señor.* Thank you. Cleaning maid. I thank you. Nice lady. Ciao ciao. Do as she says. Scuttle out the door. Through reception. Check out. See ya Miguel. Good luck Raul. Au revoir other Miguel! Realise I have eight hours to kill before I need to be at the airport. Two hours on the curb outside the hotel. Six more sitting in Subway. Getting my lifetime's worth.

So eh . . . yeah. Past few days have been a right old flutter of fun. Although is fun really the word I'm looking for? Should it be funny? Maybe in a . . . it would be funnier if it wasn't happening to me but one of my friends, kind of funny. Fun . . . Not sure yet. Funny enough though. Funny enough to keep me laughing all day. Upbeat. Keeping my mind off other things. Great flight. Distracted. Queuing. Calm. Loose. Fun. Agreeing. Yes. Surfing holiday. That's it. I'm a surfer. Nod. Noddy. Nodding. I'm a dancer. You're a dancer. We're all dancing! Dancing! DANCING through immigration!!! Back. Back! BACK IN L-HEY!!! Wuu duu! Mighty sprung broke, go on the Mee-hee-ko! Fun times ahead!!!

Bang Smart Stop Dumb Go Flow!

Now. How shall I get back to WeHo? Bus? Cab? Another car rental? No no, my friend. Moving up in the world. Picked up from LAX, by my buddy. Yes, you read that correctly, a *buddy*. Go on the Chowder. I have friends. Not the kind of friends that I've only ever met once. If at all. Got an odd amount of texts from randomers just before I left telling me . . . 'Don't leave LA! I'll miss you too much!!! We must hang out when you're back!!!' Sure you do. Sure we will. Sure. Seeing as we never have before. Fake on! Odd and pointless. Anyways, I suppose I've made some sort of progress since last time I landed in LAX! Baby steps. Time to get straight back into the groove. Productive. No more dumb running around like a headless drunk gibbering chicken. Time to get smart.

Rocky start. Home. Hi Jess! Miss me?! Here. Before I spend it . . . Rent. Funk. Blow to the stomach. At least it has decreased by a few hundred. Layla is chipping in. A bit. Finally. Bum. Hot bum. Still a bum. Still hadn't spoke to Jess since the night before I left. So, eh, about that night be– pardon, oh you're rushing out. Cool. Where are you off to? Oh right. A date. Guy you met at a gig. I know that band. The lead singer is the guy you're meeting? Him? The guy who's been in a few class movies. Yeah, he is a good-looking bastard. Yeah, I'd pick him over me too. Cheap blow to the mid-section. At least that's sorted. Moved on to sort out other basics. Gym. Jaymes! High-five! Did I tell you I just watched *Milk*? Super movie. Go, Harvey, go! Pump the air. Pump it, Jim. Yes. Wuu! Free again, smile? Pardon? You can't? Nooo. Really? Cheaper rates only. What if I go put on a smarter shirt and then ask? Comb my hair? Throw on a bit of cologne? No! Jaymes! I swear, I really did like *Milk*! No. Balls. No more free gym. Blow to the kidneys. At least I got to go for free one more time. Back to people-watching.

Started off on some perplexing machine. Clueless. Trying to figure it out. While doing so, a guy asks can he jump in. Sure buddy, work away. I jump back in. Struggling. And for some reason, humming. 'Umh, umh umh, umh umh be ummmmhumh?! Umh umh umhum umh, umh umh umhum umh – When, will I, will I be famous?! I can't answer that, I can't answer that.' No clue why that song popped into my head. Until the guy asked if I had a problem? Yeah bud, can't figure out how to use this machine properly, is it for my arms or legs or what? And then I copped on it was one of the guys from Bros. Amazing. Time for me to move on. Bench press. Again, sharing. This time I did recognise the rapper/actor guy who was spotting me. Common fellow. Forgot how dime-a-dozen famous heads are here. Finally, I shared a machine with a random Joseph Soap. And guess what happened? Just like the other two guys earlier, Joe Soap didn't wipe his sweat off after him. Amazing stuff.

Rent. Must now pay for the gym. Tough start to the return. Capped off a great day by punching myself in the groin. Decided to stay in on my first night back. Smart plan. Dodged the girls. Dodged calls. Dodged Copelando. Next day. Rang Copelando. Apologies, phone was on silent last night. What did I miss? Balls. Big game of poker. Robbie Williams' house. Balls. What? No way?! Slash was playing! Slash?! How many times do I get a chance to play poker with a Guns 'N' Roses?! Uppercut to the chin. Reeling. Let's ignore the little part of the amount I would've needed to buy in. Not sure if I'm dumb enough yet to put over two months' rent on the line. Not the usual $10 games

I might play. (Still though, Slash?!) Staying in, smart plan? Starting to look a tad dumb. Looked dumber when I spoke to the girls. Declined their offer to join them for jazz night in Teddy's. No no, first night back, early night. Smart call. Even if you don't have to wake up early for anything. This is what smart people do, right?! Girls informed me that I missed a great night. Don't care. They sang a song. With who? Do I know Prince? Not personally, but yes. Why so? Oh. That was who ye jazzed it up with? I prefer Michael Jackson anyways.

Poker with Slash. Jazz with Prince. Declined both opportunities. Unwittingly. Still, declined. Trying to be smart. Use my head. Think things through. Economise. Save money. Plan ahead. Not really what LA had been about for me before I left. Now resisting her charms. In fear of getting a bout of the Fear. Afraid to keep living the dumb dream I got myself into. Rent was paid. Bought time if nothing else. Hobo heaven. Poor man's paradise! So what if E.T. was calling me to go home. My parents had been cool when I told them my plan to stay on. Seeing as I might have the coolest parents one could wish for. Proper cool. Not hippie cool. Cool. Time to embrace the LA! Back to basics. Back to being dumb. Keep it simple. Stick to what I know. Go. With. The. Flow!

Every Man Needs an . . . Orgy?

Realised something today. I can see into my neighbours' clearly from my bathroom window. About two arm-lengths away. Look into their living room. Meaning. Logically. They can see me clearly. Which is what I realised. While I was naked. Just out of the shower. Brushing my teeth. As I went to the toilet. Multitasking. Like an idiot. Realising. As they started to wave and chuckle at me. What are they all chu— Hand-towel grabbing. Toothbrush dropping. Toilet bowl splashing. Neighbours now laughing. Ha. Funny all right. Can I subtly reach down and pull out my toothbrush? Can I? No. Obviously not. Seeing as they're still looking. Flush. Good luck. Run on, headless chicken, run on!

And I actually did start to run. As I was late. Meetings. Projects. Two words. People use a lot here. Always on their way. Always working on. Used to annoy me. Probably as I never had any of my own. None pre-arranged anyways. Today. Tables. Turned. Meeting. Fred. The writer. Used to be my neighbour. Moved house. Still my mentor. Happy days. Happy that I made it back in. Not so happy that I haven't made a plan for myself yet. Breaks it down for me. Either I show him I'm serious. Or he isn't interested in helping me out any more. Knocks some sense into me. Unexpected. Surprising. Needed. Kick. Hole. Brilliant. Spur. On. Bullet points. What I need to be doing, in order to get where I want to be. Ranging from small: stop procrastinating! To big: start stand-up! Everything in between. Outline. Map. Bullets. Stones. Baby steps. Every man needs a plan!

Left the meeting, pumped. Time to get cracking on my

projects. Plan is on! Quiet night in. Hang on, text . . . Cat Woman, long time no gibber! I've been dodging you. Ever since the hippie. Party in your house tonight? Lots of Europeans? Directors? Producers? Come along? Let me mull. Actually, you know what, no. New plan. Focused. Off the booze . . . How many is lots of European girls? Lots. Mull. Hmm. Can barely remember what Cat Woman looks like. Let me check. Hello Spacebook, fill me in. Cat Woman is kind of looking hot. So are these girls in her photos. Eh, Cat, I'm back. I'll call around for a while so. Sober Joe though. Just to say hi. See you in a while so, ciao ciao Cat Woman!

Head down around eleven. Find the apartment. Cat opens the door. Looking all bohemian. Good call coming. Come in. Cross the threshold. Quick scan of the apartment. Just as I remembered. Sitting room, come kitchen. Bedroom. Bathroom. Balcony. Weird vibe. Party? Music? Maybe that's the weird vibe. Roasting. Sweet Jesus. Why is the fire blaring? Sweats are on. Not the weird vibe either though. Relax! Have a seat. L-shaped couch. Four guys sitting on it. All look up. All give me a smile. Huh-yup smile back. One girl. Sitting on the floor. Back to the fire. Howdy, smile. She just looks back. No room on the couch. Sit down next to grump. French, it seems. Unsurprisingly, for LA, quite hot. Not half as hot as the fire burning my back though. As I sit down, literally just as my buttocks hit the carpet, the girl stands up. Seeing as a guy came out of the bathroom. They hold hands. Kiss. Whisper. And leave. All in one fell swoop. Now just the four lads. Cat Woman. And me. Eh, Cat, where are those hot European girls?

Cat introduces me to the lads. Swiss. German. French. Austrian. Wuu, Euro. Great. Emm, women? Music? Why's the fire on? And why am I still sitting on the floor like an idiot?

Everyone else is sitting on the couch. Smiling at me. I'm on the ground. Smiling uncomfortably back. Like a dope. What the funk is going on? Random questions get thrown at me by the dudes. Want a beer? No thanks, man. Are you on something? No. Want to be on something? No. Are you single? No. Weird smiles. I add that I'm married to God. Cat pipes up. I told you he was chilled. Funny Irish man. Irish Mark. Yes, weirdo woman. Just relax. This is a good place. We're going to have fun tonight. Eh, say what? Why are all these dudes smiling at me so much too? I just thought they had a Euro vibe going on. Now guessing they're all gay too perhaps? Where are those hot women, Cat funking Wo-man!?!

Cat pipes up again. Hey, chill out Mark, you need to relax, it's not always all about the women you know. Some Austrian dude named Klaus purses his lips at me. Eh, what? And what the funk is Cat on about. Yes it is. If you're straight. What the funk is this? Yeah, Mark, you need to relax. Are you sure you don't want to be on something? Klaus, give Mark a pill. Klaus, funk off. No longer sweating because of the fire. Kind of start sweating when I see Klaus take off Gunther's jacket. Cat rubbing thighs. Not her own. Now realising this is not a normal party. To my naive eye, starting to look a wee bit more like an orgy. One girl. Four dudes. And if their plan goes well, me. Or am I . . . Wait, my mind is just running wild. Chill out, just being presumptuous. Not an orgy. Ehhh . . .

Thing is, I've never been to an orgy. And did not really think this was one. Still not fully convinced. Active imagination? Let's just check with the Cat. Are there any women coming? No. Why is there no music either? Oh, there's music in the bedroom. Want to help me pick a song? I wasn't asking you, Klaus, funk off. In reality, I didn't tell him to funk off at all. In reality, I was planning my escape route. Trying to play it cool. Outnumbered. Don't want to startle anyone. Cause a scene or anything. Unsettle them. Make them do something rash. Definitely don't want any rashes. Looks like they're all now taking pills. Probably just E. Hopefully not Viagra. Don't freak them out with being freaked. Time to get out. Before it's too late. Shouldn't have drunk the water Jurgen gave me. Oh Jesus, what if I've been spiked. Got to get out. Jumped back up. Time for me to leave. You can't leave, just got here! We're going to have a fun night. You're not leaving. Sit. Down. Jesus, Andreas, no need to serious up the tone. Of course I'm not leaving. Just going outside to make a quick call. I'll be right back. Line up the tunes Klaus, let's get a jig going when I get back, yay!

Before I could be stopped, I was out. Gunther was in the middle of unbuttoning a shirt. Cat was taking off her headscarf. Hot weirdo. Time to giddy up. Dodge. Didn't want to risk the elevator. Hurtled down the three flights of stairs. Ran the few blocks home. Run, headless chicken, run! Got home. Freaked I might've been followed. Told the girls. Laughed. Realised I was serious. Stopped laughing. Hugged me while I wept and rocked myself to sleep in the corner of my room.

To top it all off, I got a flurry of feline texts. Why did you just disappear? We all thought it was very rude! Should be more open, maybe next time? No. No next time. Not into orgies, you muppet. Well, not ones with four dudes. Might have to alter my plan of embracing LA, trying everything and all that. Everything? Bob Hope. New plan starts tomorrow. Now, I do need to sleep. Meaning I must go brush my teeth. With my finger. Which was surely not part of any plan.

In the Shower. Singing.
In French. Crying. Go!

Acting. Classes. Are. Bizarre. Fun though. Slightly different from the lectures I used to go to back in Éire. Acclimatising is all that's needed. Lee Strasberg has served me well lately. Thank you, talented accent of mine. Thank you, girl at the front desk who loves my talent. First-class. Must've started early. Walk in. Big room. Look around. Immediately worried. Freaked. What's wrong? Everyone's crying. Making weird noises. What the funk? What did I miss? What did I do? Eh, might just leave. Swivel. Quietly open the door. A Woody Allen lookalike grabs me by the arm. Pulls me back into the room. Now I'm starting to really freak. Should I cry for help? Oh Christ, is this a cult? Scientology has a new wing?

Woody sits me down. Gives me a calming smile. I assume that's what it's meant to be, anyway. Too calm. Deadly calm. Drink the Kool-Aid. That kind of reassuring smile. It'll all be OK. Just observe the class. Soak it up. Dahling. Take it all in. Dahling. Eh, OK . . . darling? Walks to the other side of the room. When I say he walked, I really mean he pirouetted. Seriously, four twirls across the room. Swivels between two crying, wailing girls on his way, arms in the air, flamenco-style. Repeats. Bit more flamingo this time. Back in front of me. In a ballet stance (on his toes on one foot, arms up in the air, other foot wiggling around, gracefully, like a posh-little-tea-cup stance). 'We're just warming up. Have a seat.' He points, with the toe that's in the air about neck height, to where I should sit.

Cheers, Woody. (I. Am. Freaked. Re. De. De!)

Did a quick scan. Not sure why. Maybe because Woody is still looking at me. With Kool-Aid eyes. Scan on. I'm lucky number thirteen. About twelve other students in the class. Warming up. Some staring intensely at the wall. Some walking around with their eyes shut. Others with their arms out and fists clenched. Majority are crying. Minority wailing. Pausing only to say 'HUU-UUHHHH, HHHUUUHHHH. HHHUUUHHHHHH.' Then politely crying or wailing on. One guy is sitting on the floor. In the corner. Saying nothing. Doing nothing. Just rocking. Wonder if he's new too? Will I be like that soon?

In the opposite corner, a girl with a massive afro. Shaking her head. Spitting out random French words. Crying. Rubbing her hands all over herself. Freaky as funk. Reminds me of a voodoo scene. Although . . . started to notice something else the more I looked around. Amongst all the tears, wailing, huhing and general oddness, the women here are pretty funking hot. Top-dollar. Thinking about it. All women cry, wail and are a bit odd as it is, right? Maybe I'll stick around for a few more minutes. Rude not to. Follow Woody's toe and sit in the corner. Observe. Soak it all in. Dahling.

As I observe the asylum, an older Australian dude (thirty-seven and a half, maybe?) sits two seats down from me. Huhing away. Softly at first. Eyes closed. Arms out like a cross. OK, huh on buddy, as you do. While he is huhing to my left, an extremely hot girl sits two seats to my right. (People were walking around the room, changing places.) Forget about the dude. Let's see how good an actress the girl is, do I *really* believe that she's crying? Is she *really* as hot as I first thought? Sobbing away. Looking well. Very well. I believed her. Hot. Notice the huhing getting louder to my left. Turn back around. Aussie dude is staring at me. Or through me? Into the distance? Not sure. Just huhing for dear life. Getting louder. More intense. Veins popping out of his neck. Eh, Woody, Wooood-e, what's going on? Is that his chick next to me? Should I move seats? No, looks like the girl is on the move. Gets up. Eyes closed. Starts to laugh. Ah good, you're getting better, did I tell you I'm Irish? Suddenly lets out a loud, grunting 'HUUUUHHHH'. Whacks me on the head with her arms. Reverts back to laughing. Rambles off on her merry way. What the funk is going on? Sweet Jesus, I'm surrounded by nutters! And did she hit me on purpose?! Your eyes peeked open!

Woody skips back over. Explains how they were seeing what emotions they had in them today. Releasing them. Strip down bare. Work off an empty canvas. Blowing on. Starting every sentence with: 'Dahling . . . Lee used to say . . . ' then say whatever it was he was going to say. At one stage I think he said 'Darling'. Didn't give him as much credit after that slip-up. First hour went on like that. Good laugh. Sitting. Observing. Soaking, Watching. Drenched. Second hour involved everyone doing a daily activity. With a twist. Showering. Cleaning the dishes. Making breakfast. Decided to get involved. Had a nap for myself. The twist part came from whatever Woody called out . . . 'Showering drunk', 'Cooking naked', 'Sleeping like an Irishman'. Or to the girl with the afro: 'Making coffee, singing a song, your national anthem, at the top of your voice.' Oddly, she wouldn't – or couldn't – stop crying the entire time. Most disturbed, I think. Therapy session needed. Or maybe this was it for her?

Woody then started to ask what emotion they were feeling. Sad! (No way!) Explosive! (That's an emotion?) Tired! (Give me five more minutes, Woody. Late night.) Really hot girl feels sick. Sick? Starts to reveal too much. While she's cooking her eggs. In the freezing cold. Eyes shut. Half-crying (half-sobbing?) . . .

'Dahling, why do you feel that, tell me more . . . ' (Sob) My stomach feels sick, I don't want to eat these eggs. 'Dahling, tell me more, what happened today that made you sick? (Sob) I was using the bathroom all day. My stomach is upset. 'Dahling, tell me more, were you getting sick all day?' No, other kind of upset, really bad . . . 'Good, dahling, let it all out! Now you're ready to act! Open your eyes.' Too much info for my liking. Thankfully it was time for a break. Which I think she spent in the bathroom. Nicely done. Must remember to bring some Immodium for her the next time.

Second half was all scene study. Guy and girl. Guy from Argentina. Girl from Spain. No clue whatsoever what they were saying. Or what the scene was. Or which movie it was meant to be. Completely lost. Bored. Went to the bathroom. Forgot to go back. Tough few hours! Got home. Had a bowl of porridge. Mulled it. Thought about it. Forgot about it. Sense of it arrived. Highly bizarre. Full of funking nutters. Too much ballet. However, I could see the logic behind it all. And I did enjoy it. You know what, I liked the nutter vibe. Maybe I just won't go as hung over next time. Ignore the freaky smiles they all have. Good laugh though. Plus, funking hot women! Spent the rest of the night practising my 'Hhhuuuuuuhhhhs'. Staring at the wall. Naked. With an upset stomach. Huh?

Pumping. Spinning. Sweating. Oh Jesus, What Have We Done, Jim?!

Things have been chugging along. Writing bits and pieces every day. Acting classes couple times a week. Fussball during the week in Mulholland, downtown at the weekend. Few nights out. Maybe that's not chugging as well as it had been actually. Mostly misses. In fact, all misses. And speaking of which, still having spoons issues in the house. Where the funk do they go?! Can't understand it. Layla has no clue. Too spaced to know what's going on. Jess is hardly there these days. Her new beau is still in tow. Life is flowing on. One other thing has been flowing along as well. Outwards. Downwards. Gushing in one direction only. Money. Which is a handy commodity to have. Can't buy you happiness. Can buy you other stuff though. Food and the likes. Which, in turn, make me happier. My, eh, movie career has yet to start paying its way. Might be a while. Luckily, I think I might have a few slim leads. Slim. Line. Tonic.

Looked like my master's might actually be of use, might keep me puttering along. Such as . . . design a website for my nightclub promoter buddy. Asked me when we were out one night . . . 10 percent chance. Night out, booze involved. Still no start date. Breath. Held. Next offer . . . fix and update a film festival's website. 100 percent guaranteed. Big enough job. Lot of work involved. How much payment . . . Pro bono. Pro funking bono? Right here, right now, I am big-time anti-bono myself. Nothing in return? As in *nothing*? Is there anything besides money that I might gain from doing it, girl who asked me? You'll do what to my what now, pardon me? Will you do that anyways? No. Eh, sorry, you're kind of hot, just not that hot. 0 percent chance. Thoughts were ill-guided once more. In LA, I have realised, 99 percent of the time, favours are done or asked for, with sex in mind. Seriously. To be James Blunt. I'll do this for you in the hope I'll get to do, ahem. In any case, my leads were bringing me to frustration town. Especially as I kind of let myself assume twice that they were both in the bag. Seeing as they had asked me. Lesson learned. Nothing certain until it's in writing! Looks like my master's, as good and all as it is, might not be useful here. *Or.* I'm just useless.

Although there is one random shimmering knight flickering through. Very random. Would never even have considered it myself. Again, I was asked. Not entirely sure yet what exactly happened. Or if it was even a job interview. Kind of shook. Kind of rattled. Kind of feel used. Kind of slightly abused? Kind of better go back to yesterday. Headed up to the gym. Foot in the door. Balls. Forgot my earphones. Why does that never become apparent as your foot leaves your house? Dose. Music. Dire. Dull. Crap. Jim, what's the story with the music being so bad? Sorry, my bad, Jaymes. Pardon, do I think I could do better? Yeah. This is crap. Am I a DJ? Well, I have always thought that I would be good at it, but I've never actu— actually . . . hubbula, hubbula, and what I was saying was, yes, yes I am a DJ. Obviously. Yes, I will make a quick demo and drop it up tomorrow. Be ready though Jaymes, as I will rock your pink knee-high socks off!

Now. Time to make my demo. Google, what is . . . no, how does . . . wait, keep it simple. Demo? Demo. Burn five separate songs onto a CD. Done. And. Dumb. Quite the DJ wizard. Facebook chat. Perfect my DJ buddy Neil was online . . . I need a quick rundown of how to DJ. Or at least how to speak like one. No problem. Feeds me all the jargon and lingo I could possible need. Mixers, soundcards, song bits, soundchecks, bits of card, plugs, wires, blenders. Too much. OK, I'll just keep rambling and confuse them if they ask too many questions. Up to the gym I go. Pumped. Rocking songs! Perfect for the gym. Demo on Jaymes, you shall be dancing! Thanks Merrick, I'll listen to it later. Funk that Jaymes, I need a job to keep me sane and fend off the Fear! I need to know if I need to keep trying to flog my master's or not. Listen now! Sign that line! OK Irish Merrick, let's go to the spinning room. Listen to the demo there. Demo we go!

Up to the spinning room. Jaymes, with a Jay, asking me do I spin anywhere else? No, never tried, hear it's tough. Oh, you meant spin records, eh . . . (my buddy never mentioned that term to me!) . . . just listen Jaymes, shhhh. Tells me to take a seat. Only bikes in the room. So I take a bike seat. Jaymes sits on the bike at the top of the room. Next to the CD player. Facing me. Loads up the CD. Hits play. Demo on, we're on the road! First song is brilliant. An indie electro remix, go on the Franz. Savage. Gets me toe-tapping straightaway. Jim cocks an ear to the music. Closes his eyes. Head starts to bop as the song trundles on. Feeling the tune! Realise that I've started to cycle the bike I'm sitting on. Music got me going. Feeling this tune too! Song is really kicking in. Pedalling a bit more. Jaymes opens his eyes. Starts pedalling. Liking the song. Giddy up!

Next song is even better, Jim! He flicks on to the second song. Even more rocking. We're both pedalling a bit. His head is bopping like a toy dog on a dashboard. Fingers clicking, shoulders waking up. I'm pedalling faster. Jaymes starts to pedal faster. Look at us go. Greatest demo ever! DJ on! Beat slows down a bit for the start of the third gem. Jim opens his eyes. Exhales. Deep breath. Wait for it, wait . . . song kicks in and Jim is funking loving it! Shrieking as if Madonna just waltzed into the room! Clapping his hands, pumping them out, gay head bopping around, he's pedalling, the music has me pedalling, this demo is too good! And now we're in a race. Pedalling in synch. Faster and faster with each song. Go on the demo!

Jim and I are now picking up speed. Not sure what's going on, but I'm not going to lose. Jim must be thinking the same, staring at me intently. Winking. Let's see if you're winking with the next one. You wanted a European vibe. Here's a French gem of a remix! French lyrics come on. Jim squeals like a girl/pig, almost chokes with delight. Starts pedalling away furiously. Shoulders shrugging full on, like a gay robot. Pumping the air with his hands, loving it! I can't stop pedalling either, the music has me hooked. I defy anyone to sit on a bike and not pedal with that music playing! At this stage we're pedalling in synch, to the music, to the beat, faster, faster, oh Jesus, this is the best part of the song, it's really going to kick in here. Jim is now staring at me. Pursing his lips. Fingers pointing. At me. In time with the beat. Hips start grinding on the seat. Oh Jesus. What's going on? Is this a race? Oh Jesus, quick, change the song before it climaxes. Change it, Jim, change it!

Final song. Almost there. Keep going. Interview is going well. Just keep it going. You're winning this race. Oh Jesus. Why is Jim grinding the bike? Standing up. Pumping the air. Is he breathing out? Or blowing kisses? And why can't I stop pedalling so furiously?! Beat of the song is building. Legs flying. Gripping the handlebars. Now remember what the last song is. Oh no. Not a good song. 'If U Seek Amy'. Britney. Great remix though. Britney. Same level as Madonna. Start to feel very nervous.

Almost afraid. Beads of sweat forming on my forehead. Jim is not yet aware who it is. Must stop pedalling in synch. Like we're one. Oh dear Lord, why did I make this demo so good? Slowly but surely Britney's voice can be heard. Jim's eyes widen. Lips suck in the air. Legs pumping. Hands in the air. Slow motion. Britney fully kicks in. Jim screams. YEESSSSS . . . YEEEEEESSSSS, MERRICK, F**K DO IT!!!! Oh sweet funking Jesus, turn it off Jim, turn it off, I didn't know this was going to happen, it was only meant to be a demo!!!

Why can't I stop cycling?! Chorus comes on. Jim starts mouthing the words straight at me. If. You. Seek. Amy. Grinding. Staring. Pointing at me. Pointing at himself. Licking his lips. Repeating the chorus. Stupid chorus. Singing it out loud to me. If. You. Seek. Amy. F. *. *. K. Me. Merrick. Oh sweet Jesus. Oh dear mother of God. What have I done?! Before I can stop myself, the song kicks in for the last time. Final hurrah. Race is back on. Can't resist any more. No energy to hold back. Just give in. Go with the music. This race is mine biatch, you're going down Jim!! My hands gripping the handlbars. Legs pumping to the beat! Gritting my teeth. Biting my lip. This is the greatest remix ever!!! Head bopping, wuu!!! Eyes shut tight, working it out, one with the beat, feel it!!! Open my eyes. See Jim with a euphoric look on his face . . . This is no race, turn it off, stop the music, stop it Jim . . . I said no!! Jim is shaking his head. I give in. Yes!! Feel the music!!!

Song ends abruptly. With me pumping the air. Shouting 'Yes!' Keep it going Jim, please don't stop the music!!! Realise there's silence. Open my eyes. Sweating. Red head. Flushed. Panting. Dizzy. Feel naked. Exposed. Jim is looking at me. Standing next to me. Sparks up a cigarette. Tells me he enjoyed himself. Ruffles my hair. Are we meant to hug now? Want to go for breakfast, Jaymes? I'm kind of hungry. You look like a French-toast kind of guy. Can't. Too busy with work. He'll call me later. Maybe tomorrow. Sometime this week. OK Jaymes, I know you're busy. It would be great to hear from you though. You have my number. Call me! Promise? Promise me, Jaymes! Scuttles off. Leaving me on the bike. Shattered. I'm sure he will call. What the funk just happened? Did I just somehow pleasure a gay man?! Oh my God.

Left feeling violated. Still hasn't rung. Bastard. Used me. Feel like such a cheap whure. Why did I go all the way the first night?!

Call Me, Bridget. Call Me, Prick!

Monday: Why hasn't he called?

Tuesday: Bastard.

Wednesday: Still nothing. Still? Nothing!?!!

Watched a documentary today. 'Married to the Eiffel Tower'. Women who are in love with objects. Married. To objects. Having sex. With objects. Their 'husbands'. Are inanimate objects. Such as the Eiffel Tower. The Berlin Wall. A rollercoaster called 1001 Nacht. A bit out-there. Although in fairness to the married couples, at least they looked happy. Kind of. Got me wondering . . . am I happy? Actually, I know why they might look happy. Seeing as they were having sex. And I was watching a documentary, showing them grinding on a fence. Not happy with that. Time to go. Get drunk. Left my house. Off to My House . . .

Hot waitresss. Coming gome. Wit me. And den. Hoboo tok er. Ho bo. Tom Greeene. Woulldd be beetterr fer her carear, to go wit hiim, she saiid. Car ear? Whure. Didnnt reealy like herr anwyays. Why wo nt Gymp cal mee?!

Thursday: Hung over. Need to get back on track. Be the bigger man. Head to the gym. Head down. Funk you Jaymes! Ignore him. Which he thought I was doing. Never returned the voice-mail. Which now? What voicemail? Oh right. Just seeing that now. Wondered what that icon on my phone was for. Eh, sorry Jim. DJ on? DJ on! Start Saturday? Wuu huu. Go on the gym!

Friday: DJ software. $50. Cable to connect my laptop to their sound system. $18. Google: How does one DJ? Priceless!

Nerves kicked in. First ever DJ gig tomorrow. Always thought I'd be a good DJ. Closest I've got before has been making playlists on my iTunes. Spent the day teaching myself the basics of mixing. Similar starts and endings. Or else twirl a few buttons. DJ all the way. My plan. Press play. Play remixes. Mix songs with my mouse and new software. Dancing, Jim, we'll be dancing!

Saturday: Debut. Yeah, here to DJ? Pardon? Yeah, today, Saturday. Not today? Not actually meant to be until Monday? Oh right. Monday it is so. Trial run? Yeah, I'll have it rocking. Actually, how much will I be paid? Eh, pardon me? DJs here don't get paid? Free membership. Good exposure. Exposure for what?! No pay?! Seriously? For funk's . . . Dazed. Confused. Dizzy. What is going on? Is it me? Have I got the whole concept of working in LA completely wrong? Society, I know your rules seem to be different in LA. Still though, do they no longer apply for the whole work-and-get-paid scenario? As far as I can see, the rich get paid for doing very little, while those struggling to make ends meet are expected to work for free. Maybe I'm wrong, but . . . Oh sorry Jaymes, rambles kicked in. Yeah, I'll still do it. Yeah, I'm a gimp.

Hollywood. Fight. Club

Just got back from trial. Not court. Fussball. Went well. Really well. Almost too well. Wuu to the huu-ugh. Just going to sit by the phone now. Should be dringing any second now. Seeing as it went so swimmingly. Starting off with that old Mexican lady screaming 'Rape!' at me. Not my fault if the men's bathroom was locked. And I was bursting. Just need the bathroom! Gimps. Trying to fight me before the match. Do me in. Little did they know I was already a cripple. Of the highest order. That incident was probably an indication of how the match would unfold. Suppose I'd better pre-empt tonight's trial for Hollywood FC with my regular game last night.

Sunday night ball is flying. Kind of. Myself and Chowder are flying at least. The rest. Hit and miss. Every third player is a hit. Rest seem like they have been abducted by aliens. Tied up. Blindfolded. Stripped naked. Plonked down onto a pitch. Blindfold is taken off. They see a football coming near them. Take off their heads. And just run around for dear life. Not having a clue what to do. Or where they are. Kicking air. Kicking player. One guy seems to be always kicking me. Same team. Keeps forgetting this. Nice guys though. Sound dudes. So can't complain. Except when they give rousing, clueless, baffling half-time speeches. And also when they ask me to place the left side of the ball on the right corner of their foreheads from a free kick in the lower left corner on the third quantrant. Come on to funk, I think I'm good, but not that good, lads!

Although Hollywood FC seemed to think Chowder and myself were good enough. Which is why they asked us to go to a trial match tonight. First things first, usual game downtown on a Sunday. Last night. Regular game. Nothing game. Where I chased a lost cause of a pass given to me. On my own. Ball going out of play. Grass. Running track. Idiot. Not wanting to slip. Tried to stop. Foot, clipped. Idiot, slipped. Sliding away. Falling. Jerk. Yank. Pop. And there goes my knee. Coach ran over. Poured water on my knee. Diagnosed it as my cruciate ligament. Oh sweet Lord, no . . . Actually, you just diagnosed that from standing there and looking at it. Please funk off. Just let me lie here for the next twenty minutes. In pain. Cursing the abductee who gave me that pass. Cursing the idiot for chasing it. Ape. Home. Ice. Bucket. Pain killers. Give me more. Actually. Now. Woah. Hey man. Feel's fine now. Can't really feel it. But that's OK. I feel . . . I feel, I feel it all. What was I saying? Ah, I'll be grand. Knees and kidneys. One will do, right?

Tonight. Trial. Hollywood FC. Big shots. Hot shots. Ex-pros from England. Actors. Movie stars. Porn dudes. Name-drop. Name drip. The works. Manager on the regular team told us that this could be our chance to shine. Incentives. Travel around California for matches. Expenses. Paid to play as well. Yes, payment. As in real money. Not the make-believe kind I've been dealing with lately. Re de de, could be a big one! Money. Contacts. Two big birds. One ball. Time to get the game head on. Take off my spaced-man helmet. Painkillers still tipping me over. Get to the pitch. Meet the other players. All think I'm Russian. No clue about my accent. Head to the bathroom. Locked. Women's. Empty. Actually. Hysterical Mexican lady. Calm down lads. Five on one. Great. Chill. Simmer. Gibber. Sorted. Back to warm-up. Slowly. Very. Slowly does it. Walking slowly. Knee felt grand. Just as long as I don't use my left foot. My good one. Just as long as I don't move any direction but forward. OK. Felt grand if I maintained that. Must just make sure not to be tackled either. Fine. And don't run. I'll be flying. I'll be grand. I'll be captain? Probably. Purely. As I'm closest to the halfway line. Decided to play, eh . . . that way. Game. On!

Playing in the hole. I knew I wouldn't last long. Plan was to score a goal. Leave the pitch. Impress and go. One burst forward. Swing with the right foot. Hit the crossbar. Unlucky. Decided to stay up top. Better for my plan. Another chance. Swivel. Feint. Flick. Hit the post. Horrendous miss. Horrific. Continued on. Numerous near-buckles of the knee. Pain making my eyes water. Also known as something else. My eyes were dying! Guy runs past me. Brushes off me. Knocks my knee. Buckle. Flop. Hit the ground. Sack of spuds. Yaaarghhh. Cry out like female yeti. Hollywood dude who brushed me, comes over. Tells me to get up. Stop faking. Does it look like I'm faking? It does. It doesn't. It does. Nooo! It doesn't. Pushes. My eyes die some more from the pain of going back on my knee. I ask the ref to hold my handbag for one second, please. Punch. Hollywood dude. Porn star. Down. Not out. Mêlée. Both sides. Eventually I'm carried off the pitch. Can't walk. Give their coach the thumbs-up. Make the 'Phone me' sign. Max length of time I was on the pitch, eh . . . I'd say ten minutes. Probably five. Time flies when you're out there having fun. Digging an early grave for yourself.

Still waiting. For the call. Still waiting. For the painkillers to kick in. Definitely going to call me. Better call. This was a chance as well. Funk. Ha, I'm joking. Not like I expected to get on the team, make buddies with a few actors and the likes, hoping for some sort of route to success that way. Not like I'm that dumb. Obviously. Funk. Could've been the way. And there we go. Waiting is over. Phone off. Thankfully. Painkillers. Kicking on in. And then, Merrick was gone.

Chancers, Prancers, Dancers!

Hands up. Who here has pleasured a gay man!? OK, now who here has pleasured a room full of gay men?! Aw yeh, me too! Along with a scattering of ridiculously hot women. Obviously. Nay, didn't accept another orgy invitation. Today, I went dancing. In the gym. Not actually able to dance myself. With my baboon knee holding my twirls back. But at least I had the rest of the gym heads rocking. Gyrating. Screaming for more. DJ. Debut on. Popped mine in a gay gym. Wuu to the huu. Something to tell the grandkids. The day I did some DJigging.

Remixes, bootlegs, curveballs . . . check, sorted, dancing. Playlists . . . brimming. Software . . . set up. Practising in my bedroom for a few hours . . . done. DJ T-shirt . . . buckets. $18 lead . . . waste of money. Not needed. One already there. Pretend I know what I'm doing. Chance on. Setting up. Eh, just keep looking busy. Plug the lead in. Laptop hooked up. Headphones slot. Being used. By that lead. Headphones? Plug into a slot in my laptop. Which no sound comes out of. Prop. Wearing the headphones now was actually blocking out the sound. Blocking the music. I'll just leave them around my neck. Prop. On. Funk it. Time to shine!

'Smells Like Teen Spirit'. Let's try out a bit of rejigging and remixing. Press . . . Press . . . Press it . . . C'mon play . . . And a one, and a two, and a three, and a four, and an up and a down and away we go! Play. Dung dun, dung dun, dunga dung, duk a dun dun. Or however that opening riff sounds, when hummed. Scan the gym. Ears perk. Puzzled look of recognition. I know that song. Kind of. Remix? Remix! Toes. Tapping. Hips. Popping.

Asses. Shaking. Heads. Bopping. Started well. I had a feeling I knew what it would lead to though. Song kicks in. Right on cue . . . Big gay Jim comes flaming out of nowhere 'Arghhhh, I love it, turn it up!' No problem Jim! Actually, where's the volu— oh, there we go! I step aside. Music takes over.

Place is soon rocking. Although maybe I shouldn't have played MIA's 'Boyz'. Where my boyz at?! Brought a flurry of them over to me. Decided to try the same with Beyoncé's 'Single Ladies'. Brought even more guys bounding over. Screaming. Yelping. Britney! Madonna! Cliché! On! Complimenting my music. Not actually my music, but cheers lads. Now who wants an Elton John remix?! Yay! Mixing went well. Mostly. One songs ends. Slipped into a new one with similar beats. Dancing. DJigging all the way. Even if I was bluffing slightly. Headphones being used to full prop effect at times. I prefer to mix visually. Innate. Laptop did freeze once for a few seconds. Actually turned out well in the end. Group of guys thought I purposely paused the music, just to pump up the crowd. Fake chanting 'We want more! We want more!' And more ye shall have lads. Simmer! Hurry up laptop, c'mon, unfreeze . . . and we're back!

First hour flew by. Few guys even asked for my DJ card. My what now? Or maybe they just wanted my number. Unsure. Amazingly, even a girl was impressed. A girl?! DJ lark might have good side perks. Bouncing up to me. Bubbling with compliments. Ditzy. Dizzy. Dumb. As funk. Enthusiastic at least. Popping off walls. Rar diddy rar. Are you from France? No. Why, do I look French? Hee-hee, no, just wondering . . . England? Nope. I know where . . . Liverpool? Closer. You do know Liverpool is in England? No, is it . . . ? What's your name? She asked this just as a song was ending. While I was mixing. Focused. Intensely. Matching those beats. Two secs there. Held up two fingers. As in . . . hang on. Two minutes. While I do this mix. And I will tell you then. Two secs there. She obviously understood me word for word. Responds with 'Tsector? DJ Tsector? What an awesome name! I love it! OMG, are you Russian!?! You *are* Russian!!!' Before I could say anything else to her, she was off bouncing around the gym again, exclaiming . . . DJ Tsector, he's Russian! Love it!!!

Two-hour set finishes up. Pumped! Did an extra half an hour. For free. I'm nice like that. Encore. Sensed I had a new-found respect from the employees. Although one guy blatantly wasn't a fan. Must not be gay. Straight prick. Don't mind though. New-found respect for myself! Finish up my debut. Pack up my gear. My laptop, lead and headphones. Pack all that up. Hobble down the stairs. High-five from Jim. Followed by a grave look of concern . . . What happened, hobbling? Soccer. Saaawker? Oh my gosh, what *don't* you do, my little Irish man?! Well, Jim, for one, sorry to say, I don't do men. Look on his face was payment enough. In gym land. In the real world, with real money, emm, yeah. No.

Let's ignore the little thing about me not making any money from it. Besides once again having free gym. Just not exactly what I thought was going to be a job. A paying one. Seeing as I need money to survive. Actually more like me being up there doing a new hobby. Ignore that. And that even though I'm in the gym, I'm not working out. Ignore *all* that. Focus on the positives. Seeing as I *delivered*, if I do say so myself! And I know, I know, self-praise is no praise. However, the praise of others works fine for me. Have to start somewhere I suppose. Might as well be a gay gym. Lot of prancing. At least they were dancing!

The Passion of Christ

Us Irish. We do like to complain. Which is why I won't be complaining about the heat. However, it is *roasting* beyond belief! Now I know how Steve Staunton must've felt. Past few days have been fun-funking-real hot. Sleeping is tough. Particularly with no A/C. Waking up from the heat. That kind of hot. So I did know it was roasting outside. And I do know that the acting studios here are all *roasting*. No air conditioning in any of them. Cutting costs, tut tut. If I paid money for these classes, I'd be outraged. Anyways, with all that heat, you'd think I'd have copped on. Didn't even think about it though. Just threw it on. Rushing out the door. Studio is close to my house. Yet I was rushing not to be late for an acting class. Just threw it on. That light blue T-shirt. Again. Again? On the hottest day I've experienced in LA. Coincidence? Maybe. Stupidity? Definitely.

Skipping along. Dodgy knee. Hobbling along. Attempting to scuttle. Hurry. And hurry I did. As fast as I could. Not so fast that I started to sweat or anything. Just fast enough for me not to see a dog. And its owner. Almost hobbled straight into them. Outside the acting school. Hob, skip and a jump around them. In the door. Up the stairs. Into class. Not yet started. On time. Wuu huu. Go me, go my knee! Full class. 'Acting for TV and Film'. Now we're dancing, this is the stuff I want! Squeeze into the seat between two girls. Sit down. Breathe out. Breathe in the dead air. Roasting studio. Sauna-like. Hot flushes. Sweet Jesus. Some heat. What's tha . . . sniff . . . what the funk's that smell? Some stink of something. Jesus. Smells nasty. Mixing with the heat. That's *horrendously* disgusting.

Girls seem to notice it too. Noses go up. Faces scrunch. Teacher walks in. Looks at us. Coughs us quiet. Ready? First scene good to go? All the time the girls and I are looking at each other. Shrugging shoulders. Do you smell that? Yeah, me too. What the funk? Who, or what, is making that smell? Why are they both looking at me? Sniff. Sniff. Does seem strong. Weird. Crikey, so hot as well. Sweats. Why did I wear baby blue?! Smell is overpowering. Where is it coming from?!! Why have both girls tried to move their seats away from me? In it together, girls. We'll find the culprit. Let me check. Oh that's it. Good work. Big pile. Dog shit. Sole of my runner. Balls. Funk. Class has just started. Everyone's hushed. Can't leave now. No washing it off. Maintain low profile. Maintain free classes. No fuss. Unique attention. Can only sit. In the heat. Sweating buckets. Stinking the place out. Well, my runner. Four-hour class. No break until midway. Sorry girls, it's going to be a tough two hours. Apologies in advance!

Thankfully, a distraction was on the way. Jesus. Arrived on stage. Long-haired Spanish dude. Took everyone's minds off the smell. Warming up. Yoga movements. Flailing arms. Wearing jocks. And a shower cap. That was it. Teacher gives him an action. Jesus just stares. Action. Keeps on staring. Intensely. As if it's a battle of wills. Go! Action! Still nothing. Camera man stands up. Waves at Jesus. Go. You're up. On stage. Come on to funk! Action! Jesus Christ, come on Jesus! Finally snaps out of it. Then takes off the shower cap? And puts on his clothes? Now ready to go. Wait, what. Jesus, why were you stripped down?

Lights. Camera. Action. Go. Weirdest. Scene. I've ever. Seen. Putting on make-up. Lipstick. Tights. Rambling out Spanish words. End scene. Teacher. Eh, Jesus, explain. Playing a Spanish transvestite? Jesus. Insulted. Disgusted. Explains. Goes all *Tropic Thunder*. Speaking English. OK. Playing the role of a woman.

Who is pretending to be another woman. OK. So. You're a guy. Pretending to be a woman. Who is pretending to be another woman? OK. Teacher asks another question . . . Why did you choose this role?! Hummmmmm. Jesus is pissed. Don't piss Jesus off! Rattles back. I did not *choose* this role. The role chose *me*. I do not *choose* to be an actor. Merely an instrument for this art. The art chose *me*.

To be honest, I was impressed with his waffling. Horse manure spewing out. How could you not admire such crap? Bit of a muppet though. Did the scene again. Probably worse. Which led me to believe that my theory is still right. Bad actors are apes. People must think I'm a muppet. Moving on. Next scene was highly boring. German guy. Australian girl. Kind of boring. Bored me senseless. Also seemed to bore the girl next to me. Who was quite hot. End scene. Small talk. Fairly brutal, huh? German dude was fairly lifeless, boring as funk you might say. That is my bruder. Oh. Right. You're German. *Wie geht's?* Ah well, your bruder wasn't really bad. Just boring. Maybe it's the heat. Probably his monotone voice. Pardon me? No, that smell of shit isn't from me. Actually. There was this dog outside, and . . . She doesn't care. Tells me to fuck off in Deutsch. What do I really think of your bruder's work? Here, look at the big lump of it on my runner!

Break. Runner. Clean. Back. Teacher. Questions. Me. Ape. I have the answer. This scene might be what you were thinking of. Why is the cameraman now filming me? Why did I put up my hand? Oh Christ. Why is the air conditioning not on? Midway through my answer, I realise that while it is the right answer to the question I thought he asked, it's actually the wrong answer to the question he *did* ask. Not the type of scene he wanted. Oh. Great. Spoof. Trying to make a new one. People can't understand me. Camera. Recording. Sweating. So yeah, that's my wrong answer. Teacher starts to laugh. Asks if I'm OK? Look hot and bothered. Sick? No, no. Fine. Low profile. Am I Irish? Yes. You're hung over, man. Crazy Irish fucker! Eh, yeah, that's the one. Jameson. Guinness. Sweating out of me. Crazy Irish! Too much whiskey with me leprechaun last night, holy begorra, us Irish huh? Top o' the morning. I'll be fine. Go back to the scenes. Toora-loora. Everyone stop looking at me. Toora . . . finally.

After class, people no longer looking at me like I'm a sweating weirdo. Now giving me a knowing smile. He's OK. He's Irish. Just sweating out the drink! You know us Irish. Not going to complain, if that's what ye want to think! Kind of dizzy after the four-hour session in the sauna. Not sure how it happened. But a Swiss dude. Asked if I want to see a stand-up show with him. Sounds good! I must try that myself soon actually. Who's going? The two of us. Only? Another man-date? Oh Jesus. No, not that Jesus. Didn't get the invite. Must dodge that man-date. Although, you know what. In fairness to Jesus, I'll give him credit. At least he was highly passionate. A passionate nutter. Believed in what he was doing. Going for it. Got me thinking on the walk home. Need to find my own passion. Not sure if it's acting. Not sure what it is really. Must mull that over. First, I need a shower.

Wow Factor

Pondering. Has being going on. What is my passion? *Sister Act 2* happened to be on TV the other day. Whoopi was giving advice. If you wake up thinking about singing, then you are a singer. Pondering. When I wake up, what am I thinking about? Lately. Writing. DJing. Plus, sometimes, women. Using Whoopi's logic, I must want to be a writer, a DJ, and a woman. Logically. Passion on. Although I do have a passion for dancing. Not the dance-floor kind. The dancing kind. DJ. Writer. Dancer. Woman. Might've found another passion. This weekend. One of my childhood dreams came true. So many people to thank. Don't know where to begin. Lifelong goal. Achieved. Finally. My true passion . . . carnivals. I became a carny. Wuu huu! Living the dream. This is what Tinseltown is all about. Pinnacle. Dizzy heights. I mean, wow. Specifically, I mean selling Shamwows. Shammys. Selling dishcloths. Look at me go. Sweet Lord.

How did such a dream come true? A friend of a roommate. Layla is seeing this guy. Rusty. Sound dude. Compared to some of the other guys, big-time. Rusty runs a franchise. Selling Shamwows. Dishcloths. The best kind there is, apparently. Big event on this weekend. Last minute, Rusty found out he needed a hand. Usual guy bailed. Now stuck. Did I want to make some easy money? Two days. Maybe come out with $400. Maybe even more. You know what . . . let me mull. Even though initially I thought not a hope said the pope. What with having a master's and a blind sense of grandeur. Realised I could do with some extra bobs. Big-time. Subsistence living is fun and all, but I'm more broke now than when I was eighteen. Way more broke.

The navy might, *might*, be pulling one more bit of work out of the bag for me. Until then though, I need to start making some cash. Money. Losing weight, need to eat. Losing out on boozing sessions, need to drink. Two days outdoors. Get a tan. Plus, free ride on the big wheel. Happy days. I'll do it! Sham. Wow. On!

As it happens, I recently watched a documentary about carnies. And their daily lives. Highlights included incest, fighting, and an even more hubbula version of English than mine. Carnival I was working at over the weekend did not disappoint. Full of them. Bizarre group. Although nice people, in fairness. Majority at least, once they realise you're one of them now. Sweet Lord, I am one of them now. Dream of mine, shine on. Carnival itself consisted of dodgy-looking rides. And even dodgier-looking stalls. Selling goods. Shoes. Looked fifth-hand. Bottles of water. Which sprayed you in the face. Ornaments. Made out of hazelnuts. Tailored suits. At a funking carnival?! Someone is actually going to buy a suit at a carnival? Sweet Jesus, no way . . . Hang on, that large chap seems to be . . . just bought a suit. No, just bought two. Without trying them on. Suit up.

Noticed that the competition was giving us envious looks. Mixed with respect. Apparently Shamwows are the kings of the roost. Main men. Golden boys. Shammys can sell. So good, they can sell themselves. Hottest of hot cakes. Two-day festival. Over thirty thousand people expected. Rusty started breaking down the figures. Sell twenty. Make $100. Reckons we'd easily sell twenty to thirty per hour at the peak times. We'd clean up! Dancing around the carnival. New kid on the carny block was in town! Wuu huu. Funk my master's. I am a born-again Sham! Time for me to go sell! Now, let's wait for the people to start pouring in. Patience. Wait. Wait. What? Rusty? Five hours later. Not one sale. As in zero. One last time, to clarify. I made zero sales per hour. As did Rusty. Seasoned pro. That made it slightly easier to take. Not just me. Still brutal. Seven hours on the clock. Not a nickel to show for it. Rusty called it the 'biggest bummer of a show' that he's ever done. Mighty stuff. Handy that it coincided with being my first-ever show. Wuu. Roll with those punches. At least tomorrow can't get any worse. Can't make less than zero. Surely!

Fantastisch!

Woke up. Thinking about Shamwows. Please do not be my new passion. Please no. Determined second day. Stayed up all night perfecting my sales demo. Hey folks, gather round. We've all had that problem, spilt drinks, disaster! What to do?!! I have the answer! Shamwow! Cover the stain, press down on the shamwow, soak it right up! Roll. Squeeze. Now can you see that difference?! Wow! That's right folks, it has the wow factor. The Shamwow! And so on. Until I had it down! Practised that more than I did the DJ mixing. Pumped for some car salesmanship. Time to shine. Twelve hours of constant sales. Let's do this, carnies, let's rock this whure! All those thirty thousand people would *definitely* be coming along today!

Just in case they did, I was hooked up with a microphone and headset. Gibberish voice rambling out over speakers. People looking at me. As if I was speaking Russian. Erra shur come over here folks, let me show you the wow! Giddy up them steps!!! Few punters started to shout obscenities at me. Irish loser. Go home loser. Fuck ye. Pricks. Forgot I was wearing a microphone. So a big group of dudes heard me call them pricks. Aggro. Luckily, us carnies stick together. Instantly backed up. Flocking over. Hubbula. Get out of here, ye pricks!!!

Four hours later. Something finally happened. Finally, after a combined nine hours of trying, I made my first sale. Very pleasant chap. Nice guy. Small talk. Did the demo. Seemed very impressed that the Shamwows were German. Picked up on it. Pressed that point home to him. You know how the Germans make the best things, right?! My pitch was perfect. Started asking me if I liked Germany. Blew his mind when I spoke German to him. Used to live there. Played up my love of all things German. Women. Food. Fussball. Cars. Rap. Ha. Everything. Never seen someone so impressed. Jesus, I might get two sales out of this. He is gripping two rolls rather tightly! Yeah, I am a fan of Germans. Yeah, good beliefs. Eh yeah, good values. So eh, up for buying a couple? Ja? Go on. Ja? He will. Shout out a joking 'Ja Voll' to him! Pleases him immensely! Ridiculously so. Gives me a knowing nod. Taps his nose. Em, OK. Tells me that he's like me. OK. Hand over the money. Then I will like you more. Cash in my hand. Felt good.

As I start to wrap up the roll of Wow for him, he mentions that he has something to show me. Briefly panic. Please don't pull down your pants. We're not in WeHo any more Toto, leave your pants on. Not to worry. Only lifting up his T-shirt. Covered in tattoos. Probably going to show me a shamrock one. No, no shamrock, look at the big one on his back. Which one? Oh sweet Jesus. That big one of Hitler's face? Now I see the other tattoos. Most are Nazi-related, it would appear. Hmmm. Shaved head. Hmmm. Not really sure if this was the banter I thought we were having after all. Maybe not the best idea shouting out 'Ja Voll' at him. It being kind of a Nazi statement if said in a certain way. Now that I think about it. We are in Venice Beach. Now that I quickly piece together, wasn't . . . ? Yes, *American History X* was based here. Makes sense. First sale. Neo-Nazi. Fantastisch.

Puts his T-shirt back on. Turns back around. Waits for me to say something. Eh, cool, that was a nice tattoo you had of an angel on your shoulder. Oh, you weren't showing me that one? Didn't really notice which one you were on about. How about those Lakers, huh? Looks at me oddly, smile fading. Eh, did I mention the Shammy holds twenty-one times its own weight in water, ja? Asks did I not like the tattoo? He expected me to be impressed. Ehh, emmm, *oh mein Gott in Himmel,* don't curb me! Thankfully, on cue, his girlfriend had seen enough of the carnival. Comes back to drag him off. Neo gives me a suspicious look, then the rock fist to say goodbye. Rock, paper, scissors. I wave paper-style back at him instead, finish on a lighthearted note. Accidentally, must've looked like a Heil Hitler salute. Neo loves it and me once more. Big smile back. Oh funk. Oh wait . . . buys another roll of Shamwow from me. Two rolls. No curbing.

Looking back at it, I should really have taken the Shammys back and refunded him his money, after he revealed his true nature. Went for the money over the moral stance though. First sale and all. I need the bobs. Weak man. Made one more sale after that. Total sales for two days of work? Two. Total amount made for nineteen hours of work? $15. Food expenses? $30. Net total money made? Minus $15. New kid on the carny block really shone this weekend. Great weekend of work. Dreams came true. Finally I can call myself a carny. I wonder how much I'll have to pay out when we get our yearly bonuses?

Decided to go to the gym when I got home. Banish some of the frustration. Did not really go as planned. Opposite. Forgot gym closed early. Sunday night. Super. Chump. Walking home. Waiting to cross the road. Gave a homeless guy a dollar. Saw that his can was almost overflowing. As in brimming. Asked how much he makes. So far, in the last two hours, $35. Pardon me? Two hours. Compared to someone I know, that is good work, if you can get it. Nice iPod too by the way. Can I have my dollar back by any chance? Interesting to find out at least. I know where I am on the scale. Homeless guys are making more money than me. Way more. Something to think about. All good for the soul. Fan-funking-tastic.

Stand Up. Sit Down

Boiled eggs. I like mine runny. According to *MrBreakfast.com*, they'll take four minutes. Not too long really. For my stand-up debut, I was told three minutes. Three. Minutes. That's all. Three minutes of jokes. Or stories. Or silence. Whatever I wanted. Just don't go over the three-minute mark. Big taboo. Not good. In the stand-up world. The world I am now part of. Wuu. Go me. Every man needs a plan. Another baby step, in the right direction. Well. A baby feint. At least it's in the right direction.

Being honest, stand-up was not a venture I ever thought of doing. Or trying. Never even crossed my mind. Until I was told it would tie in well with the rest of my plan. Fred. Necessity. OK. Let's do it. I have a feeling I know the reason why I never thought of doing it before. Easy really. My. Jokes. Are. Horrendous. I might have a bit of wit. Or might be able to whip out gibberish of a funny nature. Or have dumb, funny incidents happen to me. Jokes though? Nay so good. Usually I assume the person hasn't heard what I just said. Repeat. Still nothing. Oh right. No laughter because you didn't realise I was attempting a joke. Oh. What about this one? And now you're walking away. A duu to you!

Personally, I think my jokes are brilliant. Then again, every mother does think her baby is beautiful. Got to work on making a few beautiful babies for myself. Spent a few hours getting three minutes' worth of material ready. Hours. Into minutes. Should be easy. Balls. Key ingredient. Lines that punch. Wherefore art thou? Sat and thought and wrote. Put together a bucket of stories, anecdotes, gibber and jokes. Tried out a few of the jokes on my roommates, subtly slipping them into the conversation. Rar diddy rar, joke . . . Nothing. Odd looks. Try again, rar diddy, joke . . . Silence. Quizzical looks. Pretended they were just one-line stories I felt they needed to hear. Didn't tell them the real story. Headed off for my debut.

Fred had advised me to start away from Hollywood. Try the beach areas first. Work on the routine. Perhaps. Practice does makes perfect. Then do the Hollywood circuit. Perhaps. If I had a car. I don't. Time is also of the essence. Let's try one of the big three. Laugh Factory. Comedy Store. Improv. Open mic. Give Improv on Melrose a whirl. Tough to get a slot. Over a hundred people show up. Only about twenty get to go on. Names on slips of paper. Hat. Raffle. Balls. Not in. Funk that. Now or never. Manager. Top o' the . . . any chance . . . I'm Irish . . . I'm in. Duu! Told I had a slot towards the end. Started at five. Finishes at seven. Followed by the pros. Towards the end, am I? That, to me, sounds like I'm headlining. Wuu duu. Let's just convince myself of that. While I calm my nerves. Listening to my iPod. Strangely choosing to play Elton John and Kiki Diamond on repeat. 'Don't Go Breaking My Heart'. I wouldn't if I tried. Singing on nervously. Heart was fine. Stomach started to get a few flutters.

As I made my way from the bar to the club part, I realised something. Not only would this be my debut, it was my first time ever in a comedy club. Ever. Pretty pretty pre-tty cool place. Always imagined it as having the red-brick wall. Microphone. Bar stool. Spotlight. Cool little tables. And guess what? Exactly the same. Walls covered with photos of all the people who had start-ed out there. Performed at various stages. Still performed there now. Bill Cosby. Richard Pryor. Steve Martin. Robin Williams. Jay Leno. Jim Carrey. Jerry Seinfeld. Chris Rock. And everyone of note in between. Needless to say, an impressive list. Which I was about to join. Oh Jesus, stomach is flubbering. One more listen to Elton. 'When I was down, I was your clown.'

First few acts had me fired up. No offence to them, but they were bruuuuutal. Jesus, they were bad. At least they taught me a few lessons. Long jokes. No dazzling punchline at the end. Not a good idea. If a joke starts off horrendously, more than likely it's a horrendous joke. If your punchline gets a laugh, don't try to get a cheap add-on laugh with an extra horrific punchline. Making the first one seem like a fluke. And finally, they showed me that there are a lot of racist comedians. White on black. Black on white. White on Jewish. Jewish on white. One girl had a white Mum and a black Dad, who were both Jewish. Could say whatever she wanted. Everyone had a pop at Tyler Perry. That man is not liked. I'm sure he's gutted. Heartbroken. While he rolls around in all his money.

Few funny comedians were on. Big fat gay guy. His description. Funny. Next guy. Black albino. With alopecia. Blind. Certifiably at least. Funnily enough. All true. As far as I could see. Couldn't see if, eh, he was able, eh, to see or not. (See, an attempt at a joke, not so funny!) Two other things I noticed. Everyone gets a snippet of a song played before they went on. En route to the stage. Book of songs. Choose. And secondly, as it got later and later, people started to leave. Most of the audience was made up of comedians. Either those going on or those that got shafted in the raffle. Numbers dwindled every five minutes. So by five to seven, there were very few left in the crowd. As in a handful. Which is roughly the time I heard Elton John's 'Rocket Man' come on. Oh Jesus. That's the song I picked. This is it. Time to shine!

Up on stage. Nerves. Don't worry. Speeches. Easy. Small crowd here. Shine on. Dance on. Stand up. Gulp. Eh, how's it going? Ploughed into my opener . . . about the pig I had sex with on spring break in Mexico . . . and away we go! Few laughs. Few confusions. Irish accent. Americans. Banter. Mocking. Banter. Horrendous attempt at an on-the-spot joke. Great laughs for next joke. Although they came before I told the originally intended punchline. Say nothing, remember that for next time. Flashing light. Time almost up. Gay-horse-joke time. Heeeeeyyy!!! Song comes on. Off I go. Waving. Cheering. At the five people in the audience. High-five from dude next to the stage. And I was pumped. Victory lap!?! No.

Those were my impressions at least. Probably biased. Had a booze beforehand too. One good sign did come from the manager. Came over to me afterwards. Congratulated me. Good set. Thanks. Told me a story about Jim Carrey. Apparently he was brutal when he did it for the first time here. Thought I did well. Better than Jim. Delighted to hear! Safe to say I was the first and will be the last to hear that. Told me to come back next week. No problem. Cheers! A paying gig, I assume? Ha. Ha ha. He said. Good one. He said. Good one indeed. I said. Good joke by me. Call me Joe King. He didn't get it. Neither did I really. So I left before I could say any more. Skipping home. Singing Elton John. Delighted.

About two streets away from mine, coming up to a junction to cross the road, I saw a homeless guy I'd had banter with a few times. Waiting to cross at the lights. I'll play a little joke. Tapped him on the shoulder from behind. Ducked the other way. Only joking. My buddy turned around to see no one. Great joke by me. Quickly swivelled back around the other way. Where I was standing. Smiling. Funny guy. Comedian. Huh? Instinctively swung. Clocked me, in the ear. Knocked me, to the ground. Dumb. Down. Off my high horse. Who's laughing now?!

Oblivious to the Obvious

Empathy. I felt it all around. Air was dry. Numerous plants scattered around my house were going through a bit of a dry spell. Girls have been neglecting them. Poor plants. I felt their pain. Personal dry spell going on for far too long. One thing I knew for certain: something needed to be done. I knew this much, at least. Other things, maybe not so clued-in on. Oblivious. To the obvious. Although it never is obvious until you get told.

Such as . . . bikini bars? Assumed it was a beach-themed bar. Sand . . . sangrias . . . *sans* clue. Presume on. Ended up at a party the other night with five girls who worked at bikini bars. Cool. Ye wear bikinis to work. Mighty. Myself and Chowder randomly met them in a weird after-hours bar we randomly ended up at. If you want an odd night, Thai Angel delivers the goods. You can always get an indication of what an unknown place is like from the look of the people you meet in the queues for the bathroom. If I wasn't a tad drunk and oblivious, I might say it's a dodgy spot. Seeing as I was a tad of both, it was a great spot. For some reason bellowing 'THAI AIN-GEL!' over and over made it even more fun. Which I think brought the girls over. Curiosity and cats. Fans of Irish accents. Fan of their various American looks. Single fan, seeing as Chowder fell asleep at the bar. As he likes to do, every now and again. Party still on? Party on. Five girls. One me. Wuu huu.

Although it turned out I wasn't the only guy at the party. One other dude floating around. Friend of the girls. Assumed he was a beach-bar bum too. Except he dressed like Carlton from *Fresh Prince of Bel Air*. Bit of a nutter. Full-on muppet. Found out I was Irish. Not a fan of Irish people. Probably just not a fan of the girls liking my accent. Accused me of being a criminal. Seeing as my ancestors were all criminals. Fun 4 AM chatter. Bit oblivious to his tone. Took no notice. So he moved on to having a pop at me for being white. Mighty stuff bud. Let's be honest, as a white man I have rarely experienced racism being hurled at me. Off the top of my head, I can think of one other time. Only that time. Also in America. When a girl kept calling me a dumb white Irish boy. Which, in fairness to her, could be seen as an accurate first impression. But the fact that she was white as well, and constantly emphasised the word 'white', confused me big-time. Not sure what triggered it off. Must've pushed the wrong button. Might not have been so oblivious to her tone. Might've kept on pushing.

Back to Carlton. And his pink sweater over his shoulders. Trying to push my buttons. Red wine was flowing. Tad more oblivious. Until one of the girls asked why my friend was saying all this to me? No clue . . . wait, pardon, who? What friend? Carl? Don't even know him, thought he was *your* friend . . . Nope, never met him before in my life. Seemed like Carlton was a mere randomer. Even more random than I was. At least two of the girls brought me back to the party in a cab. Girls assumed. I assumed. We all assumed. No buddy. Sorry buddy. Time to go. Big scene. Not only was Carlton a bit of a racist, dabbled as a bigot on the side. At one stage, while he was being kicked out, he moved on to some Catholicism gibber at me. Guessed I was a Catholic. Which I think was the insult? Good one. Carlton. Boot.

Back to me and five girls. Too many cooks. Three of the girls were really quite hot. One was ridiculously quite hot. Daisy. Did not look like a cow. Or a duck. More like the lead singer of the

Pussy Cat Dolls. Seeing as she had no interest in me, I obviously thought she was even hotter. Gibber. Jabber. Toora-loora.
Nothing. Except for me digging a hole. Finally one of the other
girls told me she was a lesbian, was it not obvious? Eh, no, not
at all. Would've been handy knowing that twenty minutes earlier.
Chatted to the blonde girl instead. Drank some more. Jigged a
little. Went to bed.

As it happened, that girl also went to the same bed. Ahem.
Ahem. A duu. Woke up. Still feeling a tad drunk. Drank the glass
next to the bed. Wine and coke. Mank. Funk. Definitely. Drunk.
Realised the girl next to me looked a bit different than I had
remembered. Transformer? Her hair is way different. Something
else . . . skin colour . . . What the funk?! Was she not white? Oh
Jesus, what exactly happened with Carlton again? Memory playing tricks . . . He was the one saying all that stuff, right? I didn't
have one of my 'reality dreams', did I? Can I subtly ask her if she
was not white last night? Can I? Will that sound racist? Oh Jesus.
Can't really ask the girl. Just in case I was the racist bigot? Surely
not. No. Just say nothing. Said nothing. Never asked. Still no
clue. Probably never find out.

What I did find out that morning was that they all work at
the top of my street. Really? Where? Which club? Place at the
top of the street. Had been shut because of renovations. Now
back open. I was not aware. Although I did hear something
about a garage opening up. A body shop. No. I was wrong. *The*
Body Shop. Which is not a bikini bar. In case you thought it was.
I did a bit of sussing. See, a bikini bar is not a beach-themed bar.
It is, however, a club where girls dance. On tables. And a stage.
In their bikinis. Which are kept on. All of which means, the club
is still allowed to serve booze. The Body Shop is not this kind
of place. No booze in the Body Shop. Not allowed to serve

alcohol. No bikinis. Not a garage. No mechanics. Only apple juice, and naked dancing. Dancers. Girls. Strippers. Strip club. Top of the street. My street. Open until the wee hours of the morning. After hours. Which is handy. Just to know. Obliviously.

Implosions

Open mic in Improv was on once more. Working away on new stand-up material since my debut. Didn't want to reuse the same material. Fresh batch, spice it up. Pumped. Ready. Prepared. For three minutes. Asked would I like an early five-minute slot. Bring it on. Bigger crowd. Ready to go. Only have material for three minutes though. Two minutes longer. Sounds like nothing. Sweet Lord, it's far longer than one might think. Particularly when the new material was barely understood. Not sure if it was cockiness or cluelessness. Either way, Cutting Crew started blaring inside my head with about two and a half minutes gone. At one stage, I tried to sing a line or two, to kill the last minute. 'I just died in your arms tonig– ' Throat. Mouth. Dried up. Armpits. Forehead. Sweating down. Raining. Pouring. Insides shrivelling up. Parts dying inside. Swallowed up. Until finally . . . five minutes. Oh sweet Jesus, that went well. In a *horrific* way. Not a fan of that bombing exhibition. Air badly needed. Dizzy. Almost said nay more. Seriously. Bombing is brutal. Decided to leave it for a week. Rebuild the confidence. Finally built a bridge. Got over it. Only my second time. Back to basics. Which, eh, were what again? Google, YouTube, fill me in!

Giddied back up. Did a stint in the Laugh Factory. Three minutes. Back to basics. First routine again. Went well. I think. Shone at times. Crowd laughed. With me. Maybe *at* me? Who knows? Who cares? They laughed. I had a good laugh. Bombs were avoided. Got the bug again. Stand-up is needed. Try everything, and all that. Practice on. Hunted down more venues. Found another good spot tonight. IO West Theater. Hollywood.

Emailed the manager. Got a slot. Sorted. Dancing. Sunday night. Meant to be good. The Andy Dick Comedy Box. Assumed the comedian Andy Dick would be at it. He was. Great detective work by me. Headed along by myself early. Do a bit of pre-gig mingling. Network all the way. Recognised one guy who was waiting outside, directs episodes of *The Office*. Must do stand-up as well. Pity I didn't have my spec script on me. I'm sure he would've loved me giving it to him then and there. Common practice, I'm sure. Actually having something in writing as opposed to just storylines in my head might be a good start for that plan to work though.

Seeing two people of note in the audience did make me realise that stand-up could be a good way in. Fred is a wise man. Just need to get good at stand-up now. Practice on. Also gave me a good kick that they were in the audience. My Irish gibberish would wow them! Invited Chowder along as well. Who brought along a date. Who brought a few of her friends. So they were also in the crowd. People I knew. People I knew of. All in the crowd. Pressure. Time to shine, get over that hump. Two-hour show. Ten bells. Sit down. Show starts. Wait for my turn. Wait. Twelve o'clock. Shows up. Show is over. Still waiting. Still sitting. Still down. Never got called up. Manager. Apologies. Ran over. Had to accommodate others. Maybe next week. Ape. Even worse. Chump for inviting people along. Apologies Chowder, not the greatest of first dates. Although turns out they all enjoyed seeing me getting so worked up about not getting to go on. Oh. Cool. I don't feel as bad so. As long as you're laughing. All that matters really. Well, besides not bombing. Brutal buzz. No bomb, laugh on.

In the Name of the Father

Taxi men. I think they may be sabotaging me. Coming back from bars or clubs in Hollywood, they insist dropping me at the top of my street. Which is when I remembered. The Body Shop. Taxi men. Only reason I remembered, I swear. First night it happened, I decided to pop in for a second. Just to say hi to the girls from the party. Personally, I'm not a fan of strip clubs. Well, as in one-on-one lap dances. Think about it. Just teasing. Personally, I prefer to have banter with the girls. Have a laugh. Or else dance for them. Added bonus if they happen to be hot. Or show interest. Make them laugh. And opposed to them making you give them more money for another frustrating song.

Another reason why I'm not a great fan of the stripping aspect. Waste of money. Particularly when you're surviving week to week. So it kind of all worked out nicely when I was in there my first night. And a girl sneezed. Achoo. Bless you. Thank you, oh my Gawd, do you have an accent? Yes, I'm Irish. Achoo . . . Bless you. Oh my Gaaawd, are you a priest?! Eh, yup. Well, kind of. Almost one. Yet to be ordained. This is my last hurrah before I must go home and be ordained. Father Merrick. Until then I was told to enjoy myself. Would I like a dance? I would, however, I can't really get one-on-one dances. As that would be a sin. To spend all that money.

Let the mind run free, and the words will just ramble out. Turned out to be *mighty* drunken gibberish. No hounding me to get private dances. Banter on. Leading me to realise a few things. One. All strippers go to UCLA. Claim to go. Only stripping to pay their way through college. Sure. You. Are. And I'm a priest.

Another thing of worthwhile note . . . Just because strippers work together, doesn't mean they're buddies with each other. Not in the slightest. Leading me to my third discovery. That really hot girl from the party, Daisy, Pussy Cat Doll . . . not a full-on lesbian. Bi. And. Clever. Ish. Copped on I wasn't actually a priest. She knew the real story. Which is why I think she said good-bi to women for a night. Knew that I was in fact doing research for a role. Movie role. Tried to tell her I wasn't. She knew the truth. Put two and two together. Living on the same street as the Irish movie office? She knew what was going on. She wasn't dumb! She was going to UCLA! OK . . . you got me. Now, want to go see where I live? You do? Daisy Duu!

I'm pretty sure most of the girls had a deep-rooted priest fantasy all along. Although they might just have a million fantasies and want to try each and every one. American girls do like to embrace sexual adventures though. Far more fun. Far more vocal. One thing they constantly say is 'Daddy'. Daddy this, Daddy that, do it Daddy, and so on. Trying to be sexy, I think. Not too sure. Personally, I'm not a huge fan. First time I had it said to me, I was highly confused. What are you meant to say back . . . Mummy? Not a hope said the pope, way too odd. Not that I'm complaining or anything. Better than just lying there like a dead fish.

Now and again it can get odd though. Especially combining certain aspects. Funny at first. Weird is a close second. One banter dancer I met really liked saying Daddy while we were off on an adventure. Issues. I assume. Asked her to stop saying it, please. So she did. Apologised. Profusely. And instead started to call me Father. Ahem. Me. Father. Ahem. Harder. You. Irish. Priest. Father. Merrick. Ahem. Me. Good. Ahem. No. Not. Good. Enough. Ye . . . Oh Jesus . . . Father, no . . . You're done?

Ahem Father! Faking the end of the adventure just to stop hearing a girl fake-scream 'Father' at you is a tad off. My priest background can backfire at times. On the upside. Assumptions are made that I must repent my sins. Straightaway. Feel bad for corrupting me. Eh, yeah, I need to start saying Hail Marys. Send them on their way with ten Our Fathers.

Fair old flurry of discoveries to be true, to be true. Lot of fun discoveries. Few fun adventures. Few bizarre. (Particularly that girl who I thought kept getting a phrase mixed up. Seeing as a lot of Americans do get confused with that phrase. You want me to take a what now on you?! Ha ha, no, the phrase is taking *the* p . . . Oh, you knew what you were saying. Oh. Jesus. Sweet Lord. No. Crikey, what are you trying to do?! Giddy up and be gone! Close call.) Along with all those other discoveries, I did also find out that there was another place at the top of my street, which may be beneficial: the Irish Film Board office. Just across the road. Obviously. I knew that all along. Just like I know where I'll eventually be going. Straight. To. Hell.

Googling. Crawling. Running

Running. Looking for clues. Big loopy circles. Running and running. At least I know I do this. However, I'm now beginning to see that it's better than not running at all. For example, I have been DJigging in the gym now for a while. In exchange for membership. No actual payment. No cash. Just membership. And a fan-base. Grow on. People who own bars and clubs go to that gym. Asking me if I play anywhere else. Like to come see me play. Mostly dudes. Saying they will come find me. Hunt me down. Bit odd at first, but it did get me thinking. Perhaps I could spread my DJigging wings. Saying this to Chowder one a night out in Barney's. Bar manager comes over to chat with Chowder. I remembered her from my first ever week in LA. Interviewed me for a bar job. Rejected. Could barely understand a word I said to her then. More or less the same thing now. Chowder translates for me. She asks what do I do? Chowder mentions that I DJ in a gay gym. Is this true? Well, not actually a gay gym. Just a lot of gay men. And a few hot women. Oh, the DJ part, yeah, that is true. Circles collide . . . She's looking to hire a DJ. Would I be interested? Surely I would! Giddy up them there steps!

Happy days. New DJ gig in Barney's now. Jim Morrison's old watering hole. Used to perform there as well. I'm in good company. You could say that the Doors are opening for me. But it wouldn't make much sense. So I won't say it. Moving swiftly on, I've realised that from playing soccer up in Robbie's house, I know a lot of guys. However, no clue what most of them do. Never really asked them. I know what Chowder does. As I asked him. Runs a marketing agency. He knows what I'm trying to do.

As I told him my plan. Every man. Needs a plan. Chowder has offered his marketing expertise if needed. Informed me that I actually know a fair few people who could help me with my plan. Cameramen. Lighting guys. Sound engineers. Who, as it turns out, would be interested in helping me with part of my plan. The part where I shoot a few scenes to go with the script I'm writing. Not only would I have a script, but also a few visuals to go with it. All part of the plan! Amazing what you can find out once you ask. All pretty good to know. Plan is forming, even if it is in a roundabout way.

More running went on yesterday. Literally. Sprinting to a coffee meeting, which I was late for. Seeing as I decided to have a quick cup of tea before I headed off. Dumb. As. Funk. Quick cup? Tea? Before going for coffee? Chugging. Spitting. Burning mouth. Late. Well done. Running up the hill, top of my street. Meeting with the head of the Irish Film Board. Sit down. Small talk. Coffee. Grand. First-date feeling, with one highly uninterested party. Needed to start sparking interest quick. What are you doing? Well, I'm doing this, this and that. Oh really. Stand-up, writing, acting classes and DJing. Technically . . . yes. Grand. Still not really that interested. Until it came out that I supported Everton. As. Did. He. Happy days, common ground, more relaxed. Banter on. Now recommended that maybe I should meet this Irish girl who works in BAFTA. Could put me in touch with a guy who is part of the committee that helps out newcomers. Might be useful. Sounds useful. Cheers for that. And after a slow, awkward start, the meeting was well worth running for. Yet another nudge in the right direction. Baby. Steps. On.

What Number Are You?

Past few days have been pretty eventful. Well, full of events. A full week really now I think about it.

Monday: Eat. Writing. Eat. Acting class. Eat. Gym. Sleep.

Tuesday: Stand-up gig. Five minutes. Not my own show. Unpaid. Obviously. Dancing and prancing in the gym. DJing. Obviously.

Wednesday: Acting class. Dinner. Drinking. Cans. Cheap. Cheerful. Save money. Before I headed out. To *Maxim*'s Top 100 party. Living a dual life. Eternal student. Getting invited to these events. An event that was big enough for everything to be free. Wuu duu. Fan of the free. If you go past a certain level with these events, everything is free. Like when you get so rich that people start giving you free stuff. Not sure how that logic works. I can't wait for it to happen to me. Can. Not. Wait. Got the invite from Zen, who was DJing at it. Come along, free booze, good-looking women, should be good. Sounds good. In fact, that sounds funking mighty! Although – and this might surprise you – it actually sounded better than it turned out to be. In LA, it is all about personality. Seeing as everyone is good-looking. Hot blondes. Hot brunettes. Hot redheads. Even girls with shaved heads are hot here! All hot. Which is why personality is more important. Party was lacking personalities. Everyone was ridiculously hot. Just ridiculously hot though. Little life in them. I thought it was meant to be a party?! Bored people looking hot. Or hot people looking bored? Hot bores. Where are the wild boars?! Or, the wild whu— eh, what what?

On the upside, there were more than a hundred hot women. Another thing struck me while at it though. Plenty of the girls who were working at it seemed far hotter to me than some of the girls I was chatting to that made 'The List'. Not one girl on this list got my horrendous attempt at a joke either . . . I'm number 167, how about you? 'Aren't there only 100? And you're a guy?' Died a death. As did I, when speaking to a girl called Mandy. Getting on well. Barman was ploughing shots into me. Maybe that was the dumb reason I thought she said her surname was 'Whure'. What? Whure? Mandy Whure?! At least she laughed. And then walked away. Barman told me who she was. Well done Merrick. Number 39 would've been nice. Would've made the event as good as it sounded, to be true!

Thursday: Writing. Shamwow show during the day. First DJ gig in Barney's. Well, first paid gig since my trial run last week. Almost lost my mind when I found out the trial-run payment would only be a free tab. Unlimited food and drink for my buddies and me. Why not give me the money?! Kept it together though. Drank through the pain. Another chump DJ job where I don't get paid. Manager liked the music at least. Rock on. Asked me back. Money. Crossing. Hands. Wuu. Now, not only am I a struggling writer (did get paid for articles for Irish publications, after all), I am also a struggling DJ. Struggling in general. All about it. Struggle on.

Friday: Day of rest. Mull over my conundrum. A big Shamwow event was happening over the weekend. Surprisingly, between the last navy contract I got, and moonlighting as a Shamwow salesman, I was just about making enough money to keep me tipping over. Barely. Tipping still though. Subsistence all the way.

Shamwow event might let me earn about $400 for the two days. Probability? Actually high. Which would give me some sort of a comfort buffer. Haven't had one of them in God only knows how long. Constantly living in fear of waking up broke. Fearing that the $10 I have hidden in my suitcase would be my last bit of money. And, as a result, homeless. Not great for one's state of mental well-being. Could do that. Sell Shamwows. Money money. Buffer buffer. Or . . .

Take up my buddy's offer. Copelando. Invited me along to Rob's house on Saturday. Watch the big fight. Private party up there. Reason I was invited along: game of ball on beforehand. Drafted me in. Wanted to win. Somehow, I was seen as an asset. Game of ball. Followed by a party. Big party. Private party. I had heard who had been at these parties before. Copelando dropped a good few hints. Couldn't say much though. Wanted to ensure it'd be low-key. Asked me to keep it quiet. Not many other 'regular folk' had been asked along. Was I up for it? Hmmm. Go to a party in the Hollywood Hills in Robbie Williams' house. With a load of people I presumed were going. Chance to mingle. Network. Baby-step it up. Or sell dishcloths. What was I up for? Money is money. Which I would need badly in about two weeks' time. Especially with my man-period due soon. Unless I somehow landed a big break before then. Using that logic, the party would be a great place for this to happen. Funk, what to do? Money, memories. Memories, money. I know what I *should* do. I know what I *want* to do. And I know how many lives I will be living. Party on!

Do It for Me, Ricky, Please!!!

Woke up with a bang. Door swung open. Not a notion what was going on. Thought I was late for the Shamwow job. Saw a scantily clad lady jumping on my bed. Jess. Kept asking me what colour to go with . . . red or black, this or that, look, look!?! Red or black which? Bikini! Pepsi audition today. Oh. Right. Go blue. Modelled the blue for me. Looked mighty. Great call out of me. Good perk of living with models. Who cares about the smoking and the mess, swimsuit modelling all the way! My sieve finally settled. Got out of bed. Gathering thoughts kicked me in the forehead. Today wasn't about Shamwows. Today was soccer day. Tonight was fight night. Today was a big one!

Forgot what I had decided I had planned to do. Forgot I needed to go get business cards made out if I could. Forgot that Saturday morning is not a great time to do this. Forgot all that. Did not forget to ring or text everyone back home about where I was going though. Just don't tell anyone. Keep it hush. They want it to stay low-key. We *all* want it low-key. Chilled. So we did. Even if I had it built up to be the greatest party of all time. At least, of all *my* time. Needed to get photos of the night. Not a fan of photos. Just handy to have in case it turns into a heavy boozing session. Stored memories. Forgot my camera was broken. Did not forget to buy a disposable one though. Forget about the business cards. Bought a crate of beer instead. Cans of Bud Light would be my business cards! I was dancing.

Won't lie, my mind started thinking of every possibility of who might be there. Copelando had the whole affair laced with ambiguity. Don't tell anyone. A lot of people over from the UK for it. Neighbours calling around as well. Seriously, my imagination ran away like a wild headless chicken. Giddy. Excited. Nervous. Pumped. Five-a-side in Robbie Williams' house. 'Special game'. Invite-only. Whatever that meant. Why hadn't Chowder got the nod? Followed by a party to watch the big fight. Mingling with Rob and his buds. If you think about it, kind of odd. Not a dream I've ever had or anything. Just surreal. Or maybe I was still a wee bit hung over. Party afterwards would be perfect for me to mingle, network and meet the right people. Hopefully pull a supermodel while I'm at it. Hopefully. This could be huge. Might not get another chance like it. Time to embrace! Layla offered me a lift to the house. Go on the Lay Diddy! Decided to have a sneaky Bud Light en route to calm me down. Layla then almost fell asleep while driving. Sweet Lord, crashing, not making the party. Not an option.

Dropped off. Waltz in. Copelando. Howdy. Small talk. Manage to keep a cool front. Restrain myself from blurting out: 'Who else is coming along?!' Introduced to my teammates. Don't know any of them. Nice guys. However, none of them were the superstars I was expecting. One girl appeared, up to watch the game. Didn't even recognise her. Until she introduced herself. Brief introductions. Oh yeah, Kelly. Seen some of your photos in magazines. Hot enou– and then get introduced to her boyfriend. Balls. Same team as me. Rugby player, Dan, or Danny (whichever I prefer), think he plays with England. Good start I suppose, but I was expecting more. Special game? Where's Robbie? Held up at a photo shoot. Might make the end of the game. OK, cool, let's play a bit of a fussball!

While warming up, I remembered that this was actually the first time I'd played since that mighty trial for Hollywood FC. Knee was still a bit dodge. Thought this was the right time to risk trying it out. Put my body on the line. However, getting second thoughts now that it's not the all-star game I'd imagined. Potential dodgy knee for life? Great call. No worries. Pretty soon I'm into the swing of things. Who cares if I won't be able to walk in the morning. Dan and myself link up well. Surprisingly good for a rugby player. Between the two of us, we rip the other team apart. One goal is so good that Kelly, our cheerleader, rushes on to hug us both. All about teamwork. Dan, keep it up. Kelly, hug on.

Game finishes up. Down to the house. Plan: shower, food, fight, party. Magic. First time actually in the house. This house. Couple more in the area. Cool house. Ridiculously cool. Andy Warhol paintings. As in originals. Not that I'd know the difference. Rooms kitted out. Savage décor. Balconies. Views of LA. Like something you'd see on *Cribs*. In fact, like it was shown on *Cribs*. Started wondering where everyone else was though. Why was that game invite-only? Nothing too special. Bar that goal we got. Before I headed off for a shower in the guest room, I subtly asked when everyone else was coming along . . . 'In a while'. Decided to stop asking. Only so many times I could ask, before I start to look like an obsessed weirdo fanatic guy. Which I wasn't. Obviously. Hee ha.

Shower. Changed. Dressed to impress. Spruced up. Sprayed down. Everyone else is already eating. Watching the pre-fight warm-up in the living room. Not really that dressed up. Haunted I didn't end up hiring a tux. Obviously, I never actually considered doing that. Obviously. Joe King. Head into the kitchen to hunt down some chicken. Kelly is on her own, slicing up a pizza. Hubbula hubbula, I make a brutal joke. Doesn't seem to understand me. Repeat it. She hears me. Doesn't laugh. Good start. Asks me to try the pizza she just slaved over. (Put into the oven . . . slaving?) Decline politely. Tell her I'm on a healthy buzz. Eat what I must, so I can drink what I want. She insists . . . I must try it! Again, thanks, but no thanks.

Appears she's not used to rejection. Shaking her head as if I've no other choice, makes a beeline for me. Trying to force a slice into my mouth. Dodge quickly away from the sink. She moves quicker, pins me against the fridge. Moment of clarity hits me. What's going on?! Why am I running away from her? Funk the pizza! Should I try my luck? Although if I show the same interest in her as I did in the pizza, she might be up for it more. Maybe I just lure her in by taking one bite of pizza. Tease her with it, play hard to get, might just work! Then I remember . . . Boyfriend. Next room. Balls. No point in trying the pizza. Sorry Kelly, I'll stick with the chicken and banana. Head back into the living room. Kelly informs everyone that she's not happy with me. Dave shoots me a 'What the funk did you just do?' look. Shrug my shoulders sheepishly.

Quick scan of the room . . . The A-list team have not yet shown up. Getting the feeling I may have built this up a tad too much. Although . . . no, the night is still young. Party hasn't even kicked off. Box of cans still full to the brim. (Minus two. One sneaky one in the shower as well. Say nothing!) My hopes are restored as I start to overhear all sorts of names. Actors, rock stars, models, producers. A wide assortment of people who I could network and mingle with. Did someone just say Slash? Paris? Tom Jones? Who else has Robbie invited?! Funk, should've really got the business cards!!! Four cans deep and my mind starts to run away on me again. Maybe I could get a producer involved with the sitcom I'm working on. I wonder if one of the Weinsteins will be coming? Might have a word with Robbie later and see if he wants to get on board as an executive producer perhaps? And on a slightly different topic, who cares if Kelly is already taken?! Plenty more beautiful women coming along soon by the sound of it. Did I just hear a supermodel's name? Did the weird French guy next to me just say Naomi? Who?! Campbell? Oh Jesus. Calm down. Play it cool. Don't want to jinx it, but . . . the greatest night of my life might just be back on!

Danny and myself are tucking into my bag of cans. At least someone appreciates the thought. Even better, I see that he is almost as excited as I am to be here. Everyone is pumped for the fight, all supporting Hatton. Someone suggests doing a pot, predicting the winner and which round. Sounds good – only a small amount – sounds even better! Yeah, only . . . $50. For funk's sake. Five dollars is a small amount when you're on my budget, not $50! Can't say no, so my fifty is in the now-chunky pot. Fight just got more interesting. I get Hatton to win in the second round. Waste of money. Fights go on, what, twelve rounds?

Fight. Start. First round. Blink of an eye. Hatton. Pummelled. Everyone is freaked about the battering he's taking. I'm far more freaked about something else which started to seep into my brain for those three minutes. What if the fight doesn't go the full twelve rounds. Never even crossed my mind. C'mon Hatton. You've at least six rounds in you! Nervously sipping my can. Sliding into the couch. Disheartened. People on their phones. Relaying the fight to people. How badly Hatton got knocked about. Calm down folks, wasn't that bad. They all need to chill. Seriously, everyone, chill out. Now sense that the mood has dipped drastically. Overhearing people on their phones saying: 'Hang on first, see what the next round is like and I'll let you know' . . . 'Wait where you are a while, this could be over soon' . . . 'I might come to you instead'. Oh sweet Jesus no. This was not part of the plan! Panic. Stations. Come on to funk Hatton, put up your fists man! Where's your defence? I need this party to go on all night!!!

Second round. Ding-a-ling. Very, very worried. Plans are hanging in the balance. Give me twelve rounds Ricky, do it for me! Edge of our seats. I'm guessing a few had big money on the fight. I'm guessing they think that's why I'm so worried as well. Mood. Palpable. Spar, spar. Shuffle, shuffle. Work the feet Hatton, shuffle shuffle! Too late. Pacquiao lands his unbelievable punch. Everyone. On their feet. Screaming. Hatton!!! Get up. My head is in my hands. On the verge of tears. 'Do it for me Ricky! Please!!!' Game over. Hatton is down. Out. Done. Little does Pacquiao know, but his punch has reverberated all the way to LA. Party is down. Out. Done. Dusted. Sucker-punched.

Everyone's shell-shocked. Can't believe it. I know. I can't believe ye're all making new plans of where to go! Let's meet X downtown instead. Let's go to where Y is playing a gig instead. Let's leave this party. Let's leave Mark here crying. Eh, can I come? No? No one is listening to me. Cool, I'll meet ye there? What's the name of the place again? Pardon? Kelly, I'll try your pizza now if you tell me! Do we get our money back from the pot by any chance? That fifty would be handy. No. Night was not getting any better. Head to the bathroom to assess the situation. Felt deflated. Sick. Almost embarrassed. Let down so many people at home. Family, friends and supporters were expecting great things. Where did it all go wrong? No excuses. Only myself to blame. Ricky, I feel your pain!

Just like that, the fun was over. By the time I return, most people have already left. Forgetting to bring me with them. Worst night ever. Dave has decided he's not even going clubbing. Feels sick too. Lost a lot of money on the fight. Pretend I did as well. Mask my true disappointment. All a front. What a letdown. What a disaster. Highlight of my night was when my camera went off by accident in the bathroom. Think it took a photo of me with a signed Beatles photo behind me. I think. A souvenir, at least. Highlight of my night. What a chump. Four Beatles. One ape. Leave the party on my own. Disillusioned. Just my bag of cans to keep me company. Ring Chowder. Clubbing? Club on. I'll tell you all about it. Hear someone calling me. My new buddy Danny runs after me. Going to the club as well. Can he come along. Of course you can! Hand Dan a can. Shotgun one each. Away we go!

In fairness, for a rugby player, he's a good wingman in a club as well. Brings them over, I gibber on, good combo. Until he heads off with Kelly. Now pretty drunk. Strip club. Telling some girl named Limber Kimber about my life choices. Party delusion all my own fault. I almost got a tux, Kimber . . . a tux?! Hang on Limber. Just got a text . . . Shamwow buddy: Had a great day. Made $500. Probably make the same tomorrow. Too late for me to find a way down to the fair in San Diego and work tomorrow? Too late. Already has someone. You chump. Turning down all that money for what? For what, Limber?! What did I expect? Meet someone who would do all the hard work for me?! Is that what I thought, Jimber? Crikey, you are quite lim— wait, what am I doing with my life?! Pardon? No, I'm not really in the mood for a lap dance. Let's chat, Kimby, I'm kinfda druunck. No, I'm OK for another drink at the moment. Unless you have whiskey? No? Well I have ten apple juices in front of me as it is. Why would I want another one? I like this table. Why would I move? Wait, what, why? No, I'm fine. Get out? Why? I have ten! Ten apple juices! I don't want another one! Ah come on. There's no need for that . . . Come on now . . . Big Jim?! Jim? Argggggggghhhhh! Let goooo!!! Jesus, I'm drunk.

And then. I was kicked out. Of a strip club. Over a glass of apple juice. Great moment. Personally. Definitely one of the highlights my life. Up-and-coming what now? Down-and-out chump. Lying on the curb. Outside the strip club. Funk it . . . decided I might as well go all the way. So I did. Rolled over. Into the gutter. Looking up. Cursing the stars. Ye whures! Why did ye not show up for the party?!

Breakdown? Breakthrough?

For the past three nights I haven't slept much. My brain is going deep. Wading through the swamp. Burrowing into my muddled marsh of thought. Thinking about trivial stuff. Which seems to be playing on my mind . . . Is everything in LA just a performance? Daily life. Day to day. People you meet on nights out. Especially. Nightclub folk. Best buddies. Fake smiles. Trying to suck you dry. Until they realise you're not the person they assumed. You're just some dude. With an Irish accent. Maybe that's why LA is so soulless. All a front. Everybody wearing a mask. And then, to make it worse, am I just like them? Or, better still, even worse than them?!

At least that's what I was thinking when I woke up this morning. Another bout of the Fear had flared up. Finding a couple of fifty-euro notes in my suitcase settled me down a bit. Helped my fragile mind. My gut has been telling me to start making my choices wiser. Time is ticking. Money and visa are having a race. Who can run out first? Added to these thoughts, I kept getting woken up in the middle of the night by something else, far more annoying. A fly. Past few nights have been the same. Constantly buzzing around. Landing on my back. My ear. My face. Making me smack it away. Yet it just keeps on coming back. Freaking me out. Leaving me with two choices. Ignore that small, innocuous buzzing noise. And try to sleep. Or open my eyes slightly to see what it may be. And end up chasing a fly. That disappears whenever I turn on the light. Making me wonder. Is there any funking fly at all?!!! What am I chasing. Up the walls. Out one window. In the other. Running around. Circles.

Madman-style. In boxers. Chasing a noise.

I finally passed out at about seven in the morning. Alarm went off only a few hours later. Oddly, sprang out of bed. As if I was late for an exam. First go. Standing. Like a madman. Crouched. In my boxers. Waiting. Listening. Hearing. A little buzz. You F**KER fly, leave me alone!!! Once again, starts to taunt me. Darting around my head. Buzzing in my ear. Whispering insults. Ridiculing me. Getting bullied. Close to tears. Lands on my right shoulder. I swing blindly for it. Miss. Obviously. End up hitting myself in the shoulder. Again, the fly taunts me by staying close, moving to my lower left back. Once again. Like a dumb fool. Swing. Miss. Wallop. Myself. Slap to the kidneys. At this stage, my lack of sleep is kicking in. Think I'm close to losing my mind.

Sweet Lord above . . . Let it go. Just a fly. Close my eyes. Lift my head towards the ceiling. Start taking deep breaths to calm down. Ears perk . . . faint sound . . . whispering . . . bsss . . . bsss? Buzz, buzzzz. Feel it brush off my nose. I swing inwards with both hands. Flailing wildly. Miss my own face. End up slumped back on my bed. Beaten. Distraught. Close to tears. Open my eyes. Look up. See the fly. Other side of the room. Buzzing at me. Must have thrown his voice. Ventriloquist-style. Just to make me looker stupider. Had enough. Leave the room. He wins. Let him celebrate. Leaving me a broken man. Not yet even had breakfast. Slowly eating my porridge. Staring down the barrel of a gun. Should I bother even leaving the house today?

My exile in the cave didn't last long. Meeting was pre-arranged. I couldn't pull out of it. Coffee in a place called Urth Café. Bizarre place. Everyone just staring at each other. Freaking me out. Trying to look through your sunglasses, see who it is underneath. Are you famous? Are you worth staring at?! Go funk yourself, muppet with the chiselled looks! I'm a nobody, stare elsewhere!!! Meeting with a guy from BAFTA. Who I thought initially was Larry David. Spitting image. Made me get out of my seat a tad quickly when he said my name. Jumped up. Knocked coffee all over myself. Jumped away from the boiling stuff dripping off the table. Knocked into the guy at the seat next to me. Balls. Apologise. No worries, man, it's cool, we're cool man . . . Realised it was Lenny Kravitz. Sorry, Lenny. No worries. Nice songs by the way. Cheers. Yes. Cheers to you too, Leonard!

Rocky start, but I pulled it out of the bag. Mr BAFTA asked me what I was doing? What was my plan? How did I intend to make it happen? Wanted to read my script when it was ready. Would like it even more if I could make a few scenes myself. He might be able to show it to the right people. Go get it done. Then get back to him. What was I doing about a visa? Working on it. Money? Working on it. Well, trying to work on it. Asked me a bit about Ireland. Turns out he was born in Cork. Spent the next twenty minutes chatting about Cork. Delighted to meet another Corkman like myself out in LA. Handy little perk, giddy up the Rebel county! Left the meeting pumped. Knowing what I needed to do. Getting it done. Then getting back to him. Targets. Walked home. Thinking. Walking. Must finish off my script. Decide which scenes to shoot. Organise a crew. Get it done. Pass it around to all the people I've met. Before my money and visa run out. Thinking. Hoping. Praying. Please God. I hope that the fly will leave me alone tonight.

Hmmm. That Is Interesting

So I thought last weekend was a horrendous weekend. But you know what. Not really so bad. At all. Actually a good weekend. I just had it built up too much. Hence, only one person to blame. Thought I would reach new highs. Sank to a new low. Lying in the gutter outside a strip club is never great fun. Unless a stripper is lying on top, perhaps. And not Big Jim. Pinning you down. Go on the Jim! Looking out for me really. Went back up the next day. Apologise. No worries, Irish guy. Although that was my second strike. Forgot I had been kicked out before as well. For dancing with a girl. *For* a girl. A stripper. On stage. Spotlight. In my defence, I did think my name had been called out to come up. Actually someone called Matt. A stag. Groom. Not calling me. An ape. Forgot about that one. Apologies again, Big Jim.

Anyways, at least I've been more determined since then. I've been working on a couple of scripts. Trying to improve an older script I wrote before. Send that into RTÉ back home. Also been working on a new sitcom script. Involving some idiots gallivanting around LA. Great new script! BAFTA dude is interested. Fred wants to see it. People are waiting to view it. Unfortunately, I am kind of an idiot. Whose head gets turned easily. So I still haven't nailed that yet. Learning to write by numbers is taking me a while as well. No clue of length or format. I'll get there though. Google, hook me up!

More hooking has been happening. Yesterday I met a buddy. Who has produced a few indie movies and the likes. Works in an acting studio on the Warner lot. Did not know any of this. Only found out through a buddy. Interesting to know. Met him.

Interested in working with me. Putting a crew together. Who could help me shoot a couple of scenes. In this day and age, scripts are no longer enough. YouTube and all. People want visuals. I don't need a TV company to give me permission to do this. Some of their money would be nice. Nice and handy. However, until then, I'm going to start doing things on my own. Only person I can blame or thank in the end. Crew being formulated. Wheels being oiled. Good to know, for my soul anyways. Productive on!

Did you know that I've yet to play soccer with Robbie Williams? Perhaps not. At the start, he was away a lot. Followed by me funking up my knee. So I missed him when he arrived back. Assumed he was going to be playing last weekend. I assumed a lot that week. Presuming no more. Anyways, last night, I met the big man. Didn't even come into my head that he'd be there. As opposed to building it up to myself on Saturday. I could feel a surprised look glowing on my face like a baboon when I saw him stroll up. Hiya boyo! Small talk before the fussball kicked off. Trying to get rid of my big saucer eyes and open mouth. International man of success, after all. Global superstar! Although you know what, straightaway I realised two things. 1. He was a sound guy. And 2. He was just a guy. Not saying that in a bad way. But if you were to forget about the fact that he was someone whose songs I'd listened to, who I'd seen numerous times on TV, in magazines, in the papers . . . Put that to one side. He was now just a guy I was playing soccer with. As you do, kind of thing.

Enough players showed up for there to be three teams. Roll on, roll off. Playing on the same team as Rob. Having great chats between the games. Giving me advice on writing. Songwriting techniques. Might be applicable to my gibberish writing. Telling me he always has to get out of LA when he needs to write. Focus himself. Centre himself. Too many distractions here. Likes to go to the middle of nowhere. Desert. Somewhere quiet. Recommended that I should do the same for the script. Should've asked him for a loan of his private jet. You never know. If you never ask. Should've. Funk. Asked me what it was like doing stand-up in LA. Comparing that with his concerts here. Hang on now Rob, different level I do believe. True and not true, Rob retorted, still just one guy and a mike. Same nerves, no matter what size crowd. You know what, that is true, you're dead right. Same, just vastly different levels of success. Sound dude. Gave me great nuggets of advice. More the merrier! Only ape thing I did was that I might have implied I'd seen him in concert. Kind of. Didn't actually lie. Said he was great in Slane years ago when he played. I *had* bought a ticket. Meant to be going with my buddies. Slept in though. Missed the bus. Didn't get to go. Still have the ticket. So when he asked was I at it, I replied with: 'One of the first people to buy a ticket!' I'll have to fess up next time!

Must say, it was pretty cool to finally meet him. Good soccer player too. Although we disagreed over the penalty-taking duties. In the end he buckled. I nailed it top corner. Ran off jokingly celebrating. Running around like an ape. Some guy jumped on my back joining in. Looked over my shoulder. Big man! Up on my back! You only sing when you're winning! Running around a pitch up in the Hollywood Hills, yelping like a cowboy. Yee-haw! Like a scene from *Brokeback Mountain*! Rounded off a funny old week. Interesting, to say the least. Cherry on top: two more things were revealed when I got back from fussball tonight. First, Jess is no longer seeing the rocker/actor/handsome dude. Interesting. And secondly, later on, I discovered that Kimber – remember her from last weekend? – turned out to be true to her name. Limber on! All those apple juices were well worth it . . . wuu duu!

Adaptor

Every good plan needs a bit of flexibility. Mine has just been flexed a wee bit. On the upside, I finally figured out a mystery that has been plaguing me since I arrived in L-Hey. And in doing so, a load more things started to make sense. Thinking about it, I must've been walking around with my eyes glued shut the whole time. Originally, I was meant to move out by now. However, the girls like having me here, and I like being here, so we just worked it out. I'd stay in the room. Just now Layla and I would share my en suite. Nay bother, work away. One night. Middle of the night. Layla. Knock knock. Bathroom. Work away. Sleep. Morning. Wake up. Bursting. Bathroom. Layla. On the ground. Passed out?! Layla?! Holy funk. Are you OK? Jess! Quick. Run. Big panic. Jess. Calming. Turns out Layla's OK. Actually just half-asleep, half-passed out. OK. Bit odd. Something amiss. And then. I finally found one of the missing spoons. In my bin. Black. Burnt. What the . . . ? Oh. Right. Jesus.

Eyes. Wide. Shut. Now that I copped on, everything clicks in. I did get the feeling that Layla hadn't been too happy for a while. Not getting the breaks. Not really chasing them either though. Other personal stuff I had no clue about. Never even thought about the fact that my missing-spoon problem might be related to a problem Layla had. Hid it well. Ish. Always said she was fine when I noticed she seemed out of it. Didn't like it when I tried to find out more. At least that half-passed-out incident made her decide she needed help. Which is why her parents were now flying out to LA to look after her. Wondered if they could stay in the house for a few days. No worries. Myself and Jess decided we would make ourselves scarce. Give them space. Maybe a week away. Jess decided she would go visit her family for a while in New York. Cool. Where should/could I go? Actually, you know what, I'll go visit family too for a few days.

See, the thing is, I have cousins in San Francisco. Colin and Kevin. And Colin had rung me the day before. Told me he'd got engaged. Party on this weekend. Did I want to DJ? At the time, I said, as much as I would like to, I couldn't really. Must stay in LA. Write. Stay focused. Shoot some scenes next week here hopefully. Colin had tried to twist my arm by saying I should write up in San Fran. Quieter. After the incident with Layla, San Fran sounded like a good plan. Could be my cabin. Like Robbie's desert. Get out of LA. Colin knew a visa lawyer up there as well. Helped him with his visa. Could set up a meeting for me. Free. Plus, could also DJ on the Saturday night in the local Irish pub. All sounded like a tidy plan. Quietness to write. Make the engagement party. Two nights' work. Paid. Added bonus, return flights available for only $50. All right. I'm in. Makes sense. Few days up there. Back down to LA then, ready to shoot. Dancing!

You know what they say. Every action has an interesting funny old side effect. Decision to go was on the Monday. Booked my flight up on the Thursday. Between Monday and Tuesday night, I got a few texts from various girls. Asking if I wanted to meet up? Eh, can't really, dodge on. Must, emm, tie up a few loose ends before I leave LA. Which made them all slightly freak out. And wanting to call around to see me before I left. Not all together, but they all had the same reaction. Must see me before I go. All because they presumed the same thing. That I was leaving LA to go back to Ireland. All wanted to wish me off. In the same way. Funking nuts. Four in the space of about forty-eight hours? Day and night. Day. Good morning sunshine!

Handy that I don't work a nine-to-five. Another good thing about that. More time to get things in during the day. So to speak.

All in all. Mental stuff. Should've thought of that earlier! Besides that adventuring, I managed to tie up a few loose ends. Producer buddy, Frankie, round up the folks . . . He had them lined up already. Say when? Happy days. Actresses that I know, next week sound good? Dancing? Wuu. Jess, up for karaoke before we both leave tomorrow. Booze. Duet. Booze. Duet. Blank. Stumble. Fumble. Wake up. Turn over. Déjà vu, how are you? Ehh, see ya in a week, Jess. Always the night before I leave! Adapt on!!!

Brad, I Feel Your Pain!

I now know how Brad must've felt when he had to leave the set of *Mr & Mrs Smith* and head home to Jennifer. Leaving Angelina behind. I can now relate. See, I used to love San Francisco. Since I've arrived up here, however, all I can think about is LA. Wondering what I'm missing out on. Why did I not stay put? Will it be the same when I go back to her? A lot can change in a week. What have I done?!!! I keep waiting for someone to stop me on the street. Pretend to be my friend. Try to con me out of something. They could at least try! Unlike LA, no one glances twice or tries to stare you down. Peering into your soul. Or at least under your sunglasses. Nobody's looking to see if you might be famous. Simply don't care. No mishaps waiting around the corner. Only people who are off-kilter are the millions of homeless people, but what good are they to me?! None even try and knock me out up here. Just wailing at me. No famous people to bump into. Just regular, sound people. More importantly than all that though, where have all the fake smiles and fakes breasts gone to?! Tut. Depressing. What a crap city.

People get my name right in San Fran as well. I'm mumbling more than ever now. Grasping at straws. Trying to bring back the memories. Omar! Merrick?! Why doesn't anyone Google my name here either?!!! Pardon me, who am I? That's the spirit, now we're talking *at* each other, not *to* each other! Oh, you did actually ask me how am I? Not so good! Anyone offering or wanting coke? Tissue? Anyone? I have a load to spare! Where have all the perks of a gay neighbourhood gone as well? I'm in the gayest city in the world now but there are no free-gym perks here. I'm paying like everyone else. No celebs in the gym for me to chinwag with. Only commoners like myself. Big pink heads. Sweating. Not posing. Sweaty, grimy machines. Tut. What a crap city!

Presume LA is struggling to cope just as much as I am. Misses me too. Definitely. Obviously. Stood still since I left. Moping around. Watching *Scrubs*. Drinking tea all day. Not that that's what I've been doing or anything. Obviously. Not. On the upside, I did have a savage laugh with my cousins and their buddies at their engagement party. Forgot how sound Irish people can be! Not the likes of funking Timmy! Proper people. No crap. Genuine. Still though, I can't wait to play Jen's Lekman song as I leave San Fran next week. 'I'm Leaving You, Because I Don't Love You'. Apparently Brad played that to Jennifer as he drove off. Although personally, on a serious, realistic note, I'd definitely pick Jennifer over Angelina! Seriously. I would. Just in case she might be reading. Just. In. Case. You. Never. Do. Know.

Procrasti Nation

Ever walk into a bin? Walking down a busy street? And the person walking behind you falls into the back of you? Making you spit out a mouthful of Red Bull. Pouring the rest of the can all over yourself. I managed to do that today. Good old hoot. Probably the highlight of my day. Mighty. Productive old day. Almost too productive, some might say. In fact, I think it's time to name and shame. Ensure I never have such an unproductive day again. Managed to do absolutely everything to procrastinate my way through my first day of writing. Anything but write my script. Hopefully this list will slap me in the head. Cop me on. List on!

1. Watched *Days of Our Lives*

2. Watched *General Hospital*

3. Bought more pens (takes the total up to four fully inked pens)

4. Bought more paper to write on (takes the total up to two notebooks, an A4 pad and two hundred index cards)

5. Brought my disposable camera to the shop to get developed

6. Cleaned my already-clean runners. Three pairs

7. Walking around aimlessly. Looking for my phone. While on the phone

8. Went to the gym

9. Collected the photos from the shop

10. Wrote this list

Procrasti. Nation. No. More. Time to grow up! At least in the writing world. Time. Ticking. Like. A. Tock. Running away from me. Like a whure. As I said before, I am anti-pro. Anti-crastination all the way.

Write, Said Fred

Tip, tap, tapping away. Two days. Non-stop. I. Am. Dancing! A ridiculously productive burst. Turn up the flame. And eventually I'll get going. Words are flowing. Although I did get a bit of a kick-start. Fred. Send me an email. Reminder. Just sit down. And start writing. Get something out on paper. Which has being happening. Good timing by Freddie! Even better. My buddy Frankie has a full-on crew lined up, literally all ready to go. Even better again. The actors I need for the scenes are all interested. Ready to do it this week. Some are full-on actors/actresses as well. Up-and-comers! Pulling out the favours. Favours being offered. Happy days all round. A lot to be said for networking! Even have a couple of strippers willing to do one big scene that I have planned, wuu huu! Now. Must keep my productivity levels high. Deal with some real-world stuff before I head back. Money. Just DJ one last gig here. Legality. Meet the visa lawyer. Fly back to LA. On my birthday! The day I am going to start shooting scenes. Crikey, that shall be a mighty present to myself. Pumped! Write on!

Ninety-nine Red Balloons

Visa-lawyer meeting tomorrow. Hopefully he can pull a few things out of the bag. Seems to have ideas. Did a bit of DJigging tonight. Needed the bobs. Ridiculously bad. Nice chunk for a DJig too. Although everything does come at a cost. Money included. Earned those few hundred bills. DJed in an Irish bar close to where my cousin lives in San Fran. To say that the bar was Irish would be a bit of an understatement. Pub, in a little village, somewhere in west Cork. That kind of feel. Pre-tty Irish. And as if a few American tourists are after wandering in. More Irish than any bar I've been in at home. I was asked to stop the music at about twelve o'clock for ten minutes so a raffle could take place. That Irish.

Arrived in. Saw my name. Lit up in lights. Moving up in the DJ world! Decided to go with 'DJ No Requests. All the way from LA!' Technically. True. Ish. Had been told to expect requests. Jukebox-style. Which is why I had jokingly requested one of my own . . . 'I have one request that you have none!' Worked well. Even though the bar was far from full, the requests started bombarding in from the word go. First song. Barely pressed play. Nice chap comes over . . . 'This is s**t. Play me Lady Gaga.' Thick country accent, GAA player, thick as muck – in fact, bit of mud on his face – spitting out requests at me all night. Yeah, this is the song you actually want. Listen. Playing. Right now. Yeah. Listen. OK. Come back again later altogether. Flooding in non-stop, thereon in. Wide and varying range . . . 'Play some Scooter' . . . 'Play some heavy-metal rock, then some Scooter' . . . 'Play that band I loved back home, Cascade?' . . .

'Do you know this song – Do do doooo doo do dooo dada – that dance one?' No, sing it again for me . . . 'La la laaa la le da da doo da – you do know it? Everyone knows that, what kind of DJ are you?' . . . Eyeballs me. Up and down. As I shake my head. Laugh at his attempt . . . 'You're some s**t DJ.' Cheers bud.

One guy in particular grew an immense dislike for me. *Immense.* In such a short time too? Usually takes longer. Hazarding a guess. Forty years young. Small. Bald. Swaying. 'Play me some rock, willya? Some heavy s**t. All my friends are DJs. It's cool, I know what I'm on about.' (Incidentally, this was at my highest point, when I started to play the gym remix section, which had the crowd pumping.) Hang on two minutes, I'll play it in a while for you, just hang on. 'Play it now, I want to rock out before I go home.' Chugged back his bottle. Pretty drunker. Gripping the empty bottle. Looking me up and down. Complete. Disgust.

Dance floor died down a bit. Last call. Died down some more. Smoke and drinks were needed. Died some more. Only person on it was my new buddy. Threw on a Metallica song for him. Started rocking on. Air-guitaring his heart out. Not in a piss-take way. Life-and-death stuff. Until he realised it was not the version he was expecting. Remix. Forgot it was. Better suited for clubs and bars anyways. Not that he cared. Flipped out. Straight up: 'For f**k's sake, you prick, play me a rock one!' Wringing the neck of his empty bottle. Eyeballing me. So, obviously seeing as I am so obliging and all, I played him another rock song. Which was also a remix. Obviously and on purpose.

'You f**king prick, you're a c**t, you know that, let me rock out!' Came into the DJ booth. Told me he never liked me. Never liked when I played here. First time? Fuck you, you queer. Added he would bottle me if I pissed him off again. No worries, bud.

Smile. Wink. Nod. Thumbs-up. Demanded I play him one more rock song. Tried to shake my hand. Declined. Gave him another thumbs-up instead. Left the booth. Started walking back to his buddies at the bar. En route, I decided I would play him one last song to rock to . . . 'Ninety-nine Red Balloons'. Rock on, you funking gimp . . . Muppet went a tad mental. Turned around. Smashed his bottle off the bar. Started having a fit of rage. Deep within him. Anger that had built up over years. Somehow now was the time to unleash it all. On me. Roaring with his back to me. Swivelling around. Roaring again. Gearing up to attack. Friends spotted this implosion. Jumped and held him back. While he grabbed random bottles and started smashing them. Nice chap. Thumbs-up, buddy!

Eventually he calmed down. When he wife showed up to take him home. Very quiet then. End of the night. Packing up my stuff. Random mucker buddy of his comes over. Also giving me dirty looks after that incident . . . 'You're not Irish, *are* ya?' Sorry to disappoint you, but yup, I too am Irish. 'Well, you're not from Cork.' Again, apologies, but I actually am. 'You're not from wishht Cork anyways. Because that's where *I'm* from!' You got me there bud, well done! Delighted with himself. He knew it! 'Thank God this quare isn't one of us too!' Yeah, thank God.

Besides these minor incidents, coupled with the sound system almost blowing out, which nearly blew out my eardrums, all in all it was a good night. Money is money! Did make me realise that I was delighted to be in America. And not back in Ireland. Bubble of LA, all the funking way. Packed up my DJ gear. Laptop. Wires. Headphones. Headed back to my cousin's apartment. And then. Something really unexpected . . .

Not So Happy Day

Kind of spaced. Out of it. Not on drugs or anything. Not even drunk. Maybe I should be. Not too sure of my surroundings. Well I am sure of them. Just a bit surreal. With everything being so real. Which is maybe why I am out of it. Somehow ended up here. Time-travelling. Lack of sleep has me all over the place. Lagged. Numb emotions too. My brain is processing everything in unreal slow motion. I think. Or else the opposite, zipping through it all so quickly that it's just one big blur now. My body is here. Not sure where my mind is at though. Pixies song running around my head. Besides that, not much else in there. Just a black abyss. Better explain.

My cousin Colin got a call from my Mum. She couldn't get through to me. Preoccupied driving little bald angry men wild. Asked for me to call home. Got back from the DJig. Rang home. Bad news. Sad news. My Gran had passed away. Knew that she had been sick, but didn't really know how bad. I always find that whenever I'm told sad news, my brain straightaway blocks it out. Doesn't like to process it. Turns off whatever part of it might be in charge of calculating what has happened. So when I got off the phone to my Mum, I told my cousin what had happened as if I was just reporting a story. Didn't even think how it would affect me. Until Colin asked me: 'What are you going to do?' Oh yeah. So, I did what I knew I had to do after I spoke to my Mum again. Told me I should stay and get my stuff done in LA. Only two weeks left on my visa. Shoot the scenes. Would obviously prefer if I was home, but everyone would understand. It's my

Gran. Nana Ryan. All my grandparents are legends. Only one choice.

Booked my flight. Slept. Packed my bags. Got on a plane. Sat next to a girl who I think was a Jordanian princess. Or else a drug smuggler. Fun flight. Read *The Road Less Travelled*. Listened to Sigur Rós. Not sure if I wanted to be sad or to be inspired. Sigur on. Flight over. Arrived home the next day. Back in Cork. Drove up to Tipperary. Got in just in time for my Gran's funeral. All pretty sudden. All pretty surreal. Numb. Spaced. Sad. Glad that my Mum was delighted to see me. Made the right call. LA can wait. Real world needed to be visited for a while. Real-time. My Mum reminding me what day it was in the real world: my birthday. Completely forgot. Not such a happy day. Although that country pub we went to that night did kind of pick up my spirits. Far cry from L-Hey. Old men. Tweed jackets. Paddy caps. Guinness. Muddy wellies. Walking sticks. Dogs running around. Fire blazing. Bathroom broken. Sign saying: 'Go outside against the wall'. Women getting flustered. And me almost being kicked out for asking the barman if he had any light beer. Eh, Bud Light . . . 'Era, arr ouu quare?' A birthday I won't forget, I suppose. The day. I arrived back. In Ireland. Just. Like. That.

Wallow and a Plough

Last couple of days have been spent reacclimatising. Sad. Down about my Gran. Finally all kicked in. Surge of unexpected emotions had me well and truly lagged. Odd to be home. Really bizarre. Everything seems alien. Colours. Buildings. Tones. Daylight. Air. Grass. Weird dumb stuff like that. Mind has been rambling away from me since I got home. Ramble on. Reflective mode the past few days. Unplanned. Unexpected. What now? Ever since I knew my visa was running out in LA, I constantly felt a bit freaked about the thought of having to go home. Planned on doing another visa run. My hopeful plan, at least. With what money, I don't know. Just wanted to keep going. I always thought that coming home meant that that other life in LA would be over. One shot. Dream. Done and dusted. Back in Ireland. Everything would just immediately revert back. Return to the life I lived. The person I was. The way it used to be. Fine.

Thankfully, I now know, this is not true. Dumb to have thought it, perhaps. Good to know I was just being dumb. Far better to know, than not! Dumb on. See, I've realised that just because something doesn't work out you had thought it would, doesn't mean it's a full stop in your journey. Just a comma along the way. Keep stumbling forward. Dance around the obstacle. Get back on track. *The Road Less Travelled* has shown me one thing clearly: there are good times, and there will be bad times. Easiest thing to do during the bad times . . . throw in the towel. Give in to whatever bad stuff you're going through. Or take the other approach. Harder but better option . . . plough on. Keep battling through. Because once you get out the other side, which you will eventually do if you believe it enough, you will appreciate the good times even more. At least that profound cheese is swimming around my head. Mirrors have been aligned. Reflections everywhere around my empty chasm. Profound. Horse. Gibber.

Last night I decided to get out of my head. First night out back in Cork. Hadn't even told a lot of people I was home. Out of the blue and all. Maybe I just wanted to pick and choose who I told. Met with my brother and buddy Jimmy B. Boozed on. Good laugh. Great laugh actually. Went clubbing. Mixed laugh. Met a few buddies who didn't I know I was back. Delighted to see me. Asking how long I was back for. Must meet up properly before I go back again. Good being back. Few randomers I didn't know came up to me as well. Which was odd. Read my blog. Different articles I'd done. Just said well done. Keep going. Other randomers came up to tell me I was a muppet. Which was funny enough, cheers bud. Thumbs-up. Also met a load of prefrenders. Delighted to see me. Well, delighted to see that I was back in Cork. Failed. Couldn't even get fifteen minutes. Delighted. Stuck here now. Just like them. In prison. No hope of getting out. Only choice is to get my cynic hat on. Wuu, great seeing ye lads.

Club ended. Brother went to his girlfriend's house. Jimmy B. was taken home with some lady he had been grooving with. I decided to slip off and head home on my own. Decided to walk home. Good fifty-minute walk. Maybe phrased that part wrong earlier. Didn't really decide to walk home. Fifty-minute walk when it's funking freezing would just be a dumb decision. However, I was kind of left with no other choice. Cab. Flag. Down. Cash. Needed. Cabbie. Hang on. Hello ATM. Can I have €50, please. Beep beep. Must not have €50 notes in this machine.

€40 . . . beep beep. No to €40? €30? €20? €10? You have insuf-
ficient funds. Oh no, what? What what? Bollocks. Maxed my
credit card out on booze earlier. Student limit had done me
proud! Still. Now. I'm broke. Broke as funk. Cabbie, will you
accept dollars, I have a few $100 bills at home? No. Drive off.
Cheers. Time to walk. Time to think. Mull things over. What to
do? Wallow. Moan. Concede. Complain. Stay. Or. Accept.
Embrace. Head down. Plough on. Prison break? Funk. Freezing.
Never freezing in LA. If nothing else, I could use heat as my
motivation? Eventually got home. Watched *Into the Wild* while I
boozed on. Decision made. Two possibilities. Only ever one
option. Wallow off. Plough on!

How to Tie a Tie?

When I found out I was leaving America, it was all a bit of a rush. Quite the blur. Now needed to sort out the life I left behind. Most of my stuff was still down in LA. Bar a small bag of the clothes I brought to San Fran. No time to fly back to LA. Would've missed the funeral. And that would've been pretty pointless. Barely had time to say goodbye to people. Texts mostly. Tried to ring Jess to fill her in. Couldn't get through to her phone. Broke it first day back in New York. Handy. Tried to ring Layla. Found out she was in rehab in Malibu. One month. Seclusion. Seems to be getting better. Jess rang me a few days later. Told me she had decided to stay in New York for a few months. Wanted to get out of LA for a while. Plus, she got a few big modelling contracts. Happy days. New York for her. Mailbu for Layla. Cork for me. Wuu.

Thank funk for Chowder. At least he was still in LA. Seeing as nobody was living in our place any more, everyone decided to say goodbye to it. Landlord said we had to get our stuff out pretty soon. Chowder sorted me out big-time. Collected all my stuff. Stored it in his apartment. One loose end sorted. Tied up another one quickly. Producer. Frankie. Who had rounded up the crew. Told me not to worry. Completely understood. Things have to be done. Would be there waiting whenever I got back. No pressure. Still wanted to do it. Just let him know when. Happy days. Same situation with my writing mentor. BAFTA contact. All the people I had meet and could help me were as helpful as ever. No full stops. Just commas. Plough on!

Another tie which was flapping about was the meeting I was

meant to have with the visa lawyer in San Fran. What I never even thought about, dumbly, was a wonderful device which could still make this happen. Device. Called. A. Phone! Had a long chat with him. Gave me two options. He could do all the work. However, wouldn't be for free. Give me a good price. But it would still cost a couple of grand. Emm, I can't afford a day pass to the gym at the moment . . . Plan B? He could point me in the direction I needed to go. Give me a list of options to exhaust. Go it alone. More work. Frustrating. Free. Alone it is! Gave me a list. Pointed me this way, that way and the other way. Actually, that other way might hold a glimmer of hope in it. Other way on!

Alone, it is. Different possibilities, waded through. Endless forms, filled out. Countless US embassy information phone numbers, rang them all. Eventually, I applied for a visa. Nervous. Tick. Waited. Tock. Confirmed. Interview time. Set-up. Balls. Further away than I had expected. Now need something to kick in. Something which I struggle with big-time. Patience. Giddy up. And while I'm calling on the Ps, you too perseverance. Both needed badly. Let's do this hubbula! Another tie, not tied, but gripped hold of at least. Managed to get through to one, two or ten other ties I left behind as well. Weirdly, ye were right, girls. I *was* going back to Ireland after all! Kimber, hang on, stay limber, I'm going to find a way back! Heat and duu!

Bring Back the Bubble

Feels like I've been home ages. Days are slower here. Plenty of time to think, at least. Starting to see that if you're happy, or at least not complaining, when people think you should be, it makes them suspicious. Looking at it, LA is perhaps the biggest bubble of optimism I've ever lived in. You can bounce off other people's bubbles. Fill up with optimism. Rebound some to others in return. A good cycle. Just as long as you don't fill up an annoying amount. Bubble on. Bubble's burst now. An odd thing I've noticed is that everyone in LA is telling me I'll be back in no time. Cork is the opposite. 'Ah, being realistic and all, it's not likely, is it?' Ah, being an ape and all, funk that, unrealistic seems to be the only option. Since I've been back, I keep getting asked if I'm freaked. Must be freaked. Freaked. Home. Freaked, I'd say. Freaked. No. I'm not. You freak. Cork isn't a prison. Not like I was out on probation. Not physically stuck now. Mental barriers are the only things holding me back. Well, along with money. And a visa. Still though. Pointless being freaked. Although I'm getting the feeling you'd be freaked. So you need me to be freaked as well. Sorry bud. New me. New freak.

Easier just to smile and nod . . . Why bother? Give up. Better yet, why start? Fooling yourself . . . I know, freaked! Not saying that you should be fully delusional. Maybe just not think all the time in realistic terms. If you were, you'd never break new ground. I must have heard or read all that gibberish somewhere.

Probably would be easier to complain, moan, join the sheep, carp about the weather, how life is against me, dealt a bad hand, always the same, always only happens to me, I never get a break.

Decided this might be a waste of time though. Might just be a hunch. Could be wrong. But I'm going to try and avoid going down that route. Obviously I wouldn't mind being on a beach in the Caribbean. That can wait for now though. Further down the line. Keep the faith.

My sides are getting spurs into them, keeping the faith high. I've been talking to my Mum recently about my Gran. Telling me stories about what was going on since I'd been away. And my Mum told me my Gran told her numerous time of how happy she was that I was off in LA, trying to do what I was trying to do. Plus, how she knew I'd eventually get there. Said to say how proud she was of me. If that isn't a spur in the side, then I'm not too sure what is. Spur on! Being honest, you can either be looking for inspiration, or not. My eyes have been peeled wide open. Anything. Pull me through. Not too sure where I got this from, but I jotted it down. Probably thought it was profound and written specifically for me when I read it hung over: 'Nothing in the world can take the place of perseverance. Talent will not; nothing in the world is more common than men with talent. Genius will not; unrewarded genius is almost a proverb. Education will not; the world is full of educated derelicts. Perseverance and determination alone are omnipotent. The slogan "press on" has solved and always will solve the problems of the human race.'

See, any old talentless, dumb, uneducated fool can do it. Obviously, instead of 'press', I'm using the word 'plough', but the gist would be the same: Plough. On.

Gigging and DJigging

Money. Visa. Holding me back. Mentally, staying strong. Tough to do here. Has to be done. Whereas weeks and months zipped by effortlessly and with worrying speed in LA, life is a bit slower back in Ireland. While I wait for my visa interview, I've been doing a few things on a regular basis. Sleeping. Gym. Eating. Reading. TV. Hibernating. DJigging. Stand-up gigging. Over and over. Building my pot of gold back up. My LA fund. Grow up fund, giddy up them steps!

Getting DJ gigs was handy enough. Easier than I thought as well. Lucky I had a few contacts from my promotional-company days. Owners of bars and nightclubs. Giving me a trial run. Liking what they heard. Ask me back for more. Happy days. Some have been good. Others have been very good. And some have been, ehh . . . brutal. A learning curve. Fail forward! Keep getting back up on the horse. One time in particular I almost threw in the towel. Packed nightclub. Full to the beams. Big crowd for someone who just started DJing a handful of months before. Showed up as usual. Plugged in my stuff as usual. Started to play as usual. Bombardment of requests followed along. As usual. Numb to requests at this stage. I've realised the only thing to do is smile, nod, give them a thumbs-up, and say it'll be played soon. Most are too drunk to remember. A few are so drunk they don't realise they're asking for the song that's being played right at that moment. While others are just a bit slow and want you to play them the song that was just on when they were in the bathroom and missed the start. Patience, bear with me.

Anyways, this particular night, one guy came up to me. No request. Just to tell me it was crap. Sounds s**t. Do I know what to do? Pardon?! Do you know what you're doing? Threw me off. Finished up the set. Went home. Not sure why. Any good stuff. Forgotten about. Funk that. Funk DJing. No good. Need to start looking at other ways to make money. Quite the ape. Slept it off. Hopped on the horse. Went back the next night. Rocked on. A savage night. Compliments flying in. More importantly for my dumb brain, that same guy came back up. Told me it was way better this week. Cheers bud. Sound was crap last week. Yeah, off-night. Not sure what happened. Couldn't hear any music by the bar or on the other side of the club, sound was so bad. Pardon? Sound was crap? Or I sounded s**t? The sound. Oh. Really. Right. Found out afterwards that only half the music system had worked the week before. No one told me. Nice one. At least I still had my towel. And was giddying on the horse!

Same kind of thing with the stand-up gigs. Decided to go straight to the hub of stand-up in Ireland. Temple Bar. Rang up a few places. Told them the truth. I had been doing stand-up over in Hollywood. Technically, this was true. Just hadn't been paid for any of it. Booked a few gigs in Temple Bar. Paid gigs, funnily enough. Handful of change. Still though, paid for my train tickets up and down every week. First gig enabled me to pop another cherry as well. Room was full of my buddies. Eighty percent were my buddies, I think. First time doing it in front of an Irish crowd of people I knew. Nerves. Few shots. Dancing. Up I go. Goes surprisingly well. Congrats afterwards. Shots. Pints. Shots. Woke up. Sobered up. Cold light of day. Maybe the gig wasn't so great actually. Maybe it was just me having banter with my buddies. With the only difference being I was on a stage and had a microphone in my hand. Maybe I didn't actually tell one of the jokes or stories that I had prepared. Perhaps the set was just all inside jokes. Mocking my buddies. Mocking myself. Still though. Had a laugh. People laughed.

Next couple of gigs were misses. One hit. Followed by a few maybes. Couple more hits. Another maybe. A flurry of hits.

At this stage I was doing a fifteen-minute routine. Moving up from the lowly three minutes! Had a great gig then which almost stretched to twenty minutes. And then . . . and then . . . I did something dumb. See, there was a woman who saw a few of the shows I did. And one night, the night after my best show, she came up to talk to me beforehand. Liked it. LA. All that. As she was going back to her seat, she said she hoped I had all-new stuff for her tonight. Couldn't keep doing all my other material. Eh. Maybe. Yeah. Putting thoughts in my head. As did the smell of fake tan off her. Which is why I decided, as I walked up to the stage, to try out new material. Straight off the top of my head. Mocking fake tan. Load of orange Irish women in the crowd. Not one laugh. Bombed. How do I try to save this? More new stuff off the top of my head. Decided to compare Irish women to American women. Mighty. Bombed. Digging. Hole. Dug. Some more. Bombing. Bombed. Worst show ever. Last few minutes I could barely get a word out. Throat dry. Swelling up. Even broke into German at the end. Bruuuutal. Cut the fifteen minutes short. Get off the stage. Funk that. Don't like stand-up. Not doing it again. Train back to Cork. Down. Chump. What was I doing? Up there like a fool. Bombing. Not sure if I'll bother any more.

As it happened, on that train ride home, I watched a DVD I'd been given. *Comedian*. Starring Jerry Seinfeld. Showed how he started with zero material. Built up a new set. Constantly practising the jokes. Took him a year to get an hour. Didn't just chop into a new set because of some drunk girl in the crowd. Practice makes perfect. I'll give it one more go so. Plough-on time. Originally told Tony the organiser I wasn't sure if I'd be around the next week. Time to change that. Made the call. *Dring dring.* Tony, about what I said the last time, I've . . . before I could say I'll be back, he cuts me off . . . Pardon, money issue? What do you mean? You want to pay me even more money now? Eh, what? What what? OK. I'll do it. Are you sure you want to pay me more? OK. Cool. Out of nowhere, started getting enough to cover my train up, my night out boozing and a bit to put aside. Baby steps. Persevere. Plough on. All which was helping my plan, to tip along. My little pot of gold. So proud of him. Slowly but surely, he was growing up.

Books, Shows and Rocking Chairs

Hibernation is great fun. Growing a beard. Not sure why. Just for the sake of it. Something to do. Reading. A lot. Books. Sitting in chairs. Watching TV. Going to the gym. Sleeping. Hibernating. Little duu. No duu. Great. Fun. Patience. Give me some. Long-term plan. Simmer. Duu can wait. Beard on.

The Long Tail

My parents are teachers. My Mum works in a school. Her friend works there too. She is dating a man. This man works in RTÉ. She told him. About me. He arranged. A meeting. With. A TV commissioning editor. In RTÉ. I was told. All this. Last week. Just goes to show. Sometimes you go looking. Other times. It finds you. The. Long. Tail. Bizarre. But. Fun. Anyways, this week I headed up to Dublin for my meeting. Prepared my pitch. Googled how to pitch. Re-prepared my pitch. Shirt, on. Hair, uncombed. Teeth, clean. Dance, on. Made my way into RTÉ studios. Waiting around. Finally time for my meeting. Went in. Chatted. Gibbered. Realised. I think I might be talking to the wrong man. For some reason, I had a meeting with the Regional Commissioner. Gives the green light for programmes on topics such as fish farming (true) and agricultural studies, i.e. farming (true). And you're pitching a show about which again . . . ? A show about an Irish guy in LA? Regional? Yeah. Not sure why I was sent to you. The long tail. Bizarre. Not always fun.

Left the meeting being told he would talk to a few people, put me in touch with who I needed to speak with. Sounded a bit like a good duckaduu. To me. Time to head off. At least I tried. Ended up getting lost, wandering along the corridors. Lost. And maybe a bit of hunting. A bit. See, I knew there was a new head commissioner in charge at RTÉ. In the Entertainment Department. Read this in the paper on the DART on the way to the RTÉ studios. Didn't even click at the time. Now though, I did think about it as I wandered along the hallways. Entertainment . . . sounded like the man I should've been speaking with. Maybe if I wandered along for long enough, I might bump into him. Foolishly wandering, in hope I'd meet the right man, and charm him on the spot. Did I really think this would work? Even though I only knew his name? Yes. Yes, I am that dumb and hopeful at times. Unfortunately. Alas. No sign of anyone on the corridors.

Place seemed deserted. Was it always this quiet? No. Reason the corridors were so quiet today was that everyone was at a meeting. A meeting which RTÉ arranged for independent producers. Invited production companies and producers along to brief them on what RTÉ were looking for in the upcoming seasons. I knew this as I sneaked in and sat at the back. Pretty cool, being in an actual TV studio, where they shoot shows. First time being in a proper studio. Proves how well I did on the acting side in LA! Meeting on. Sat around. Listened to the presentations being made to everyone. We're looking for this, this and that. Not really looking for this, this or that. Economy is bad at the moment. Cutbacks. However, there is money to be spent. Spend on. And so on.

Afterwards, I coolly slipped in amongst the other producers. Yeah, Tricks Productions is my production company. Done a few different things in the past, ehh, are you Eddie Doyle by any chance? Spoof on. And so on. Spent a good half an hour telling one lady all about my proposal and pitch. Turns out she was in charge of catering. Oh right. At least she pointed out who I needed to talk to. The guy surrounded by people the whole time. Waited. My time to get a quick word would come. Waited. And watched. As he was constantly surrounded by people. After far too many cups of tea and sandwiches, my spark diminished. Felt like I was trying to make a move on a girl. But had missed the moment. Lost my nerve. Lost my chance. Watched her being courted. Taken away. Left standing on my own like a chump. Pretend I'm getting a text on my phone. Still surrounded. Me standing. Staring. At him. At my phone. I can't just go over cold-turkey . . . Hiya boyo, can I have a quick word?! Couldn't do that. Actually. Now I think about it, maybe I should've just done that. Instead, I decided to go to the bathroom. Lost my nerve. Bottled my chance.

Bathroom. Mirror. Staring. Psyching. Come on! You can do it. Stomach dodge. Felt ill. Mix. Tea. Coffee. Sandwiches. Nerves. Time to go. First. Urinal. Staring at the wall. Humming some song. 'Heard It Through the Grapevine', I think. Humming. Staring. Not realising. Someone had come in. And was using the urinal next to me. Glanced. Glanced again. Looked. Laughed out loud. More of a donkey guffaw. Ha-haw. Like a weirdo. Got a look in return. That I was a weirdo. Finished off. Let him at it. Washed my hands. Subtly looking over. Double-checking. Drying my hands. Subtly looking. In a small bathroom. Where it was not so subtle. Realised it was who I thought it was. Gave out another guffaw. To myself. I thought. Came out loud. Very normal, I can imagine. Especially for an outsider, looking in. Or, specifically, for an entertainment commissioning editor, looking in. Mr Doyle. Next to me in the bathroom. Random enough. Dumb enough. Suits me, to a tee. Time to work some gibber magic!

Decided against blurting into my spiel right there and then. Obviously waited for him to finish up. Wash his hands. And then I introduced myself. The smiling idiot in the men's bathroom. Ha-hawing to myself. How's it going? Shook hands. Forgot he had not yet dried his hands. Smiled it off. Wiped my hand off my pants. Looked at me oddly. Rattled off my elevator pitch. Not as oddly. Interest. Showing. Wanted to hear more. Set up a meeting with his development executive. Could have a project that I might fit in with. Numbers, emails, hand towels. All exchanged. Ha-haw. Time for me to go. Get out before I donkey too much. Ape on. And I was dancing out of RTÉ! Can't beat the bathroom wheeling and dealing. Good old long tail. Never know where you'll end up!

On Tour

LA is pretty big. Pretty funking huge, to be honest. Mass sprawl. Luckily, I could choose where I lived. And somehow stumbled upon a little hub for myself, WeHo all the way. Every place I needed to be was a thirty-minute drive away from me. Max. Location. Key. Problem now is, I can't choose where I'm from. Cork. Mighty place. Just not a lot happens here, in the industry I want to be in. Hence, so many trips up to Dublin. Staying with my brother. Don't plan on being here long-term. (Please God, visa God, please.) Up and down. Up for meetings. Down for DJing. Up for stand-up. Down for hibernating. Up. Down. Train. Tripping. Fun. Seriously. Actually a good laugh. Unless the stand-up bombed. Then. Not so fun.

Majority of stuff happens in Dublin. Since my first trip to RTÉ, I've had a couple of meetings with a development executive in the Entertainment Department. New show coming up in a few months. Like *The 11 O'clock Show* on Channel 4 in England before. Except this would be *The 10 O'clock Show*. Original. Development executive, Mary, thought I might work well for a five-minute slot on the show. Test the waters. Gauge the feedback. Irish man in LA. Go make five minutes of magic. One a week. Might not sound like a lot. Baby. Steps. Foot. Door. Giddy. Up. Ricky Gervais. Sacha Baron Cohen. Similar starts on *The 11 O'clock Show*? I'd take four minutes!

Anyways, I put a proposal together for Mary. How I would fill up those five minutes, and so on. Also made out a short DVD of some of my stand-up. Sell myself. Flog it. Wanted to show it to her boss (my bathroom buddy) and the producer of the show. Big enough. Made sure I had it right. Had to be right. In fact, I wanted to ensure this so much that I decided I couldn't trust the post office. Mary kind of presumed I was living in Dublin. Asked if I could drop it in to her? Asked me this on Thursday afternoon. Drop it in before noon on Friday. Funk. OK. Done. I'll tie it in with all the rest of my unexpected tour.

DJing in Cork on Thursday night. Up early for the train Friday morning. Cab straight to RTÉ. Get there at eleven. Mary? Mary's sick. Meeting scheduled for next week instead. Secretary said just to leave it with her. Handed my proposal and DVD to her. Exactly like a postman could've done. Well done me. Managed to get in a stand-up gig on the Friday night in Dublin. Something to justify my trip to Dublin, at least. Average gig, at best. Out after it for a few drinks and jigs. (No duu in Dublin. Dublin is my kryptonite, for some reason. Maybe that's why I don't have the urge to move there.) Back to my brother's apartment afterwards. Checked my emails before I went to sleep. One of note. From TG4. An assistant had contacted me while I was in LA just to say she had read my blog. Liked it. Kept in touch. Emailed her a couple days ago, asking about the possibility of meeting the head of the station. Even though it was an Irish-speaking channel. And I can't remember the last time I spoke Irish. She'd let me know if a window opened up. Window. Pop. Opened. Film festival. Galway. This weekend. Could I make it there for this Sunday, meeting at eleven? Giddy. Up.

Saturday. Up early. Book a hotel. Get the bus. To Galway. Bus. Hung over. Horrendous. Seat. Next to the bathroom. On the bus. Smell. Horrific. Fun journey. Get to my hotel. Wrecked. Laptop. Music. Emails. One. Of. Note. TG4 girl. Really sorry. Head of the station has had to cancel all his Sunday appointments. Really sorry. Hope I hadn't left for Galway yet. Eh, a bit funking late now! Gave me his number. Ring him during the week. On the phone. Mighty. Funking. Berries. Touring Ireland, for absolutely no reason. Phone and postman! Complete dope . . . All these trips, for what?! Money well spent on buses, trains, taxis and hotel rooms. Idiot. Ape. Dope. Reading that email made me feel like a complete muppet. Being honest, I think I saw a nervous breakdown on the horizon. Brain. Melting. Mind. Swirling. Thankfully. Instead. I ended up just trashing my hotel room. TV out the window. Messed the sheets around a bit. Left the toilet seat up. Complete mess. Well, I did all but one of those things.

However, luckily, I can be a clever idiot at times. For some reason, my brain kicked in. Emailed a few different people. Googled this, Googled that and Googled all others. One thing led to another. Ended up being invited for drinks, a meet-and-greet, before a big dinner that was going on in a hotel near mine. Conveniently, the person I came up to Galway to meet would be at the drinks shindig. I could now meet him there instead. Wuu huu. Who's the clever idiot! Time to bring out the charm! Shirt on. Runners shined. Headed down. Managed to have an informal meeting, in the quiet corner of the packed room. Which. Thank funk. Went very well. Interest shown, more information asked for, up to me to deliver, rar diddy rar rar rar! That fifteen-minute meeting made the previous days of traipsing around the country well worth it. All about the small victories. Celebrate on. Did a bit more networking for myself while at the drinks shindig. People giving me their business cards. Directors. Producers. Randomers. Even a gay couple who reminded me of the Glitters. Head down. Tour on.

Bus trip home on Sunday flew by. Home. Delighted. Chill. Wrecked. Phone. *Dring*. Can I fill in for a sick DJ? Gig pays well.

Where? A small parish hall about an hour's drive from where I live. Parochial-church gig. Fortieth-birthday party. How much? Yeah, I'm in. Recoup the money I spent on my tour of Ireland. DJig. Good laugh. Still. Long day. Tripping all over. Finally. Get home. Really wrecked. Overtired. Space monkey. Beaten docket. Should've just gone to bed. Instead, I surfed the web. Checking emails. Usual junk mail, making me think I was popular. One. Of. Note. Book publisher. Interested in talking to me about the possibility of a book. Could I meet them at their offices in Dublin? I surely can. When, let me check . . . the tenth, Monday. When's that? Tomorrow. Well. Technically. Today. Oh right. Drive. On. Tour. On. No. Complaints. Need. An. iPhone!

Vi-Ya?

You know how some stuff sneaks up on you? Puttering along. Then. Bang. Out of the blue. Suddenly back in Ireland. That kind of thing. Well, this certainly wasn't like that. I've slept with one eye on this date for a while. Thought about. Every. Single. Day. Big day. Finally arrived. Visa interview. Make-or-break. Status quo. Or get to go? When you have access to a place, you think nothing of it. Waltz in and out of VIP in some club, and after a while, you don't know what the fuss is all about. However, being one the outsiders looking in, wishing they were able to waltz in, just for a while, or else be rejected, is another story. Imagine not being able to get into a club that you had planned the whole week to get into. Friends in there, waiting for you. Where you wanted to be. Bouncers say no. Now multiply that to a life-altering yes or no. Time to go charm the visa bouncers.

Sleepless night. Wrecked. Porridge. Eggs. Protein shake. Coffee. Dodge. Dumb. Nerves. Stomach. Rumble. Queasy. Embassy. Searched. Frisked. Entry. Early. Waiting. Forms. Letters. Photo. Photo? No photo. No joy. Start again. Start again? Go home? No! Please . . . oh. Leave. Pharmacy. Passport photo. Return. Frisked. Entry. Late. Queue. Long. Very long. Take a ticket. No. 150. Waiting. Now serving No. 120. Wait. And wait. Reading. Dozing. Thinking. Freaking. Reading. Dozing. Waiting. Bored. Over-thinking. Cramped. Sweating. Breather. Bathroom. Space. Praying. Please God. Distraction needed. Dirty runners. Thirty minutes. Clean runners. Bathroom. Knock knock. Out in a minute. Waiting room. Forty minutes later. Serving No. 130. What? Wuu. Waiting. Boring. So bored. So freaked. So what will I do if I don't get it . . . ?

Visa interview was not what I'd expected. Presumed, realistically I thought, that it would involve being greeted by burly security guards. Locked into an interrogation room. Bright white lights exposing your soul. Hammered with gruelling questions. Battered with accusations. Toughest thing you'll ever do in your life! That kind of thing. Perhaps I've watched too many movies. As it turned out. Not exactly the case. In fact, it is more like the everyday task of lodging money in the bank. Go up to a window. Speak to a person behind the glass. They then decide, yay or nay. No good-cop-bad-cop routine. Meaning no way to subtly bribe the person with a deft, *Casino*-style golden handshake. Unfolded my five-euro note.

Three hours of waiting gives you far too much time to think of all possible outcomes. Well, far too much time to think of one possible horrendous outcome. Oh God, why did I not just take those dodgy offers of marriage I had when I was in LA? Chowder's buddy who said she would marry me so that I could get a green card. She could travel round Europe then as well. Said all this to me on a night out, so I was tempted. Mostly down to the fact that I was a big fan of her name. And would want it if we did get married. Mr Cat Ching. Had a mighty ring to it! Next day, sobered up. Not a fan of getting married for the green card. Marriage is sacred. All that. Balls. Should've just done it. Funk. Freaking myself out now! At least I didn't take up that other offer. The dancer in the Body Shop. Five hundred dollarss and she'd have married me. If we'd been in Vegas, I would've definitely taken her up on her offer. A tad drunk. Made great sense. Thankfully, we weren't in Vegas. Especially as I found out the next time that she was actually Canadian. Married to a Canadian stripper. Would've been of great use to me. Bullet.

Dodged. After all. Marriage is sacred.

Visa lawyer in San Fran recommended that I build a case going down the writer/DJ route. The least I could do was try. No clue what might happen. Might work. Might not. Which is why now I have no clue. Not wanting to tempt fate, I instead managed to fully freak myself out. Sweet Lord, what happens if this doesn't work? Google Maps . . . nearest bridge? Oh my God, tick the funking tock on, clock! All this waiting and freaking was freaking me out. Needed some sort of distraction. Killed a good half an hour in the bathroom by cleaning my runners. Don't ask me why: they weren't even dirty. Just needed something to take my mind off the freaking. Although, not too sure, but praying while sitting on a toilet does not seem like the right thing to do. Doesn't really feel like a holy place to pray. Did help me though. Along, oddly, with some help from a small girl.

Number. Finally. Called. Sweating. Oh sweet Jesus. Keep cool. Up to the window. Regular guy behind the counter. Oddly. A little girl sitting on the chair next to him. Joe asks me a question . . . 'How are you?' As I attempt an answer, his daughter starts to hit the keyboard in front of her. Throws me off. Oh my God, I am . . . I don't know . . . What's the right answer?!! Notice he doesn't see or hear this. Attention is on his daughter. Asks me a visa-related question. As I divert my colon to my mouth, his daughter takes over. Starts smashing the keyboard now. Joe zones out what I'm saying again. Going through the motions. Interesting . . . Smash on little girl, smash on! Next question, same deal. This time, she's ripping up important-looking bits of paper. I could be saying anything to Joe. No interest. Rip on! Shred them up!!! Joe goes through my application and letters backing me up. Girl starts to wave the computer mouse. Joe doesn't take any notice. Until she tries to throw it away. Giddy up little girl! Seals the deal for me. Looks at his watch. Almost time for lunch. Looks at me. Looks at the forms in front of him. Stamps my application. Smiles? Smirks? Takes my passport. Must process it. It will be posted back to me.

Little girl interrupts by grabbing a scissors, waving them around like a crazy old man. Joe picks her up, puts the scissors down. Somehow, somehow, I manage not to yell out: 'Wait, what? What the holy funking Jesus?! Did I get it? Are you serious?!' Instead, I meekly say: 'Pardon?' Doesn't hear me. Realise then that I wasn't actually sure if he said I definitely got it or not. Starts to read my letters again. Oh God. I'm just standing here, staring at him. Why have I done? What am I doing? Fear and confusion kick in. Did I get it? Looks at me like I should've left already. He said I did, right? Did I? Yeah? No? Should I ask him? Might think it's suspicious if I do. Something amiss with my application. Maybe better to say nothing. Think I got it. I did. I think. I don't know. Sweet Lord. Decide to scuttle off. Just before I do, the girl looks at me. Gives me a thumbs-up. Did I . . . Did I get it?!! If so, little girl, you are a *dancer*!!!

V. Sa. Par. A. Noia

Still haven't heard anything about 'it'. Don't want to talk about it
to anyone. Not sure what happened. Think I did. Maybe I did-
n't. No clue. Freaked. Back to hibernation. Since I've been home,
I've barely seen a lot of the people I used to hang around with.
Initially, too much time wasted making plans with people to
meet up. When neither really wanted to. Live only ten minutes
away? Still haven't met up? Dodge each other. Pointless enough.
Just time to cull. Sometimes you just have to cut people loose.
No qualms in doing it. Not personal. Well, actually very personal. If the person was someone who I wanted to meet up with,
we'd have met. Saying that though, I can feel my old ways creep-
ing in a bit more. Bounce of the bubble must be wearing off a
bit. Doubt kicking in. Leaving the visa interview, I've never been
so pumped. Minor victory. Enjoy it. Until I waited for my passport to be sent to me. Never showed. My cousin got his within
a week. My buddy had gotten his three days later. I'm still in
limbo land. Had I gotten it wrong? Maybe the little girl actually
give me the middle finger?

Another thing has been on my mind as well. Let's just say, if
and when (please God) the visa does show up . . . what then? Just
go straight back? Round two? Won't see Ireland again for a
while. Putting it all on the line again. Hoped I would've been
back already. Being back in Cork for longer than a week had me
slipping into a comfort zone. Although going to Dublin did help.
Gave me belief. At least I was doing something. As opposed to
just saying stuff. Couldn't slip back to those old ways. Baby steps
had to be taken weekly. For my own sanity. Stagnating is a killer.

Had another meeting with the publisher. Tipping along nicely. Figured out that for these meetings, especially the first couple, a clever thing for me to do is . . . say less, nod more. Noddy. Nodding along. Look at me, I know what's going on. Clued-in. Yes, I do like that angle. Exactly what I was thinking too! After, I can go home and Google any areas which were discussed. Noddy on.

Same as all the RTÉ meetings. Ever since the last one I had, which went well, I've been waiting to hear back from Mary. I mean it went very well. Again, I was saying less. Letting them tell me their plans. Selling the idea to me, it seemed. Just keep nodding. Foot in the creaky door. Nod nod. Smile smile. And then I waited. And waited. My Dad told me these things take time. Patience. I wanted to call them the next day. C'mon, time is being wasted! Managed to sit on my hands. Bite my tongue. Eventually, my Dad nodded at me. Ring them. Enough waiting. Rang Mary . . . Mary, how are you? Haven't heard from me, everything still on track . . . Not too good? Why so? What? Really? You got let go? (You're funking joking me?!!!!) Part of the cutbacks? Mary, are you kidding me? No. No you're not. Sorry Mary, didn't mean to make you cry. OK, I believe you. Sorry to hear about that. Really sorry. Hopefully you'll get something else soon. Emm, can I just ask – I'm sure there's plenty of other stuff out there for you Mary, but . . . what does this mean for me? Me. Mary. What about me? Me? Mary? My development deal? Mary?! Sorry Mary, didn't mean to cry too.

When she heard she was getting the chop, she caused a scene. Didn't end well. Mary told her boss she was taking her projects with her. What? Balls. You took me out of RTÉ before I was even in?! What now? Now, *Mary* needed a break. Wanted to meet me first though. Proposal. Work as an independent producer, for me. More control than if it was direct with RTÉ. She knew the right people. Do the legwork. Push my projects. Hmm. Still feel sick from the kick in the balls you just gave me. Still though. That does sound interesting. Someone else helping me and pushing with me? Would make a change. Sounds good so. I'll just try the head RTÉ guy myself anyways. You don't have to know about that, Mary. Anyways, Mary went off. Did the legwork. Told me she was doing it. Doing this. Doing that. Doing all of it. Putting a package together. Sounds great, Mary. Where is it, Mary? That's two stand-up gigs you've missed now. Definitely be at the next one. Definitely! Five minutes before the next show . . . *dring* . . . Out of town? Stuck in traffic? Another excuse? Sure thing. I wonder why you got the chop, Mary. I wonder why. Dead. Dodo. Blind. Alley. Good. Luck.

At least the Mary situation taught me something. Well, more hammered home a point I knew already. Until something is in writing, signed and sealed, don't take it for granted. Which leads me back to a big concern. Now, I'm a tad worried. Paranoid. Visa. Paranoia. Did I get it? God, I don't have a funking clue. Chill. It'll be fine. Chill. Look, your buddy is back to keep you company. Ah, that's great. Here comes the Fear. Long time no see, buddy. And you've brought along Doubt! Wuu.

Hey Day. Not You. It's Me

Have you ever found yourself trying to pass the blame? Throw that buck around. Someone else's fault. Definitely, *definitely* not yours. Someone else. Has to be someone else to palm the blame onto. Can't be my dumb fault. Feels like things have stood still. Stagnating. Not hearing about the visa. Not knowing. Head-wrecking. Making it worse. By being dumb. DJing. Meeting people. Laughing. I thought you were in LA. Now you're here. DJing at this place. Didn't think you'd be seen in this place. Ha. Hilarious. Best of luck though. Cheers. You muppet. How's your own life going? Yeah, I thought that might shut you up. Not laughing now. All of which had me in a bad mood. Blaming other people for putting me in this bad mood. C'mon eternal optimism, don't let me down!

For the past few days, my mood has depended on the postman. Visa delivery? Yes? No. Funk. Can't stand Mondays. Brutal day. Tuesday. Visa? No. F**k you, Tuesdays. Slooow day. Dumbly, I seemed to move on from blaming people, to blaming the day. Good work by me. Pass on that buck a bit more. Which made me decide I had to go chill somewhere. Middle of nowhere. Thank funk for Ford hooking me up with cars while I'm back. Hopped in my car. Just drive. Drove. Aimlessly. Nowhere. After an hour I knew where I was going. Somewhere. Perfect place. Tipperary. Visit my Gran's house. Farm. Secluded. Closest places nearby: church, post office, two pubs. Rural life on! Except for my phone, cut myself off from the outside world. No laptop. Seeing as I forgot it. Funk it. Plough on. Stay up here for a while. Stop worrying about something that's out of my hands. Great waste of time doing that. Plenty of other things for me to waste my time on. Time to go hide. Sort out my head.

Next few days were spent wading through the swamp in my head. Trying to figure out a plan. What if. What then. Walked around the country lanes. Stepped in a lot of cow-shit. However. Eventually. Got bored. Went to the two pubs. Drank a lot. And came up with a plan. If the visa comes in the post, I'll play it by ear. Leave a few weeks after I get it. See how things are going. If it doesn't come, if I don't get it, I'll cry. And then I'll just move to Dublin. Try to start from there. Dublin. Where the likes of Mary run wild and free. Oh Jesus. Time to get drunker. Woke up a few days later. Walked outside to soak up the fresh air. Walked into some more cow-shit. Didn't matter. No more passing the buck. It was going to be a great day! Time to go home.

Home. Come On Home

Home. Driving along. Mind at ease. Whistling Edward Sharp's song all the way back 'Home, let come me home!' Home. Mighty to be back home. Home. Where my laptop was. Where the postman delivers my mail. Where I read an email. Where I opened an envelope. Where I showed my Dad. Where I pondered what to do. Where my Dad gave me the nod. Will I? Funk. Just made two plans! New plans, get out that window!! Why so, what happened? Passport arrived in the post. Visa attached. A girl I knew emailed me. Asking me to go to a party. Back in LA. In the Playboy Mansion. Would I go? Go back. With. A. Bang? From a farm to a mansion. Funk it. I'm in. Booked my flight. Dinner with my family. Drinks with my buddies. Packed my bags. Deep breath. Headed off. My other home. LA. Going back. Round two. Just. Like. That. Back on the Journey. Who, had it right all along: Don't Stop. Believe!

The Beginning . . .

Things I Don't Remember

Friday. Blur. Saturday. Black. Sunday. Out. Monday. Blank. Tuesday. What. The. Where. Am. I?! Bunnies. Boiling. America. Top. Model. Gin. Buckets. Champagne. Married. Women. Sky. Bar. Dr. Greg. Porn. Horse. Porn. Star. Eddie. Murphy. Griffin. Gibberish. Monkeys. Back. Black. Green. Evil. Suicide. Girls. Vodka. Tequila. Tila. Shots. Free. Bar. Food. Hotel. High. Life. Mind. Blowing. Now. Waiting. Bag. Packed. Private. Jet. Antigua? Mind. Going? Home. Ireland. Detox? Melt. Down? Lost. My. Scissors. Losing. My. Mind? Oh. Sweet. Jesus. Bag. Of. Nuts. The. Man? What. The. Funk?!!